SOFTWARE
AND ITS
DEVELOPMENT

SOFTWARE
AND ITS
DEVELOPMENT

Joseph M. Fox

Prentice-Hall, Inc., Englewood Cliffs, N.J. 07632

Library of Congress Cataloging in Publication Data

Fox, Joseph M.   (date)
    Software and its development.

    Includes bibliographical references and index.
      1. Electronic digital computers—Programming.   I. Ti-
tle.
QA76.6.F69   001.64'25   81-17692
ISBN 0-13-822098-0   AACR2

Editorial/production supervision by Karen Skrable
Manufacturing buyer: Gordon Osbourne
Cover design by Edsal Enterprises

Pages 35-87 previously appeared in Joseph
M. Fox, *Taxonomy of Software*, BITS,
Fourth Quarter, 1980, pp. 1-13. Reprinted with
permission of H.F. Sherwood & Associates,
Frankfurt, Germany.

Printed in the United States of America

10   9   8   7   6   5   4   3   2   1

ISBN 0-13-822098-0

Prentice-Hall International, Inc., *London*
Prentice-Hall of Australia Pty. Limited, *Sydney*
Prentice-Hall of Canada, Ltd., *Toronto*
Prentice-Hall of India Private Limited, *New Delhi*
Prentice-Hall of Japan, Inc., *Tokyo*
Prentice-Hall of Southeast Asia Pte. Ltd., *Singapore*
Whitehall Books Limited, *Wellington, New Zealand*

To four kids from Brooklyn

Jim, Joan, Jock, Pat

CONTENTS

PREFACE *xi*

1 WHAT IS SOFTWARE? *1*

Definition of a Program *2*
Software and Programs *2*
A Software Overview *4*
Facts About Software *5*
Why Software Development is so
    Problem Ridden *12*

2 THE COMPUTER AND ITS USES *14*

Definition of a Computer *14*
Definition of a General-Purpose
    Computer *15*
The Computer: A New Type of
    Tool *16*
The Uses of the Computer *18*
The Stress on the Computer and
    Software by Use *21*
Need for a Taxonomy *23*
Computer Power Over Time *23*
Software Cost Per Unit *26*

3   PERFORMANCE CONCEPTS   *27*

Software and Hardware   *27*
There is No One Measure of
    Computer Hardware Performance!   *28*
Balancing a System   *33*

4   A TAXONOMY OF SOFTWARE   *34*

Breaking Software into Digestible
    Pieces   *34*
Taxonomy of Software   *35*
Three Types of Software   *46*
Scale, Complexity, Clarity   *63*
Project Software and Product
    Software   *76*
Using the Taxonomy — Different Jobs   *83*
The Cost of Software   *86*
Vocabulary of Software   *87*

5   SOFTWARE DEVELOPMENT   *88*

Program Attributes   *88*
The Process of Software
    Development   *93*
Big Bang Versus Evolution   *98*
Requirements Definition   *100*
Change is Inevitable   *101*
Who States Software
    Requirements?   *102*
Overriding Importance of
    Requirements   *104*
In a Project, Who is the Real User?   *105*
Conflicting Requirements of Multiple
    Users   *106*
Product Versus Project
    Requirements   *106*
Design   *111*
Software is a Subsystem   *112*
The Design of Use-Time Software   *118*
Who Should Design   *119*
The End Product — What Are We
    Creating?   *120*
The Parts and the Process of
    Design   *122*

The Flow of the Process of Design of
    a Software System   *124*
Levels of Design   *128*
Structured Programming   *138*
Good Design   *142*
Design Is *143*
Robust or User-Friendly
    Programs   *145*
Documenting Design   *145*
New Design Techniques   *147*
Writing the Program —
    Programming   *148*
Managing the Writing   *167*
Construction   *170*
Verification and Testing   *184*
Documentation   *195*
Traceability   *200*
Too Much Documentation   *202*
Flow Charts Disappearing   *202*
Project History   *202*
"How" is "What"; A Requirement is a
    Design — Levels of Detail   *203*
What's Happening Out There   *204*

6   MANAGING SOFTWARE DEVELOPMENT   *205*

Systems, Subsystems, and
    Software   *206*
Inability to Forecast Development Cost
    or Schedule   *213*
The "Abandon Function Phenomenon"
    of Large Software Development   *215*
Plan to Evolve   *217*
Evolutionary Development of Large
    Systems   *219*
Project Management Tasks   *220*
Output of the Process   *223*
Development or Project Plan   *225*
Productivity and Estimation   *226*
Productivity in Software
    Development   *226*
Estimation   *240*
Organization of the Software
    Development Effort   *251*

Monitoring Progress   *253*
Control   *253*
The Key to Success — The Manager of
    Software Development   *255*
Choosing the Software Development
    Manager   *256*
Five Stages of All New Projects   *257*
Will the Real User Please Stand Up?   *258*
Audits   *259*
People and Tools   *261*
Build or Buy It   *262*
What to Do When It all Goes to Hell   *265*
Software Standards   *266*
Development or Continued Development
    as the Dominant Cost Phase   *271*
One Reason for Optimistic Estimates   *272*
Research in Software   *273*
The Inability of the Technology to
    Depict Software   *273*
Develop Software as We Develop
    Hardware?   *275*

7   SOME ADVANCED COMPUTER CONCEPTS   *278*

Multiprocessing and
    Multiprogramming   *278*
Data Integrity   *282*
Networks   *283*
Distributed Processing?   *284*
Summary   *284*

8   A PERSPECTIVE   *286*

Use of Industrial Techniques in
    Software Development   *286*
Vocabulary   *288*
Organization Imperatives   *289*
Predictions   *292*
Progress   *292*

INDEX   *295*

PREFACE

In 1620 Francis Bacon wrote that the discourses of learned men often end in disagreements about the meaning of words. Perhaps in no field is this truer than in the field of computers. The computer is still in its infancy, having been invented in the late 1940s, and the technological world is still struggling to evolve a vocabulary that is comprehensive, consistent, and clear.

In 1978 I had the good fortune to be chairman of the Navy Embedded Computer Review Panel reporting to the Assistant Secretary of the U.S. Navy for Research, Engineering, and Systems. One of the things that became clear immediately was that each panel member had a slightly different definition for most computer and software terms. Again and again we had to stop the meeting to hammer out a mutually agreeable definition before continuing.

Anyone discussing computers and software must beware of the accidental confusion caused by different understandings of even common terms.

I will posit some new definitions in this book, as many glossaries do not distinguish between close, neighboring concepts. Such glossaries are harmful; they perpetuate confusion.

The computer can do almost anything, and any tool that can do anything can somewhere be found doing very strange things—and for good reason. There is almost no statement that can be made about the use of computers (and therefore software) that cannot be contradicted with a specific, opposing example. This "contradiction by example" is not a valid contradiction. The fact that there exists a "one-of-a-kind" situation where it makes sense to do something contrary to the practice of the majority of users does not make the majority wrong.

The computer, for decades affordable only by large organizations, is now entering the home and the budget capacity of the average person. What cost $2 million twenty years ago can be purchased now for $1000. Digital electronics manufacturers have wrought an economic miracle. In 1960 a transistor cost about $20.00. In 1980, if you could isolate it, it would cost $.000002!

As a result the computer moves incessantly into new areas, not only in its guise as the general purpose computer, but also as the embedded control device in copiers, televisions, automobiles, engines, toasters, toys, and on and on. It is a ubiquitous device.

This marvelous progress in hardware places additional burdens on the software, and makes the shortage of software developers even more acute.

This book is about software, about the development of software, and primarily about the development of large scale software.

Many ideas and dictums for the development of large scale software apply to the development of small scale software; many do not. Rather than stop and try to distinguish, I leave it to the reader to decide if the idea is valid and if it is valid for a particular effort.

This book is for all data processing professionals. It deals with what will be the most important technology and tool of the next two decades—software. It is for the experienced professional who is typically very experienced in one or two areas of software, and relatively inexperienced in many of the others. It is for the newcomer, the computer science graduate who knows more than he or she realizes about the total field. It is a survey for them.

It is for the new programmer or user who knows an application and its intricate nuances and is frustrated by the jargon and the confusion of the software world. It is for the non-data processing executive who wishes to gain an overview of the field. The first part of the book is readable by those not in the computer field. And finally the book is for those who are doing research on this or that portion of software.

The first part of this text, therefore, is devoted to setting the stage for ideas on software development. In the first part I give definitions, set meanings, and make distinctions. I am completely aware that many of these will *not* agree with usage in some areas of the field, but I know no other way to be sure that I have communicated clearly. Whether the reader continues to use his or her words, or adopts the ones in this text, is far less important than that the ideas be clear and not entangled in ancillary concepts because of vague meanings.

We will go on to the development process in Chap. 5. The bulk of the text is on the development process, but the first 4 chapters are essential to the clear understanding of the rest of the book. I exhort the professionals *not* to skip the first part; although much of it is familiar, there are subtleties and categorizations presented that are valuable in everyday activities.

So many books approach the subject of software from the viewpoint of the individual programmer. Detailed discussion about recursive functions, language features, and theorems in technical language help the individual programmer cope with his/her immediate tasks.

But, too few books aim at the programming manager and the project manager, or even higher, at their superiors—upper management. What are the broad facts, the significant facts, the trends, the pitfalls, the important lessons of the past in the world of software?

I was fortunate to manage a large software house, part of IBM, for seven and one-half years. I managed 4400 people, mostly professionals, producing mostly software for large, real time systems. I learned many lessons the hard way. We were always breaking new ground; we always had over 100 contracts at any given time.

My job was akin to capping oil well fires, or so it seemed. I would no sooner get one large software project under control than another would explode, without warning, and blaze for its allotted time, seeming to defy all efforts to control it.

We had big jobs: 700 people for ten years on the manned space effort ground control at Houston, Texas; 500 people for ten years at the Atlantic City, New Jersey FAA site developing the en-route air traffic control system; 700 people for five years at Whippany, New Jersey, on the anti-ballistic missile system software; 500 people in Los Angeles for five years on an Air Force satellite effort.

A sampling of the jobs I managed during the seven and one-half years from 1969 to 1977 is listed below.

People/Years	Location	Project
700/7	Houston, TX	Apollo, Skylab, Space Shuttle
700/5	Whippany, NJ	Safeguard Anti-Ballistic Missile
500/7	Atlantic City, NJ	FAA En-Route Air Traffic Control
200/2	Cape Kennedy, FL	Launch Support System
60/3	Gaithersburg, MD	Japanese Publishing System
20/3	New York, NY	New York Police Dispatching System
5/1	Gaithersburg, MD	*New York Times* Morgue Automation
5/5	London	Nationwide Banking Systems
50/3	Gaithersburg, MD	U.S. Newspaper Consortium
200/3	Houston, TX	Oil Refinery Automation/Canada/Belgium
15/2	St. Louis, MO	Railroad Automation, MOPAC

One conclusion that springs from this list is the dispersed and nomadic nature of the contract software business. My office was in Gaithersburg, MD; almost all of the work was at the customer location. And for a good reason—software development is difficult enough when the software developers are co-located with the users.

We automated two Japanese newspapers with a team in Gaithersburg, MD, successfully, after a Perils-of-Pauline set of crises.

I had the pleasure and honor of having Harlan Mills reporting to me for the entire seven and one-half years, and there were many times when his great talents helped. Mills and Terry Baker pulled off the *New York Times* morgue automation with astounding productivity, and in its aftermatch we set up what I believe is the largest software statistics collection effort in the world. This has been underway now for over eight years and is a national resource. We'll see the *New York Times* project several times in this book.

The IBM chairman of the board told me that the Air Traffic Control System would never work, and I told him it would. And Congress was criticizing our Air Traffic Control effort for doing the same things that we had done in Houston in putting man on the moon.

Looking back, the years seem too few to have contained so many systems, crises, mistakes, and successes. The En-Route Air Traffic Control System not only worked, the United Kingdom bought $10 million worth of IBM computers and became the twenty-first En-Route Air Traffic Control Site. We put ten people in Gatewich, England, to support the site. That another country, with its own air traffic control agency (and a fierce "Buy British" policy) would pay $10 million for "the U.S. System" silenced the critics.

In addition to the seven and one-half years of running this large software business, I have taught hundreds of high-level managers the basic concepts of software in a series of seminars. From the seven and one-half years managing the software group, I learned the painful lesson of the doing. From the teaching, I learned how to present the ideas, but even more importantly, I learned which concepts of the computer and software were the most strange to the uninitiated— the executive. This second experience has been very valuable. Things I had taken for granted as clear and simple often were not.

For the past four years I have been chairman of a software/ development/business consulting firm. My associates and I have designed, advised, audited, and devised requirements for small systems and for some of the biggest systems developed or being developed. We have done this for DoD and some of its components, and for large commercial firms. The lessons of those activities are in this text.

Only a few of the ideas in this text are originally mine; it was my privilege to work with some of the very best in the field over the past twenty-five years.

In particular I want to acknowledge the great contribution of Andrew Ferrentino, my associate at IBM and now at Software Architecture and Engineering, Inc. Andy's insights, his deep understanding of software, and his formulations shaped many of the ideas in this book. Many of the figures and ideas in the text are his.

There is reputedly a curse which simply says "May you live in interesting times." Whether it is a curse or blessing is too philosophical a question to address here, but I believe that the last quarter century and the next ten years will be recognized as the time of breathtaking change in intellectual automation. We are lucky to be involved in this time of discovery and accomplishment.

I want to also thank Laura-Ann Charles and Janet Dalcher for their help in making this book appear.

Washington, D.C.   **Joseph M. Fox**

SOFTWARE
AND ITS
DEVELOPMENT

1

WHAT IS SOFTWARE?

A result of the phenomenal progress in computer hardware is that we talk of a large universe of things when we speak of "software." So diverse is the field of software that few statements about it are true across the whole range, and seemingly contradictory statements can often be true.

Software is becoming larger, more difficult, and more risky. Software is getting easier, smaller, and more manageable. *Both* statements are true, because software is moving in two very different directions simultaneously. Software *must* be divided into categories before we can start saying things about it that are more than oversimplifications. Vocabulary is key to our understanding.

Things that are important to people get words assigned to them—be they things or concepts.

- Snow   Eskimos have 20 words.
                             Aztecs had none.
- Cattle hides   Gauchos have 30 words.
- Flying thing   In the Hopi language, one word depicts both mosquito and airplane.

The software field is in sad shape indeed. What words it has are loose and overlapping.

DEFINITION OF A PROGRAM

A program is a series of instructions or statements which when decoded by a computer, or by a computer and a translation program, will cause the computer to do work.

There are subtleties in this definition that we will explore throughout this book. The words *instruction* and *statement* call for a precise *language*, in contrast to *user commands*. User commands are perishable, for the moment at least, while statements and instructions lead to reusable object code.

In Chap. 8 I will explore this difference between user and programmer, as it is one of the future areas where we will obtain a productivity increase in software development.

An *object program* is a program in machine language. A *source program* is an assembly program, or a higher order language (HOL) program in a language that will be translated by a machine-and-translator-program to machine language.

> A program is a series of instructions or statements which, when *decoded* by a computer, or by a computer and a translation program, will cause the computer to do work.

SOFTWARE AND PROGRAMS

We do not yet have words to make some of the important distinctions in software that we need to consider daily.

The words "neighborhood" and "city" quite clearly refer to two different things. Although we make sense of them and can distinguish between them, they do not have sharp boundaries.

What makes a neighborhood a neighborhood? How do you separate one neighborhood from another? When does a "town" become a city?

So too with *program* and *software*. Although we can not distinguish crisply between them, we can recognize them when we see them and recognize that they are different from each other.

A *program* has tight cohesiveness; *software* is more loosely connected, a *set of programs* that runs as a whole.

A program is "small"; software is "large." There are fundamental differences in their development, which we will explore.

> Software is a set of programs that interact with each other.

2

This is not a definition, as it does not clearly distinguish between a large program made up of many modules and a set of rather independent programs that feed each other and tie into each other. Despite this inability to draw a crisp clear line between a program and software the distinction between the two is useful, just as the distinction between town and city is useful. Therefore, in this text I will use the word *software* to denote a large group of interrelated and interacting programs, and the word *program* to mean a much smaller, more tightly related list of instructions that performs a more unified function.

Excluded from the Word "Software"

Many people use the word *software* to include diagrams, requirement statements, development schedules, user's manuals, and other associated byproducts of the development phase of a set of programs. We will *not* include these in our meaning of software.

This is not to imply that those items are not very important. As we shall see, they are very important! The wiring diagram for a car or the blueprint for a machine are critical items to the correct use and upkeep of expensive devices. So too with all the supporting documents for software.

But the wiring diagram or the blueprint is *not* the product. The car is the system that gets the work done. It gets me from there to there. Important to but *not* part of the car are a user's manual, a maintenance book and level upon level of more detailed drawings for repair, or for reproduction! But all of this is *not* part of the car. Essential and important for different reasons, but separate. They are produced *with* the car.

The same is true with software. Software is our car; it is the "thing" that gets the job done. We'll spend a good deal of time on supporting documentation to software, and on peoples' interaction with a system using software.

One of the most mischievous phrases abroad at present is that one "writes software." It makes software sound like a letter.

One *may* write a program, but not software. And even with a program the difficulty goes up rapidly with size.

"Writing software" is a phrase that underwhelms the description of the effort of software development.

We create software. I choose the word "create" deliberately. The manner of creating software involves many activities that are not yet part of science or engineering. The formulation of the requirements, of a solution, and the design of the software require ingenuity, imagination, and creativity. Once these phases of the process are finished, the process become more like engineering.

Software development can be broken into six parts:

Requirements definition
Design
Writing the instructions — programming
Construction
Testing
Documentation

A relatively new word, *firmware*, has been used frequently to denote software, or a program, that resides in and is executed from read-only memory (ROM). Although the fact that the memory cannot be written into creates some differences in how one would design and create the software, firmware is not different enough from software for normal memories to be singled out and treated separately. The same rules and practices apply. Therefore, we will treat *firmware* as a part of the software. We will deal with programs that fit the read-only mode of storage.

A SOFTWARE OVERVIEW

We have today a software crisis that is going to get worse. Part of the crisis is that few outside the field even understand what software is. Software is an isolated, esoteric field, fraught with semantic casualness and a paucity of terms. And its practitioners are too often focused on software, rather than on the system that software enables.

Too often, software producers cannot deliver reliable products on schedule or on budget. The supply of software producers is growing much more slowly than the need, with no real solution in sight. Software failures are experienced not only by the small newcomer. The biggest, most prestigious and most technologically advanced organizations suffer severe setbacks in the software area. The very month they were to begin shipping the new system 138, IBM announced a 1-year slip because of software difficulties. A year before scheduled initiation of the Advanced Communication Systems, ATT announced an 18-month slip.

Software use is not difficult; software development is. Software development has become the malevolent genie that has escaped the computer hardware lamp and roams the world bedeviling the lives of systems developers everywhere.

One of the major reasons for many difficulties of software development is that the scale and complexity of the efforts undertaken — and successfully achieved — grow every year. New and bold uses of the "old" tool — the computer — are put on-line constantly. The progress of the electronic circuit in speed, size, reliability and economy is simply marvelous.

It is only when we look at some of the things we have done that we see we have made gigantic strides. Airline reservations systems work — and work beautifully. The American Airline System in the spring of 1979 handled 13,500 connected terminals and up to 10.6 million messages per day. The Air Traffic Control System works — both in the U.S. and abroad. Satellite systems work. These are not accidents. They took tremendous resources and efforts, but they work.

What are the lessons to be learned from the successes and failures of the past? Where is "software engineering" now? Should we manage software as we do hardware?

This book is addressed primarily to the large system software development efforts that are becoming more common. We will examine why many large developments have hit stumbling blocks, causing untold millions of dollars of unexpected costs, years of delay, many outright failures, and not a few law suits.

Software development for small scale software is primarily a happy story of success. Many of the definitions and techniques for the large systems that we will discuss either came from the earlier, smaller efforts, or are applicable to them.

Let us list some not so obvious facts about software, and then we'll discuss them briefly. The remainder of the book will cover each of them in some depth.

FACTS ABOUT SOFTWARE

- Software is expanding in opposite directions at the same time.
- The life of any program has usually three phases, and the developers and designers should consider all three in their efforts. Usually only *the development part* and *the use part* are considered. The *support*, or *continued development part* must be addressed early in the development phase.
- Software development can be broken into six parts: requirements definition, design, writing the instructions, construction, testing, and documentation.
- Software development for large systems is often hardware specific.
- There is no one "right" set of instructions to do a given process.
- Software is abstract, and this makes it more difficult to manage.

- The computer and software are essential tools used to create new software.
- The function to be done is often not the major determinant of the difficulty of the software development; the "use-time environment," which must be "managed" by software, often is the major determinant of difficulty.
- Some software can be developed just like hardware, and some software cannot.
- Software cannot fail once it is correct. Therefore, the term "maintenance" as applied to software is a misnomer.
- Large program development is a multidisciplinary activity, not just a computer activity.
- Large software cannot be completely debugged, even after years of testing and use.
- Software development is expensive and often very difficult.
- Software is a means, not an end.

Software is Moving in Opposite Directions Simultaneously!   In the mid-1930s Alan Turing, an English mathematician, proved that any process that was describable by an algorithm could be calculated by a very simple machine, with but six possible instructions, if one ignored time. The logical extension of this principle is that the computer — *any* general purpose computer — can calculate anything that can be described by an algorithm. Software today is becoming more and more complex, handling ever larger and more complex applications, and it is moving into "trivial" products, used every day by the average citizen.

The enormous progress in digital circuit technology has been lowering hardware cost dramatically and will continue to do so. What was not feasible a few years ago because of time or cost is being done today.

This simultaneous lower cost and increased machine capacity expands the universe of applications on two frontiers simultaneously — on the high end and on the low end.

On the high end, the large scale efforts, the computer now has the capacity to perform tasks in the time required, and therefore it is put to those tasks. On the opposite extreme, the slow simple computer is now so inexpensive that it makes economic sense to automate things with computers that just did not make sense a year or two ago.

This expansion of the use of computers on two fronts simultaneously should not be a surprise, it should not be confusing, but at times it is. The software for the high end is getting more complex; the low end programs are getting simpler.

Software encompasses a host of different kinds of programs.

Software does anything that is do-able; it is small and trivial; it is large and complex and enormously expensive. We should talk about software with at least one adjective in front of it. Are we talking about "project software" or "product software"? Are we talking about "real time" or "batch"? "Interactive" or not? Are we talking about "fail soft" or "fail safe" or normal reliability? Are we talking about "support software" or "systems software" or "applications software"? Are we talking about "large scale" software or "small scale"? Each of these categories carries with it certain requirements that are peculiar to the category.

There are Three Phases in the Life of a Program.   Too often, the developers of a program focus only on the *development phase*, or that and the *use phase* of the life of the program, much to the detriment of the *support*, or *continued development*, *phase*. There are things that can and should be done during development to ease the burden in the other phases. The software can be built so as to be easier to fix, to change, to enhance. Most developers ignore this aspect of software. Too many books on the development and use of programs ignore the fact that the three phases are distinct, have different goals, and often have different managements. (See Fig. 1-1.)

Software Development has Six Parts: Requirements Definition, Design, Writing the Instructions, Construction, Testing, and Documentation. *The writing of the instructions is the easiest part.* It is very difficult to design the interactions of a large number of programs into an optimum or even a proper sequence. Most difficult of all in large systems is stating the requirements of the user and, therefore, of the

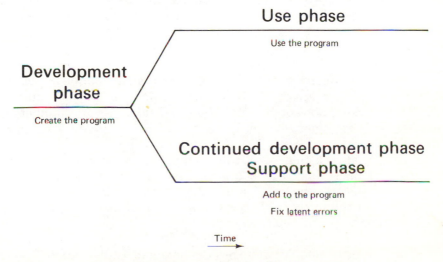

Figure 1-1.   Three phases in the life of a program.

system. Yet too many studies and books relate primarily to the writing. As we shall see, the emphasis needs to be on the requirements definition and on the design.

Software Development for Large Systems is Often Hardware Specific. Large systems usually require that the use of the hardware be optimized for economy and performance considerations. Central processing unit (CPU) loading and memory requirements must be carefully planned. This forces the designer to incorporate into the design of the program the hardware parameters and features of the system. This is usually not the case for the small program developer.

System performance — getting the computer to do the job within a specified time limit — depends to a major extent on the hardware being used, its power, and its configuration. When the hardware is barely adequate for the task at hand, the burden of making it perform *to the limit of its capacity* falls on the software developer, and especially the designer. This is the major reason that developers of large or real time systems sometimes refuse to use high order languages. We will see several examples of performance requirements complicating the development task.

There is No One "Right" Set of Instructions to do a Given Process. A hundred programmers would come up with a hundred different payroll programs, all of which would do the job. There are few optimum programs. The attributes of every program are often in competition with each other, just as size competes with speed in design of an airplane. We'll see in Chap. 5 that there are at least 12 aspects of every program, and that several are in competition with each other for embodiment in the program. The multiplicity of possible solutions is one of the stumbling blocks in properly managing the development of software.

Software is Abstract. A large software system cannot be sensed by any of the five senses. It is abstract. One can see and touch a $20,000,000 computer or a $100,000,000 bridge. As its number of instructions gets larger, the effort to visualize software gets more difficult.

Looking at a listing of a million lines of instructions is a very different act than looking at a bridge. One cannot *see* the flow, the structure of the software. One *sees* a thick wad of paper, and lines of characters, not the software. This attribute of software makes managing its development very difficult.

The Computer and Software are the Essential Tools Used to Create New Software. Software and the computer are used by software developers as the key tools to shape and create new software. Software is a "tool to make tools" in this use.

Software must be viewed either in its role of executing the job (use time) *or* in its role of helping to create more software (development time). The two uses are fundamentally different, and the fact that the same identical computer hardware can do both functions is a source of great confusion to the newcomer.

To those in the business of computers and software, this fact is so obvious that they think that everyone understands it. They think nothing of discussing, say, a VAX 11 in one sentence in its role as the operational system controlling a missile, and in the next sentence discussing the identical physical machine in the same location in the same installation in its role as the "host" machine that will support the development of the software that will run when the VAX 11 is controlling the missile. To those who have not been close to such development efforts, the language is murky, as the presenter intermixes statements about the two different uses for the same computer.

This dual role should be clearly articulated. The computer professional should be careful not to switch from one role to the other without clearly pointing out the transition.

The Function to be Done is Often Not the Major Determinant of the Difficulty of the Software Development; the Use-Time Environment that Must be Controlled by Software Often is. Reliability requirements of a system often add more complexity to the software than the function it must perform. It is easy to do a navigation program. It is very hard to do a navigation program so that it will never stop running, despite hardware, software, or human failure. Yet these environmental factors are often left unstated, to be assumed, and often incorrectly assumed. Recovery software is some of the most difficult to develop.

Some Software can be Developed Just Like Hardware, and Some Software Cannot. Software is composed of instructions, and we can write instructions to do almost anything, and in a myriad of sequences. The instruction is not a physical thing. Hardware is a physical thing and is more limited in its permutations and combinations. We find instances where software is like hardware and should be developed in the same way. But in the very large systems, the two are fundamentally different. Here, the hardware is like a piano; software is music. Hardware is a dictionary; software is a novel. There are many similarities between hardware and software, but there are fundamental differences when we are building large systems. We will expand on this later.

Software Cannot Fail Once it is Correct. Therefore, software is not maintained. It is not maintenance; it is continued development.

Instructions, once correct, cannot become wrong. They can become obsolete, because of other events. Or they can be wrong to begin with, but somehow get through test. The maintenance of a program is but development continuing, to fix errors not caught in test, to add new functions, and to improve function or performance.

This fact is important! Many programmers believe that maintenance programming is not as exciting, not as prestigious, as development programming. Continued development is often *more* difficult than the original development. We should call it by the name that is most accurate -- continued development — and take a step towards erasing the unwarranted stigma of working in maintenance.

Large Software Development is a Multidisciplinary Activity, and Not Just a Computer Activity.   Engineering, or mathematics, or weapons control, or orbital physics, or military logistics, or plan policy, or reservation policy, or astronautics, or aerodynamics, or one of many specific areas of competence is usually needed in a large software development project. The software development manager must manage the application of this discipline to the project. This means that the software manager must be capable of managing a diverse team.

Large Software Cannot be Completely Debugged, Even After Years of Testing and Use.   Small programs can be completely debugged; large and complex ones cannot be. There are simply too many possible paths through the program, or too much variation in the data, or in the users' actions.

Hundreds of years of continued testing — even if possible — would not test all the possible paths through a large, complex program. Yet some people still insist on "error-free software"!

Software Development is Expensive and Often Very Difficult. Over 20 billion dollars a year goes into software development in the U.S. That's quite a lot, and the total is growing steadily. Not all of this expenditure results in success.

In the early 1970s two major airlines each sued its supplier because after $40 million the system was not working — nor about to work. A major European bank went to court for a $70 million claim over software. And the U.S.A.F. recently spent well over $300 million in a futile attempt to automate an Advanced Logistics System (ALS).

Software is not an easy field.

Software is a Means, Not an End.   One of the finest technical groups in the world is the National Security Agency (NSA). Charged with protecting the codes of the United States and breaking the codes of enemies, it attracts and trains some of the world's finest technologists.

Recently, the man in charge of computers and communications related to me the events that transpired when, years ago, he was made chairman of a committee to define standards for acquiring software.

One member of his panel was particularly pesky, and kept insisting that the "top-down" approach espoused for software development be used by the committee. Which meant they could *not* start their deliberations with software, but with the *systems* that software was to work in and be part of.

Finally, the chairman went to the head of NSA and told him that the dissenter was right — the committee *first* had to set standards and guidelines for *systems* acquisitions, and then go on to software.

Although the NSA head felt that they already knew how to do systems acquisition, the first document produced by the committee was Systems Acquisition Policy. Then the committee moved to software!

Software is a third-order function; it makes a system work, and *the system* yields a result. Software should never be treated as an end in itself. Even as a marketable product it is an enabling factor and should be developed and marketed as such.

What do we mean "third order"? The first thing we want is a result. For example, more sales, which we will get through a seat reservation system. The result is what we are after — it is a first-order objective. The system to achieve the result is the second-order objective, and the software, as a piece of the system is a third-order objective. Important, yes. Maybe even the most important, but still third order.

Why state this obvious fact? Winston Churchill described a fanatic as one who will not change his mind and will not change the subject. We have in the industry "software fanatics," who think that software is a first-order item. These fanatics should never be systems or project managers, as they have a distorted view of the world, which *warps* the software *and* the system *and* the result.

Requirements definition is the most problem-ridden area in large software development. This area involves far more than the software; it includes all the various types of hardware, and the people, and the procedures! When software is approached as an enabling mechanism, the resulting product will be better than if the software is approached as a first order of importance item.

The Two Roles of Software

The obvious role of software is to make the computer hardware do the job! But let's probe a little deeper. That statement of role is not quite complete. The other role of software is to be amenable to change.

No one lightly considers tearing out the radar antenna, or putting up a new satellite ($50,000,000). But system managers *should* lightly consider changing the software! They should plan on it. Its very name, software, implies its additional role. This concept carries us all the way back to the idea of the stored program.

The ability to erase and rewrite memory is what made the computer a general-purpose device. But in addition it made it a very adaptable device. The ability to rewrite the memory almost instantaneously makes it general purpose *and* adaptable. To capture the benefits of the computer's adaptability, we must *control* the software with great precision, so as to be able to change it easily.

WHY SOFTWARE DEVELOPMENT IS SO PROBLEM RIDDEN

Why is software development often so difficult? For one, two, or all of the following reasons:

1. *Complexity*. The inherent complexity of what we are automating, e.g., scientific complexity (lunar gravity, etc.), or logical complexity (10 to the 3 thousandth power possible paths through the program), or both.

2. *Software is Abstract*. It is managed and created "in the blind," and complex tools are required to enable management to "see" what is happening.

3. *Requirements Confusion*. Management usually believes that they understand the user's requirements, even though the user has never seen such a system. And then there is the idea that what is wanted, even if known, will remain static. This leads to the absurd idea that a large software system can be developed in one "Big Bang" of creation.

4. *Social Factors*. Pressure is always exerted to keep the system development cost low. The software portion of the system, the least understood, takes the biggest cuts. Because software is so little understood, it is the easiest to underestimate, the easiest to defend a very low estimate for. Software is "invisible."

5. *Management by Software of the Use-Time Environment*. To manage the environment, software is created that will do the following:

   a. Assure that the system never stops running; i.e., software monitors the hardware, data *and* other software so that when errors occur, the system continues, without any human interaction.

   b. Assure that the program gets the job done in a certain period of time; i.e., the software monitors the passage of time and the status of the application, and changes the flow of work if necessary.

c. Interact with dozens of human operators in a user-friendly manner, assuring that the user will use the system efficiently and with a minimum of training.

This software is very, very difficult to develop. It is extremely logically intricate.

THE COMPUTER AND ITS USES

DEFINITION OF A COMPUTER

It is all but impossible to examine flying without examining an airplane itself. And when one does discuss flying, it is usually with the expectation that the listener understands the basic physical principles of rudders, flaps, etc. To my dismay, I often find that my concept of the computer hardware is slightly — but importantly — different than that of my colleagues. Therefore we must look at *computer hardware and its uses* before going deeper into software.

One of the meanings of the word "definition" is "to set limits." The definition we give here for computer does delineate, does set limits. It is a two-step definition, first defining computer, and then defining the stored-program, general-purpose computer.

Definition: A computer: A device that calculates automatically and continuously and that selects its future operation from preset operating options.

Let's look at these words:

Calculate: "To ascertain or determine by any process." This word can be interpreted in many ways, and I mean it in its broadest sense. To compare is to calculate. To measure is to calculate.

Automatically and Continuously: Once started by a person, the device will operate itself until "finished," until it completes its task. Theoretically, it can operate forever, if it is controlling a process that does not end. We specify here the *ability* to operate for long periods of time without human intervention.

Selects Its Future Operation from Preset Operating Options: Humans put in some number of alternative operating sequences, and the computer, based upon its own internal on-going processes, "chooses" the path to be performed. The paths are preset by the person who programs the computer.

This definition of a computer is for all computers, not just the general-purpose computer. We must distinguish between the special-purpose computer and the general-purpose computer. The clearest distinction that I have come across is found in the words of the famous John von Neumann draft memo of 1946 that attached his name to the computer architecture we now use. The memo was the first articulation of the general-purpose computer, and it stated that the special-purpose computers which had been used for many years had their instructions built into them as an integral part of the device. In other words, the way the machine operated was part of the construction of the machine. Von Neumann pointed out that the new way the computer was to control its operation was by numbers put into the machine.

> It is evident that the machine must be capable of storing in some manner not only the digital information needed in a given computation such as boundary value, tables of functions and also the intermediate results of the computation, but also the instructions which govern the actual routine to be performed on the numerical data. *In a special-purpose machine these instructions are an integral part of the device and constitute a part of its design structure.* For an all-purpose machine it must be possible to instruct the device to carry out any computation that can be formulated in numerical terms. (emphasis mine)

DEFINITION OF A GENERAL-PURPOSE COMPUTER

A general-purpose computer is a computer that has its instructions stored in a memory that can be rewritten with new instructions in a short time without reengineering activity.

Were it to take a long time (say hours) to change the instructions, we would still have a general-purpose computer, but a slow one.

This definition of the general-purpose digital computer separates the computer from the hand calculator and from the sophisticated automata that populate our technological society.

This definition can be applied to the marvelous and inexpensive devices that are coming to us from Very Large Scale Integration (VLSI) techniques of the component manufacturers. It makes a distinction between the circuit and the computer, between the calculator and the computer.

This definition encompasses all computers, whether they be micro, mini, midi, or maxi. The distinction between mini and micro is at best vague and will be eliminated by the progress of VLSI. In a few years, *all* computers will be microcomputers, in that they will all be on a chip.

To go further here about the definition would divert us from software. A definition is important, and this definition is an adequate and useful one.

THE COMPUTER: A NEW TYPE OF TOOL

How the computer is used determines what the software must do. A look at the way humans use tools is helpful here. Marshall McLuhan points out that every tool is an extension of a human capability.

Extension of a Person	Tool
Foot	Wheel, bike, automobile, the airplane
Fist	Rock, club, gun
Skin	Clothing
Eye	Telescope, microscope, radar
Mouth, Ear	Radio, microphone
Mind	Paper (memory), calculators, adding machines
Mind	Computer
Will	Computer

What faculty of humans does the computer extend; *Two* very different human faculties, as it turns out — the mind and the will.

"Nova," the public TV show, had a report on the computer called "The MIND Machine." But the computer is more than just a mind expander, and this fact has profound impact on the software we must develop as we use the computer as an extension of the will.

Mind-tool.   The *speed* of the computer allows people to solve problems that heretofore were impossible. Even thousands of people with adding machines working for thousands of years could not do the computation a large computer can do in a few minutes. This use is an extension of the mind, of the ability to solve problems, to calculate immense arithmetic sequences.

Will-tool.   In a much different way, a computer is an extension of human will. It follows orders and executes choices, whether the human is or is not present. It is the computer's ability to choose between options that makes it an extension of the will. In this mode, the speed of the computer may not be important at all.

Without this ability to choose between options, the computer reverts to merely a mind-tool! The conditional branch instruction, along with the stored program, is *the* implementation of choice.

People and New Tools.

People always use a new tool to do old things. Only after years or even decades of experience will a new tool be used for *new* purposes. The computer is rapidly moving into new areas. And it is in the new areas where the software development is most difficult.

Telegraphy replaced the Pony Express. Radio replaced the telegraph. But hopes to use the radio as a replacement for the telephone (and eliminate wires) ran into trouble because there was no privacy in its use. Anyone with a tuneable radio set could listen in to the conversation. It was not until the radio had been in use for over 20 years that it was *accidentally* found to be a great *entertainment* device — a dentist in Pittsburgh began to "broadcast" music from his garage on Saturday afternoons — and the era of broadcasting and entertainment in the home had arrived. The feature that had held radio back as the replacement of the telephone was *the* feature that made it the entertainment device.

David Sarnoff had foreseen this use of radio, and in a visionary memo, a decade before the dentist began broadcasting, wrote:

> I have in mind a plan of development which would make radio a "household utility" in the same sense as the piano or phonograph. The idea is to bring music into the house by wireless. While this has been tried in the past by wires, it has been a failure because wires do not lend themselves to this scheme. With radio, however, it would seem to be entirely feasible. The receiver can be designed in the form of a simple "Radio Music Box" and arranged for several different wavelengths, which should be changeable with the throwing of a single switch or pressing a single button . . . .

Sarnoff's memo accurately forecast what would happen. But his superiors scoffed, and others — not his company — began broadcasting.

The progress of use of the computer has followed the general trend. First, it did old and well known things — payroll, inventory, ballistics, and engineering calculations. Only gradually did it move into newer areas — inquiry systems, management information systems, and time sharing systems.

Finally, the computer moved into the area I'll call *operations/ process*, and it is here, in this *new use* of the now "old" tool, that we find most of the difficulty in developing software.

One major problem with the computer is its utter versatility — it can be used for anything! As Turing showed in 1936, any function or process that could be described by an algorithm could be done by a very simple machine, if we ignore time.

In 1910, Bertrand Russell and Alfred North Whitehead wrote *Principia Mathematica* and presented the concept that logic is the foundation of all mathematics. It presented the calculus of propositions, solving problems, in terms of statements that are either true or false. We find that the computer is far more than an arithmetic machine; it is a logic machine as well.

Documents on the uses of computers list hundreds upon hundreds of uses. One could go on and on, adding to the list of uses forever, but to no useful purpose. Instead, it is very useful to split the use of computers into categories that are significantly different from one another, different in terms of the way each use stresses the hardware, the software and the people, different enough that such categories are useful to people using or developing complex, computer-based systems.

Let us divide all uses of the computer into five separate types of use:

Type I	Data Processing
Type II	Scientific Problem Solving
Type III	Inquiry Systems
Type IV	On-Line Problem Solving
Type V	Operations/Process

The very history and vocabulary of the computer clearly distinguish between the computer used for accounting — a process labeled *Data Processing* — and the computer used for problem solving — called the *Computer*. The hardware designed for one of these two uses was quite different from that designed for the other. Only recently (1964) has the same hardware been intended to do both tasks.

The *problem solving* scientific computer was optimized around a very fast calculating unit. The *process* computer — data *processing* — was optimized as an input/output, file handling machine. For the first 12 years of computers, 1952 to 1964, IBM had a data processing product line and a separate scientific computer line.

The IBM/360, announced in 1964, came about because it had become too expensive for IBM to develop, build, and support two separate product lines.

Use Type I Data Processing

Accounting is an after-the-fact process. Billing, general ledger, payroll, and inventory are the record keeping of past events. The computer, developed to speed scientific ballistic computations, was turned down by IBM, but was made commercially available by Sperry Rand in 1952. Users put it to work doing payroll and inventory.

Use Type II Scientific Problem Solving

"Number cruncher" is the way many label the large scientific computers. Few data values are entered, yet the larger computers will run for hours, calculating fusion equations, weather forecasts, etc.

Use Type III Inquiry Systems

After a few years of use, people realized that all the accounting data was "in there," and available. Software was written so that users could type questions *into* the computer and get the data they requested typed out to them. A new way of using the computer arrived.

Use Type IV On-Line Problem Solving

When an individual uses the computer in an interactive way to solve a mathematical or logical problem, the user is "on-line," or "interactive."

When hundreds of users can all use the same computer at the same time, we have a use called Time Sharing. It is a way of using the computer to do type I or type II jobs in a different style. The difference is in the use of the computer in the aggregate; the individual user may see little or no difference.

Time sharing reduces "turnaround," the time from the problem's leaving the programmer to the return of the result, thus maximizing the human inventiveness part of the problem solving process/creation process.

The type III commercial application deals with data — files, records, policy holders, bills, receipts, customer numbers. Huge, voluminous files. The crushing work is plowing through vast files, finding *the* right one, doing a *simple* calculation — trivial even — and then plowing some more. The choke points are tape speed, disk access, the volume the disk can hold, and the structure of the file.

Use type IV deals with calculations, not with files in the sense of insurance company policy files on millions of people. There are arrays of data, but they are more arrays than files. The bottlenecks here are computer speed and the laying out of the process so that things get done on time. However, in order to do a type IV operation with hundreds of users on-line, connected to the machine in a conversational, interactive way, many of the commercial type of activities of keeping track of names and locations and time and simple things must be done. So there is overlap between types III and IV.

I list them separately because (1) the type IV use created a whole industry and use type (time sharing), and on-line use for data processing is substantially different and (2) they use and stress different hardware units, and therefore the software to run them is different.

Use Type V   Operations/Process

When a computer is used to do, or to aid humans in doing, an ongoing process, *and* we could not do the job without *constant* results, we have an operations/process use. The process can be simple, e.g., the control of traffic lights, or it can be quite involved, e.g., the system to aid air traffic controllers in the keeping of airplanes apart, or the system to keep track of an airline's seat reservations and to interact with thousands of reservations clerks simultaneously.

Operations/process uses are integral to the running of a process and usually are real-time uses. The computer must do its job in time for the process to be controlled.

A type V looks to the user just like a III or IV, but it cannot fail without major disruption of the on-going effort.

To ensure that the time response and fail-safe requirements are met requires the design of some of the most difficult type of software. A software/hardware system that must guide a missile to an intercept with another missile is doing basically the same problem mathematically as the ballistic trajectory problems that led to the development of the computer. But *now* it must be done without failing, in real time, so that the intercept takes place before the second missile is beyond intercepting. And much of the burden to do this falls on the software!

When a type III *must* run — the people's job cannot be done without the computer running *now*, then the type III has entered the operations/process arena and has become a type V.

So we have type Vs evolving from types III and IV.

A V encountered when a IV and III *combine* is a very difficult development effort. The hardware handles type Vs quite easily today! The software is the bottleneck in these systems.

The evolution of the use of the computer up the scale from type I use to type V has been continuous.

Figure 2-1. A user interacts with the software and the computer. (Courtesy of Ontel Corporation, a subsidiary of Caesars World, Inc.)

Type Is became type IIIs. The logical thing was to get the accounting data *in there*, in the computer, out on request. "How full was the average flight from Washington to Paris in the month of August?"

The type III usage is very different from the type I. *People interacted* with the computer. And the burden to do this falls primarily on the software!

In type I and II, the user is not *connected* directly to the machine. The jobs are put in via cards or magnetic tape and then the programmer or department manager waits until the run is completed, at which time they will get a set of results, usually printed.

In types III and IV, the user is *interacting* with the computer directly via a typewriter or TV-like display with a keyboard. He or she is on-line. This is a much different way of using the computer than types I and II, and the software must be there to enable the user to interact. (See Fig. 2-1.)

THE STRESS ON THE COMPUTER AND SOFTWARE BY USE

These five uses stress the hardware and software differently.

Large type IIIs have an interesting sticking point. In hardware, the disk access time becomes the limiting factor in performance. Most of the action in a type III is data retrieval, and simultaneous "seeks" are going on. The "seeks" wait in queues until the disk access mechanisms are free to accept them. The software must be designed so as to maximize simultaneous seeks. Obviously, the more disks, the more overlap possible. Some installations have hundreds of separate disks.

The Skylab software effort in Houston followed right on the heels of the Apollo XV mission. It used the same hardware as the Apollo effort did; the software was different. It was a "disaster" of sorts. It worked, on time, but the toll it took on the fine team of 700 or so professionals was exorbitant. Excessive overtime often led to the point of exhaustion and collapse.

Why? Why should such an experienced team — with 10 years of successful systems development on space efforts — all the Apollo efforts *and* the landing on the moon — suddenly run into such a problem? The answer seems simple now, but it wasn't then.

Skylab was a very large type III dropped into the middle of a large type IV — and it could not fail. The team expected *merely* another type IV going to V!

Over 100 experiments in real time were being conducted aboard Skylab, and data was streaming down in real time. It had to be collected, sorted, stored, indexed, tagged and arranged — in real time. Neither the NASA nor the IBM team foresaw the significant difference in the application, and the new software needed to do the job.

Figure 2-2 fits large type Vs, and some IIIs and IVs. It is *not* true for Is and IIs, yet it is portrayed as gospel in books and reports. It *is* true for the area from whence it came, an Air Force report about the command and control use of computers by the Air Force.

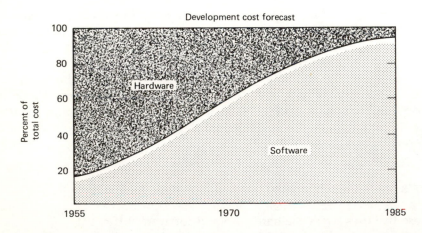

Figure 2-2.   A misleading diagram about percent of development cost.

NEED FOR A TAXONOMY

One overriding point about software must be always borne in mind. Software is too large to be discussed for any length of time without specifically stating what area, part, piece, or type of software is being discussed. The word covers too large a field to be used without qualifying adjectives.

Software is becoming more difficult to develop every day.

Software is becoming easier to develop every day.

Both of the statements above are true. The seeming contradiction stems from the broad range of the word software. Let us look at where it is becoming easier.

COMPUTER POWER OVER TIME

An oversimplified but quite valid graph makes the point vividly as to what is happening. Let's look at the universe of computers (Fig. 2-3). In 1952, there was *one*, the UNIVAC I.

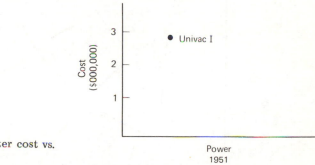

Figure 2-3. The computer cost vs. power (1951).

In 1960, the power for the price was much greater, and the computer was moving down and up and out on the scale (Fig. 2-4).

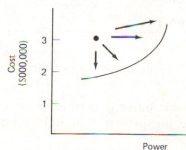

Figure 2-4. The computer cost vs. power (1960).

23

Then the "minicomputer" — which referred to its price, not its size —
pushed the computer lower down on the scale in the mid-1960s (Fig. 2-5).

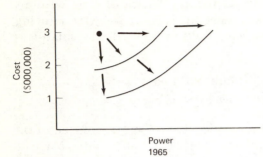

Power
1965

Figure 2-5. The computer cost vs.
power (1965).

And now digital electronics in VLSI is creating the microcomputer,
the computer in the palm of your hand. It is making us redraw the
chart again. Going to a larger scale (Fig. 2-6), we can see what has
happened over the years as the computer has come down in price and
up in capacity and performance.

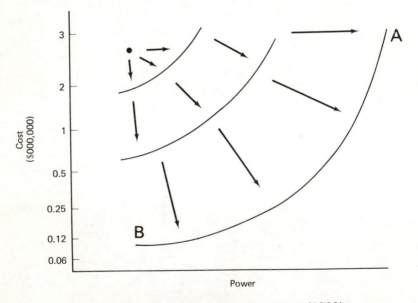

Figure 2-6. The computer cost vs. power (1980).

The computer is getting more and more powerful (A). And it is
getting so inexpensive that it is filling uses (B) that heretofore could

not afford the computer. And software of course follows the computer into (A) and (B). It is small and simple in B; huge and complex in A.

The digital circuit became a digital computer — and that means it has a program. This marvelous device costs next to nothing. As a result, the digital computer is moving into applications that heretofore could not justify such sophistication. (See Fig. 2-7.)

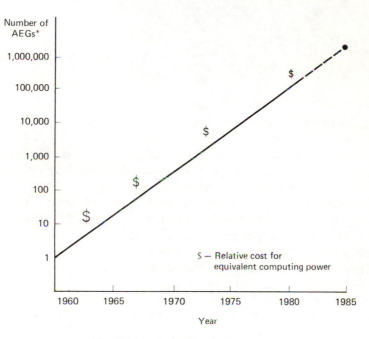

*An AEG is an Active Element Group — roughly equal to a bit or to a flip flop

Figure 2-7. Growth in solid-state technology.

As the number of circuits on the chip *doubles* every year, the price and the reliability and the power consumed stay essentially the same! Had the auto industry made this progress we would have a car that weighed half a pound, got one and a half *million* miles per gallon, and cost $2.70 (National Business Magazine).

The advent of VLSI fabrication techniques is erasing the line between circuits and computers. Is a 1-in. by ½-in. chip with a processor and 128-word memory (Fig. 2-8) on it a computer? Of course it is. And there is a great difference in how a computer is to be treated than how a circuit is to be treated. For good reasons; computers need programs.

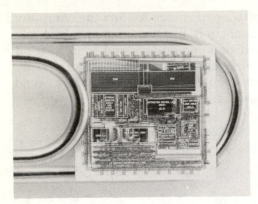

Figure 2-8. A one-chip computer. (Courtesy of Bell Laboratories)

SOFTWARE COST PER UNIT

With computers costing so little, we find them embedded everywhere. They are in toys, autos, TVs, copiers, missiles, tools, machines — everywhere. And there too is the program.

When we develop *one* program and run that program on thousands of computers, we divide the development cost of the program by the number of computers to get a unit cost for the program. There is essentially no *production* cost; we merely *copy* the program.

Thus, a program can be a trivial cost of every TV set — *one* program on 500,000 chips, one each in 500,000 TV sets! Or software can be the major cost of a satellite control system, where one computer is used to control the satellite and the communication flows. (See Fig. 2-9.)

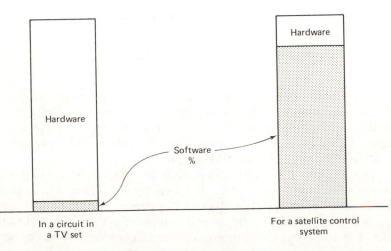

Figure 2-9. Software as a percent of total system cost.

PERFORMANCE CONCEPTS

SOFTWARE AND HARDWARE

It is the purpose of software to make hardware do work. Software without hardware does not operate and vice versa. Limited hardware can double the software development task.

There are some ideas and definitions of hardware and performance which will help us to define nuances between advanced concepts; e.g., multiprocessing and multiprogramming, between networks and distributed processing. As computers move into the operations/process area, the performance goals get more complex. We must often set the programmers to the task of eeking out more and more performance from our engine, the computer.

A large system ($40 million worth of equipment) got in trouble because the top management did not understand how the computer system (hardware and software) was to be optimized. They confused two different measures of performance: *throughput* and *turnaround*.

When we talk about the performance of a computer system, we must be clear about what measures we are using and to what we are applying our measures.

This is a critical point. Magnificent hardware can be hobbled by bad software, and vice versa. An inefficient operating system (see page 49) has frustrated many a superb, high performance machine. It is the job of the software development manager to *blend* the hardware and software into an efficient system.

The pursuit of performance is one of the things that greatly complicates software development. If our hardware is barely up to the task we have for it, then the burden of squeezing out the last drops of performance is borne by the software developer — at a great increase in cost *for the software development.*

THERE IS NO ONE MEASURE OF COMPUTER HARDWARE PERFORMANCE!

"Is computer A better than computer B? . . . faster than computer B?" This is akin to asking if the Chevrolet Model X is better than the Ford Model Y. The only response to such a question is "In what regard? Style? Cost? Performance in terms of mileage? In terms of handling? Comfort? Size? Durability? Reliability?" An automobile is a system of thousands of parts that yield many dimensions of service to the user. And the auto can be configured to optimize some of these services, but only at the expense of some others. The same is true of the computer.

Measuring Internal Speed

If we start by looking at the internal speed of a computer, we find that the time it takes to perform each instruction is one of the basic measures of the machine. Each instruction takes some length of time to execute, from start to finish. A *multiply* takes much longer than an *add.* These instructions are often grouped into "mixes" in order to obtain a rough measurement of internal speed. There are many mixes; usually there are "scientific mixes" and "commercial mixes."

A Scientific Mix	A Commercial Mix
15 Multiplies	5 Multiplies
13 Divides	2 Divides
25 Adds	25 Adds
22 Subtracts	18 Subtracts
12 Stores	14 Stores
2 Reads	8 Reads
2 Prints	8 Prints
8 Conditional Branches	14 Conditional Branches
2 Unconditional Branches	6 Unconditional Branches
100 Instructions	100 Instructions

Note that there are three times as many multiplies in my scientific mix, and one/fourth as many reads and prints.

A machine may do much better than its competitor on one mix

	Scientific mix	Commercial mix
Machine A	0.0028	0.0024
Machine B	0.0054	0.0018

Time in seconds

Figure 3-1. An example of computer performance — scientific vs. commercial mix.

comparison and do worse than it on the other comparison. (See Fig. 3-1.)

KIPS and MIPS. KIPS means thousands (kilo) of instructions per second. MIPS stands simply for millions of instructions per second. A two-MIP computer (the "S" on MIPS is sometimes dropped) can execute two million instructions in one second, based on a certain mix of instructions to be run. A machine will be at a lower MIP rate for scientific mixes than for commercial mixes.

We have been terming MIPS and KIPS as *internal* because they do not measure at all the input/output capabilities of the computer, nor the effect of memory size, nor the effect of the word size of the machine. Instruction timing has a meaning even in the most parallel of machines.

When the IBM 360 line came out in 1964, the Model 70 (it existed briefly before it was displaced by the 75) was the largest (most powerful) model; the model 30 was the smallest.

Fred Brooks, the architect of the 360 line, writing in the *IBM Systems Journal* in 1964 stated:

> The CPU's of the various models yielded a substantial range in performance. Relative to the smallest model (Model 30), the internal performance of the largest (Model 70) is approximately 50:1 for scientific computation and 15:1 for commercial data processing.

Note the significant change in the comparison when the commercial workload is measured. These internal measures of a computer are not very exact, but are widely used as a means of approximating the power of the computer.

External Measures

More useful than MIPS are the concepts of throughput and turn-around. These are measures of the entire machine, not only the internal instructions. The balance of the input and output units with the power of the central processing unit becomes important here. Too little input/output and the processing unit starves for work; too little processing

29

and the input/output units wait to move the data to their assigned tasks.

Throughput.   Throughput is the amount of work that can be processed by a computer in a given time. For example, we may have 400 jobs written in Fortran. We run them on Computer A and it does them all in 10 hours. On Computer B they are all done in 8 hours. Computer B has 20 percent better throughput than Computer A.

Throughput is dependent on many things.

1. Hardware. The machine configuration, the power of the CPU; the size and speed of the memory; the number of channels, of tape drives, of disks; the instruction set.
2. Software. The operating system manages the resources of the system. If it does so efficiently, the throughput should be good. Inefficient, it can hobble even a great machine.

Memory size has a great effect on throughput. If the memory size is small, then both it and the CPU must take time out from real work to rearrange the data within the various hierarchies of memory (disks, etc.).

Without doing anything to any other part of the computer, adding more main memory reduces this movement and therefore yields time to do real work. Memory has always been recognized as the key to the computer's performance. Von Neumann stated this in his 1946 memo; it is still true.

It is very difficult to predict throughput. There are just so many variables!

There are no metrics for throughput; there is only relative throughput. Throughput can be measured in terms of a set of specific jobs per unit of time, but only estimated in absence of a specific set.

Throughput is a measure of the total system: the CPU, the memory, the tape drives, the software, and the operators. It is a measure of the work *put through* the computing system.

Throughput versus MIPs as a Computer Measure.   Contrast throughput with MIPs. MIPs is a measure of the internal speed of the computer hardware, of the CPU and the memory. It is a measure of the time it takes to execute instructions; it does not consider at all the tape drives, the channels, or the software.

Throughput is a measure of the whole computer system and its components, and of the software driving the hardware.

Professional computer people should be careful not to mix these two concepts. To discuss MIPS as throughput is simply WRONG, as a 1.2-MIP, 16-bit machine can deliver much more throughput than a 1.2-MIP, 8-bit machine, assuming the same I/O and software.

Turnaround. There is yet another measure used with computer systems — turnaround.

The time that elapses from the moment a programmer hands in a program to be run and when he or she gets back the result is called turnaround time. The smaller, the better.

> Turnaround is not the same as throughput

Decreasing turnaround time, a desired objective, probably cuts down throughput, an undesired result. Batching jobs increases throughput, but increases turnaround time.

Emphasizing turnaround means that we are trying to optimize the engineer's or programmer's time. Emphasizing throughput means we are trying to reduce the machine cost of running the task through the computer.

"Instant" turnaround is achieved in most time sharing systems. A user, sitting at an input/output device, types in commands and data. The computer, handling up to hundreds of such users, is fast enough to switch from user to user so that each user seems to have the whole computer. A great deal of "shuffling" is being done by the computer: Input user 10's data here; get programmer 47's program; print 9's; put 197's data here; 177 wants to get on, etc., etc.) This shuffling is not real work but overhead.

In systems that are not time shared, turnaround is usually measured in hours. How many hours between the time I turn in my program and the time I get my results back? Sometimes it may be 24 hours — the computer is optimized for *throughput*.

Response Time. Response time is a concept close to turnaround, but not quite the same. It is the time it takes for the computer to "answer" me, if I am a user at a terminal, on-line to the computer. Here I am not a programmer, but a user. I am using the computer to do my job. Response time is usually measured as the time it takes from the instant I release the input button to the instant the response *begins* to be displayed to me on a TV-like scope or printer.

The New York City Police dispatching system (Dial 911), called "SPRINT," was successfully programmed by my group in IBM's Federal System Division. We were bedeviled because the corporation had succumbed to the demand to guarantee a 3-second response time. There were 96 dispatch (TV) positions manned by policemen. The

IBM Model 50 we were using could drive that many scopes only with great difficulty. Our programmers had to perform minor miracles to get the 3 seconds. We lost over $200,000 on a $2,000,000 job. The software developers knew they could not predict the response time of such a complicated system in advance. They had refused to accept the contract with the 3-second stipulation. Management had accepted it.

This "extra mile" by the software developers is very common. When the system doesn't have enough CPU or memory, the developers work harder and longer — and the cost of the software goes up. They "design" ways around the hardware slowness. They re-do programs.

Instruction Sets and Their Influence on Performance.   The Turing machine had only six instructions. It could do any job, but it places a terrible burden on the programmer if the set of possible instructions is so small. One of the economic decisions that every computer manufacturer must make is how many different instructions the computer should be built to decode and perform. The set of instructions a computer will recognize is called its "repertoire," or Instruction Set Architecture (ISA).

Today's large computers have well over 300 different instructions they recognize and perform. It is hard for programmers to master such a "vocabulary." It can take months or even years before the programmer has learned the instructions and how to use them efficiently. Only half of the instruction set of the IBM 7090 was regularly used.

There is an unanswerable question of which machine is easier to program; the large one with a big repertoire or the small one with a limited repertoire. Like so many questions in the computer field, the answer "depends" on the details. A small, simple job may be easier to program on a small, few-instruction computer. A large complicated job may be easier to program on a "rich" vocabulary machine. And it all depends on which type of machine the programmers are accustomed to using. We once had a group in Houston, Texas, very experienced with the large IBM 360 Model 75, develop software for the small IBM System 7. It was a disaster! They didn't understand the limitations of the machine, approached the problem incorrectly, used the wrong tools. It just took a year — and one hell of a lot of money — before they got the hang of it. And they were good, experienced software developers.

The opposite also occurs. Taking a group who have been using a limited instruction set and moving them to the "rich" instruction set usually results in disaster also. They can't handle the richness — at first — anywhere near as well as people used to it. Productivity is awful.

Theoretically, a large repertoire is more efficient in use, and in the development stages also. But don't assume that this is always so.

Benchmarks.   The best way to measure a computer is to run *your* programs on the machine and, with a stopwatch, measure the time it takes to run.

It is difficult and expensive to do this. Some jobs may not have been programmed yet and must be programmed to do the measurement. Representative jobs should be selected to be actually run on several computers. These runs are called *benchmarks*.

What does a benchmark measure? *Everything* in the computer system — the hardware, the individual programs (and therefore the skill of the programmer who developed each program), the compilers, the software, the I/O units, the word size, the repertoire, the operating system, the operators.

Just because Computer A beats Computer B, do not jump to the conclusion that its hardware is faster. Poor software may be holding down a superb machine in Computer B.

BALANCING A SYSTEM

To run a computer system efficiently we have to balance the system for its tasks — the right amount of processing for the right amount of input/output and vice versa. And the system must have good software. A well-balanced system will have most of its units operating simultaneously.

Figure 3-2 is a visual summary of performance concepts.

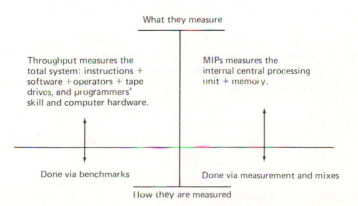

Figure 3-2.   Throughput and MIPS as performance measures.

A TAXONOMY OF SOFTWARE

BREAKING SOFTWARE INTO DIGESTIBLE PIECES

How do we cope with the diversity of the computer? By categorizing and cataloging, by breaking things into parts and pieces that are useful. And that is precisely what we are about to do in this chapter with software.

We have already seen that all computers can be broken into many categories of use, and we have enumerated five. These five are useful in understanding the stresses and strains put on the software. They can be contrasted to the catalog of software with useful results, as we will see.

Here is a taxonomy of software that will be useful in discussing and understanding the problems in the development, use, and continued development of software in large and complex systems.

As we saw, five types of use of software-driven systems are:

Type I	Data processing use
Type II	Scientific problem solving use
Type III	Inquiry system use
Type IV	On-line problem solving use
Type V	Operations/process use

TAXONOMY OF SOFTWARE

The three phases of the life of a software system are:

1. Development phase
2. Use phase
3. Continued development phase (erroneously called maintenance)

The three types of software are:

1. Applications software
2. Support software
3. Systems software

The three attributes of software applications are:

1. Software scale
2. Software complexity
3. Software clarity

The two classes of software are:

1. Project software
2. Product software
   a. The software product
   b. The hardware product with differentiating flexible software
   c. The hardware product with some software

There are some at this point who may say "Of course. This is obvious!" I wish it were. I constantly find people in the trade who do not make distinctions between many of these classes, types, and so on. The separations are useful in communication about software *and* in managing software.

We will now go through each of the parts of the taxonomy to briefly explain what is meant, and not meant, by the categorization.

Life Cycle of a Program

There are three phases (Fig. 4-1) in the life of a program:

1. Development
2. Use
3. Continued development (or support)

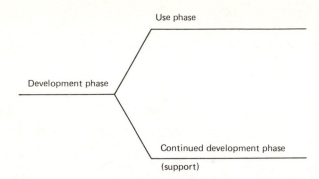

Figure 4-1. Three phases in the life of a program.

The phase that is most troublesome is the first, development, and therefore we will spend most of our time on it. Yet, in large programs the cost of the continued development phase is often (but not always) more than 50 percent of the total life cycle cost.

The use phase is the payoff, and if we have developed well, the use of the software should be smooth and harmonious. Note that the continued development phase is concurrent with the use phase. Note also that we do not use the word "maintenance." Maintenance is the commonly used term for this function. It is incorrect.

You cannot maintain software because it cannot fail, and maintenance implies failure. Instructions, if once correct, cannot fail on their own, the way a wire can. A wire can break, separate, or lose its resistance. An instruction cannot wear out.

Two things explain why the function of continuing development is necessary. First, there are some errors in all large software that will not be detected in test. We'll show why in the section on testing in Chap. 5. And the system must change. A new tax is levied and the payroll program must be changed.

Maintenance is a derogatory word. It is less exciting to work in maintenance than development, and few are content to work there. Yet in software, this area is often more challenging than the original development.

Not only must the continuing developers (not maintainers) add new functions and correct the difficult and subtle errors that slipped past the original development team, they must usually be detectives tracking down the design used, but *not clearly recorded*, by the original developers.

The reason for showing a use phase is that in many large systems a number of people are constantly interacting with the system. The system may be easy to use — user friendly — or difficult to use. It may be resistant to people errors — robust — or not. These qualities should not be accidents of the development process. They should be carefully designed attributes of the program, but they are seen in operation only during the use phase.

We shall see in Chap. 5 that there are 12 different aspects of every program. Some of those aspects relate to use, some to development, and some to continued development.

The terminology we employ to designate the use portion of the life cycle should not present us with any problem, but it does. Some people call it one thing, some others.

Some call it the "operational" phase, and "operational software." The term "run time" or "run phase" is common, as is "production phase" or "production time" (Fig. 4-2).

All three phases may be active at the same time on one computer. From one part of memory, the payroll program is being executed—use.

USE	PRODUCTION SOFTWARE
TIME	⎰ OPERATIONAL SOFTWARE
SOFTWARE	RUN TIME SOFTWARE

Figure 4-2.   Synonyms for use time software.

In another part of memory, an interactive compiler is being executed in a development effort. In a third, an "automatic build" is being performed by a support group.

This is confusing! To make sense of it we need to view the life cycle *of a program*, not of the computer installation! In this view, and for definition of the phase, it is unimportant what else is running when the program we are interested in is running.

If I am to build a steel hammer then I have the life cycle shown in Fig. 4-3. There is no repair part of the life of a hammer. If it breaks we get a new one. Yet we must design the hammer so that it is easy to use.

Build   Use

Figure 4-3.   Life cycle of a hammer.

With a bicycle we have a case where we do have a support or "fixing" part of the life cycle. Wear and tear make us put new parts into the bicycle so it will work. (See Fig. 4-4.)

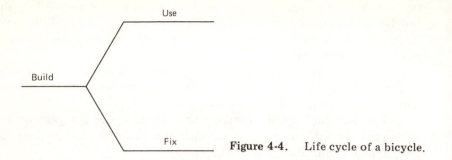

Figure 4-4. Life cycle of a bicycle.

With an office building we have a life cycle where we not only have to fix the building if something breaks, but we must *change* it as organizations grow and shrink, come and go. We must knock down walls, add walls, rebalance the heating system, rewire the electrical circuits, etc. (See Fig. 4-5.)

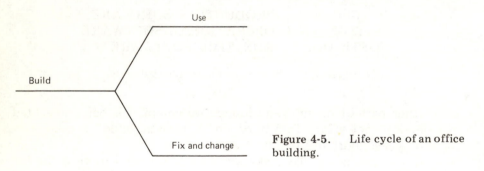

Figure 4-5. Life cycle of an office building.

Obviously if we know we are going to change the building we should take care to put into the building initially (and into its documentation) the things to make it easy to modify. This is *front-end investment* that will make change easy to fix and change.

Note that in Fig. 4-6, we switch to software and we change the label on the lower right portion of the diagram to "change" instead of "fix" and we change "build" to "develop."

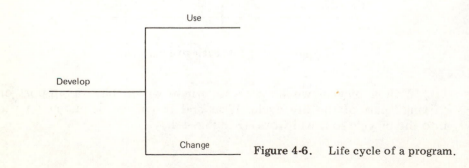

Figure 4-6. Life cycle of a program.

However, Fig. 4-7 is more accurate for the software life cycle, especially large software. There are errors that remain in the original software, persisting through the testing phase, only to be discovered when the recipient begins to use the software. Therefore the effort done is really continuing the development that was started but never really finished.

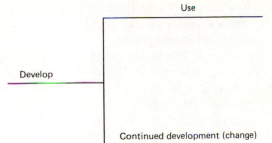

Figure 4-7.   Life cycle of software.

Contrast Fig. 4-7 to Fig. 4-8 to see the profound difference between the *hardware life cycle* and the *software life cycle*.

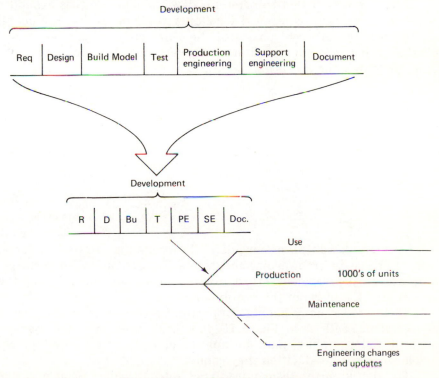

Figure 4-8.   Life cycle of hardware.

In Fig. 4-8 we see that there is a production phase, production engineering, and support engineering in hardware development.

The parts of the hardware development, especially the production engineering effort, tell us a great deal. Engineers investigate the product that is to be built and work diligently to streamline it so that factory production costs *per unit* will be minimized. Thus the product rolling off a production line is usually significantly different from the one that resulted from the development phase. But software has no production and there is no production engineering.

The other function in hardware development is support engineering. Here engineers make changes in the device that will make it easier to fix or change *when it is in* the *use* environment. The field support requirements for people, parts, training, and test procedures are minimized to the maximum extent possible by this effort. Software development also should have this support engineering as a major piece of its development effort. Too often the delivery date imposes such a constraint that *all* the development effort is thrown into achieving the date, and no effort is put forth to minimize continued development efforts. Correct development of software has a support engineering part, as we will see.

Another reason that so often no development effort is expended to reduce the future continued development effort is that the people who manage the different phases of the effort are not the same. Figure 4-9 shows that in some cases the management of all three pieces is the same. But this is the exception.

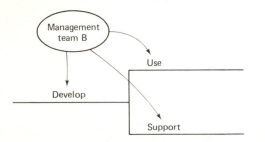

Figure 4-9. One management team for all phases of the life cycle.

In many cases, the arrangement shown in Fig. 4-10 is in force. There are three different managements, one for each phase. The management of the development effort doesn't worry too much about the support effort, as it is not their problem.

There are so many possible opportunities for error with different managements. Path A in Fig. 4-10 goes both ways, and the management of the use phase must be able to articule to the development people what is wanted. Often they cannot.

The development team must be able to articulate what it is that

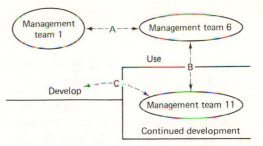

Figure 4-10. Three management teams; one life cycle.

the use-time people can use and how to use it. This is imperfect in many cases, with less than full instructions for use.

The same is true with path C, with the added problem that often the team to perform continued development is not even in existence when the development is under way. Too often no one looks out for their interests.

Path B is usually free and clear, but it too is often ignored until trouble sets in!

Pathological Software Life Cycles

Let us draw the simple model of the software life cycle two different ways in order to make fundamental points. Showing the life of software this way (Fig. 4-11), clearly shows a break between development and continued development. In many cases there are entirely separate organizations responsible for each. A group in New England, a contractor, develops; and a group in the South maintains. The dotted line between development and continued development depicts that this is not a smooth or easy transition. Indeed in too many cases we could draw the life model like Fig. 4-12.

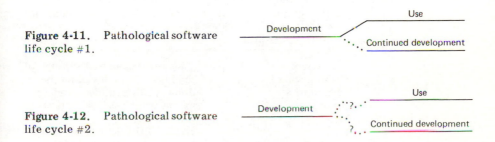

Figure 4-11. Pathological software life cycle #1.

Figure 4-12. Pathological software life cycle #2.

There is often too big a disjuncture between the developers and the continued developers in time, geographical location, philosophy, organization, talent, and staffing. And quite often a delay in time of getting the use started after development is finished.

These models imply a one-time development with a distinct finish, and this is the case in type I and type II programs.

Emphasizing Continuity Between Development and Continued Development

We could draw the model as shown in Fig. 4-13 to show that there may be great continuity between the developers and the continued developers; indeed, they may be one and the same. This is especially true in type V programs where there is evolutionary development with dozens of releases "finished" over time.

Use

Development / Continued development

Figure 4-13. Software life cycle where developer does continued development.

Is there a difference in the task of development versus continued development? Yes, but nowhere near the difference most people imagine or believe. My associate, Andy Ferrentino (who drew my attention to the Fig. 4-13 depiction), listened to a computer science doctoral applicant explain that his thesis was to be on the difference between development and "maintenance." Andy pointed out that the software generation environment should be essentially the same for both activities. These activities are only slightly different from each other. Let's look at them stage by stage.

TABLE 4-1   The Differences Between Development and Continued Development.

Development	Continued Development
1. Requirements definition for type Vs, very difficult as the system probably never existed before	For type Vs, easier, as the user now is *using* and is much more knowledgeable about requirements.
(For types I and II, the requirement job is about the same)	
2. Design wide open. Fashion what is best. Start at the top.	Easier since the system exists, much of the higher level design has been done and determines to a large extent what must be done at lower levels. Harder if the documentation is bad; An Archeological Hunt ensues
3. Programming The same	The same
4. Construction The same	The same
5. Testing The same	The same
6. Documentation The same	The same

Develop Software to Maximize All Phases of the Life Cycle

Most software development efforts, if diagrammed (in Fig. 4-14) so that the size of the letter depicted the amount of requirements and design effort that went for it, would show that development dwarfs use, and support is rarely considered.

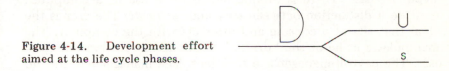

Figure 4-14.   Development effort aimed at the life cycle phases.

This is usually absolutely the wrong way to allocate development effort. It persists because the system developers continue to delude themselves into thinking that the software will be developed in one Big Bang, one effort, and it's done. This fiction persists for many reasons, which we'll get to.

What happens in most projects is that half to three-fourths of the promised function is delivered, and the project is celebrated as a success. The product is shipped, or the satellite goes up. The missing function will be added later, under the guise of maintenance. Little or no effort has been expanded in support engineering, to make the continued development easier. Not enough effort has been expended to make the system more acceptable to the user.

The USE Phase of the Cycle

Although the use phase of the life cycle comes after the development phase, it is, or should be, *the* determining part of the cycle. Its characteristics set the strategy of much of the other two phases of the cycle. Let us list a few different characteristics of *use* that help determine some of the development strategy.

Periodicity of Use.   I may develop a program to run every day, or every week, or every month, or once a year. Or I may develop it to run constantly, all the time. Or I may develop it to run once and only once and then throw it away. The efficiency with which the program exercises the hardware (e.g., memory used) is very important if the program runs constantly, and totally unimportant if it runs once, or once a year.

Number of Users.   I may develop the program to be used by my company and no other user. Or I may develop it to run in 500 of my branch offices. Or I may intend it for a thousand different small companies, each of whom may and probably will use it in slightly different ways. Once again the care and the features I insist on in my program differ greatly among these different user sets. Five hundred different users stress a program far more than 500 "same" users (my branch offices use the system in the same way).

Type of Use.   There is on-line and off-line use of a computer. Let us make a distinction between *user* and *recipient*. The user is the individual that sits at a console and interacts with the computer. The user manipulates it; he or she "drives" it. The airline reservation clerk is a user. The payroll manager is a recipient. The manager requires no interaction with the computing system as it is working on the problem of calculating the payroll and printing out the checks.

In the mode of use that has a human interacting with the system in an on-line manner, the software must be written so that the user can interact easily with the machine. This is much more than just the inquiry itself; the system must be made user-friendly in order to get the most from the human. The programs must be written so that the system prompts the user what to do when the system is given less than clear instructions.

Penalty of Failure Difference by Use.   In some systems the failure of the computer for a few hours is inconvenient, but acceptable. In some the loss of the computer for only a few minutes is potentially disastrous. In the latter case we install extra hardware. But the extra hardware is the easy part. We must also put in programs to save the critical data and to move the critical data from one computer unit to the next. This must often be done in seconds, not minutes. This is very intricate software. A program that controls traffic lights in a city is an easy task; if the program can never fail, the software is at least three times as hard to develop.

The range of complex software stretches from a $50,000,000 per year cost center servicing 460 scientists on-line, where 90 percent of all programs are run once and only once, to a control system where the software runs 365 days per year, 24 hours per day, and cannot fail and is updated very infrequently — once per year.

The Development Phase of the Life Cycle

The development phase of the life cycle can be broken into six distinct efforts:

- Requirements definition
- Design
- Writing the instructions
- Construction
- Testing, or verification
- Documentation

Since development is the area of the greatest problem in software for the foreseeable future, we will spend most of the remainder of the book on these six efforts.

The Continued Development Phase of the Life Cycle

This area is usually called maintenance, as we have seen. It is often the most ignored piece of the life cycle, left to be taken care of by some new and often unnamed team. One of the key ideas we will stress is that this piece of the cycle must be taken into consideration from the very beginning of the development effort.

Continued Development Tasks.   The effort performed by the support team is continued development. Its tasks are:

1. Add New Functions. New software functions are added to existing programs. For example, if a union is elected, we must begin to withhold dues, and the program to do that is added to the payroll program.
2. Function Updates. Existing functions are extended or changed. For example, a changed state tax law is passed, and the section of the program that performed correctly for the old law is amended with new parameters for the new tax provisions. Also, when we first delivered the software, we perhaps did not deliver all the user specified functions; we add these functions with an update, or "release."
3. Equipment Updates. New hardware is added to the system. For example, new terminals with better resolution are installed. The function does not change but we need new programs to control the new displays.
4. Error Correction. The users find "errors" in the program, and they must be corrected. For example, "When FICA withholding ceases on the same day as hospital deductions start, the two amounts get printed in each other's spaces on the pay stub."

Continued-Development Effort Product:

1. Correction programs to correct functions incorrectly implemented
2. Updates, new software, to add functions for requirements known to be needed but postponed when the software was developed
3. Updates, new software, to add functions to perform new requirements not in the original requirement documentation

The difference between 2 and 3 is subtle but very important. Number 2 says that the continued development team only needs to interpret the original, documented requirement. Number 3 requires that the continued development team *actually generate* the requirement. This is fundamentally different from just interpreting a requirement. It requires different skills, different people, and different organization to define requirements than it does to do the other efforts of continuing development.

THREE TYPES OF SOFTWARE

All software can be separated into three overall types:

1. Applications software
2. Systems software
3. Support software

The first two run at use time, and the third, support, runs at development time. Systems software also runs at development time.

1. Applications software. The programs that actually do the job that we are out to do; for example: payroll, inventory, message switching, reservations, navigation.
2. Systems software. The programs that run at use time with applications software. Systems software manages the resources of the computer, i.e. the disks, the main memory, the tapes, the CPU. The software known as an operating system falls into this category, as does data base management systems (DBMS). We will go into both of these in depth a bit later on in this section.
3. Support software. The programs that help programmers and management to create the software that runs at use time. Compilers and assemblers are the most well known of this category.

TABLE 4-2.   Three Types of Software

To make the computer do your job, you develop *application software*.

To make the computer do many applications efficiently and to fit the environment, you develop *systems software*.

To help you develop software, you use *support software*.

Applications Software

The most visible body of software is the application programs. Payrolls, inventories, bridge design, missile control, stress calculations, trajectory calculation, weather forecasting, accounting — these are just some of the thousands of computer application programs.

This type of software is (1) the easiest to develop and (2) the area in which the overwhelming majority of software developers are at work.

Most applications software is created by employees of the organizations that will use the software at use time. Some application software is created by software companies, either under contract to the eventual user, or as a product to be sold to users.

Application programs are usually written by people who understand the process that is being automated. Payroll programs are often produced by people from the payroll department, for example.

As the programmer shortage gets worse, there will be more and more "standard" application packages used by organizations. A standard package is a program written in such a way that more than one user can use it. There are limitations on the flexibility of the package, but this is often acceptable. This area of programming packages or products is one of the fastest growing segments of the software industry.

Application specialization can take place by industry, or across industry. Figure 4-15 shows a range of software entities. All users would use the hardware, almost all would use the systems software. Some piece of the application software packages, either developed by themselves or by a supplier, or purchased as a standard would be used with the systems software and hardware.

Systems Software

Systems software is used to manage the computer at use (run) time and at development time. The use of the computer to *control* itself and its environment is a logical application of the computer, as opposed to a data or numbers use. This type of use introduces a new

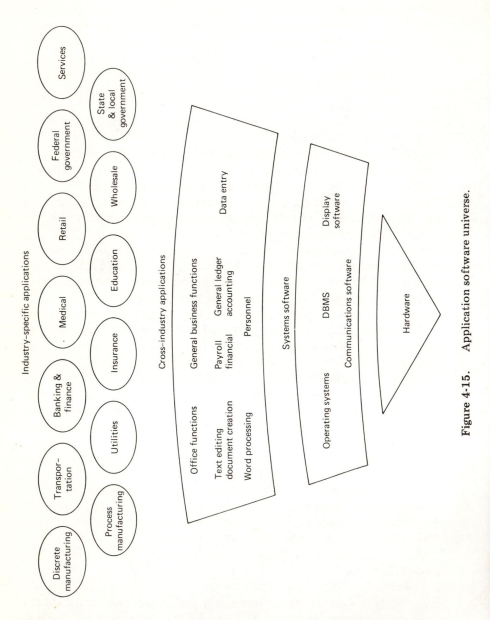

Industry-specific applications

Discrete manufacturing · Transportation · Banking & finance · Medical · Retail · Federal government · Services

Process manufacturing · Utilities · Insurance · Education · Wholesale · State & local government

Cross-industry applications

Office functions · General business functions

Text editing document creation · Payroll financial · General ledger accounting · Data entry

Word processing · Personnel

Systems software

Operating systems · DBMS · Display software

Communications software

Hardware

Figure 4-15. Application software universe.

kind of complexity into software, and we will explore this complexity later in this chapter.

Systems programs are the most difficult programs to develop and the toughest to visualize and understand. Systems programs are more complex by far than applications programs, and more complex than support programs.

Systems software is that body of programs that are used to manage:

1. The dynamic scheduling of the hardware units of the computer. Which job coming in can use which units of the machine? When? In what order or priority? A large and complex set of programs, called an operating system, running on the machine at use time, makes these decisions, and controls the use of the computer.

2. The use time environment requirements. If our working system cannot be "off the air" for more than 30 seconds, we cannot leave it up to human operators to fix problems that quickly; they can not. But the computer can, and so we *write programs* that will monitor all hardware units of the system, determine whether they are operating correctly, and if not, *the operating system* restructures the hardware configuration of the machine (it has spare units) to enable it to continue to operate even though a unit has malfunctioned.

An Operating System. An *operating system*, the most common form of systems programming, is a large set of programs.

The operating system has become almost ubiquitous. And the amount of dollars spent to create and update an operating system is staggering. IBM has probably put $3 billion into its operating systems, and is still spending.

Yet few understand the immense function provided by these systems programs, or how many programs they provide for users to run, or how much easier they make it for the user to get the computer doing the job.

The operating system has evolved over the years from relatively simple to incredibly complex software that today helps the programmer, helps the computer room manager, and helps the operator. Today, an operating system:

1. "Manages" the hardware.
   a. It (the software called the operating system) handles machine failures, routes work, handles recovery and restart procedures. It handles interrupts from other machines, clocks, operators,

etc. (This function was done by the operator before operating systems.)

b. It schedules the work on the machine, "deciding" to put job 147 on next because there are enough tape drives, or disk drives, or main memory, or printers, or any machine resources. It keeps track of what is being used and what is coming in. It schedules! In this role it manages the use of the translators, (compilers), and the input/output. (This function was formerly done by the machine room manager.)

c. It decides on the priority of the jobs to be run. (This was done by the machine room manager.)

2. Supplies programs to do functions that are required to run the applications programs.

a. It contains sorts and printouts and load programs, eliminating the need for every programmer to write his or her own version. (Used to be done by the program written by application programmers.) (Sometimes these functions are considered part of an operating system; sometimes they are not).

b. It links programs together, so that many separate pieces of programs written perhaps by different programmers will run from end to end. (Used to be done by programs written by application programmer.)

3. Manages the data storage, and retrieval, that the application programs need in order to function (called Data Management.)

a. The application programmer writes instructions that ask the operating system for data. The data may be identified specifically or abstractly, *but the physical storage details* are not specified. The operating system provides (inserts) instructions that make the computer store, get, replace, etc., the data. (Used to be done by the programs written by application programmers.) This results in information hiding and in device independence. It allows users and manufacturers to add newer, faster, cheaper physical files *without* having to rewrite the individual application programs. (Sometimes this area of software is considered separate from operating systems. It is always considered systems software.)

4. Manages the communication (e.g., via telephone line) functions of the program/computer.

a. It handles messages into and out of the computer using standard communications lines and networks. (Used to be done by programs written by application programmer.)

5. Manages the interaction with users (at terminals, TV tubes.)

a. It provides instructions that allow the computer to be used in an interactive way by users via standard display hardware. (Used to be done by programs written by applications programmer.)

6. Protects the system.

a. It protects its own programs from "pollution" by raw, new programs being entered into the system. (Did not used to be done.)

b. It does back-up functions, double storing, switching, diagnostics and other tests. (Used to be done manually, by maintenance personnel — very slowly.)

Operating systems have been evolving for some time. The *IBM System Journal* of 1966 has an article by G.H. Mealy on the "Functional Structure of the OS/360 Operating System." Mealy points out that "the notion of an operating system dates back at least to 1953 and MIT's Summer Session Computer and Utility System." The operating system "then as now . . . aimed at nonstop operation over a span of many jobs and provided a computer-accessible library of utility programs."

(The operating system got its name because at first it helped the *operator* keep the machine running nonstop by doing "set up" functions formerly performed by the operator.)

The main objective of OS/360, the author stated, was to be "equally applicable to batched-job and real time applications." (It did not achieve the real time aim.) The secondary objectives were:

- Increased throughput
- Lowered response time
- Increased programmer productivity
- Adaptability
- Expandability

All but the first help the programmer. Under productivity, we find that "OS aims to provide a novel degree of versatility through a relatively large set of source languages." Device independence is an aim; new hardware is to be handled automatically without application programmer effort! Included among the functions that OS/360 will *do for* the programmer are linking together pieces of a large program, sorts, and input/output jobs. Eight different options for having the operating system handle the data storing and retrieving are described. *Eight*! The programmer not only no longer has to create the code to do this function, but he or she has a wide range of options to tell OS how to do it.

Data Base Management Systems. There is great confusion in the field about data base management systems. They are so powerful and provide such a range of functions that many confuse their real purpose with "accidental" functions they perform.

The greatest benefit of a data base management system is that *changes to the software* are far, far easier to accomplish. DBMS makes it much much easier to change the applications programs, the data file logical structure, and the data file physical structure. In many cases it makes the difference between a change being made or abandoned.

A second reason for a DBMS is to save file space. A third reason is to enhance file integrity, that is to make it easier to assure that the files do not get "out of synch." This is a direct fall out of the fewer number of files. A fourth reason is to make it easy to retrieve data. Many erroneously think this fourth reason the prime reason.

How a DBMS Works: The Automechanic Analogy. To understand a data base management systems (DBMS) let's look at an automobile repair business. When I start the business, I have three mechanics and each of the mechanics has his or her own tools. There are no standards. As we grow to eight mechanics, we begin to get inconsistency problems. The timer that Al used to set the timing on Mr. Z's car was different from all other timers — and when Mr. Z complained, I checked all the timers and found that they didn't work quite the same! The differences were disturbing! Which was "right"?

Step 1
I decreed standards for all tools. They had to be a certain make and model. Then, as we continued to grow, I found that timers were sitting unused as we had as many timers as we had mechanics.

Step 2
I established a separate tool room, where we kept expensive tools and released them, "signed them out," to individual mechanics who returned the timer when finished with the task. This cut down the number of timers needed, and eased the task of maintaining them and calibrating them.

Step 3
I found that we had so many timing jobs that I created a timing department. All timing jobs were done in that department, even if timing were only a part of the overall job to be done.

A similar thing happened in the world of software.
Each programmer had his or her own files at first, just as each mechanic had his or her own timer. The programmer had complete

dominion over his or her files. He or she decided their size, format and content.

There were three problems with this arrangement. First, it was very hard for any one programmer to get data from someone else's files. Second, when data values changed, say a part number was changed from a 12-digit number to a 14-digit number, *all programs* had to be changed. This was painful, expensive, and impossible in many cases. Third, Programmer A's data was not the same as Programmer B's. Which was correct?

Step 1
We decided on standards for the files — sizes, formats, sequences, and we made it easier for programmers to use someone else's files.

Step 2
We created central files that had rules and regulations about what the functions were and where the data was. In addition, we put all the data into a central store and allowed programmers to get the data if they followed the rules and asked for it correctly. Their programs interacted with *my* programs, and my programs controlled the files. My programs were systems software.

This corrected many ills.

1. It kept the data in a few files, saving space.
2. It made it easier to keep the data elements current.
3. It made it possible to change data file sizes (12-digit to 14-digit part number) without changing all the individual application programs.

It did all this by centralizing the getting and putting back of data *into one* program. The programmer still had to *know* a lot about the file, the contents, what the formats were, and how to ask precisely for what was wanted. Then it was found that there was no reason to saddle every programmer with knowing so much about the data.

Step 3
Data base management systems arrived. The large program that does all the manipulating of the data got bigger. No longer did the programmers have to know the details of the files. All they had to do was give identifying data and the data base management system, a large set of programs, did the rest.

The DBMS usually has with it other programs that (A) provide an easily used *display system* and (B) an easy *language* to inquire into the

TABLE 4-3   Data Base Management System Benefits

Description of the Problem	Attribute of Data Base Management Approach	Benefit
Data duplication, i.e., size of files	One file	Less disk
Duplicate data not the same; files do not match	One file	Data is more believable
Any change in file content or structure, in the physical devices or in the application code becomes a major re-development	Compartmentalization	Easier to make changes; no longer need to change applications programs.

file content. This is usually called an *inquiry language*. Step 3 is also an *information retrieval system*. Here the functions we have seen in Step 2 are refined *to help* in *finding* data. But this is a spin-off, a side product, of the effort to make change easier. It is *not* the main reason for the DBMS.

Table 4-3 summarizes the DBMS benefits.

The Use of Systems Software.   Two questions help us to focus on the role of systems software. Why do we have systems software? Do *all* computers have systems software?

The prime reason for systems software is to maximize the use of the computer! To keep it as busy as possible. To achieve this we write software to help the operator, to help the machine manager, and to help the programmer. But all of this is to maximize the use of the computer. Each of these helps keep the computer busy. A second reason for systems programs is to facilitate change. A third reason is to maximize the output of the programming staff, by avoiding duplication of programs.

In the early 1960s, measurements of the actual use of large scale computers showed, to the amazement of most, that the central processing unit was being utilized but 50 percent of the time. Operating systems have greatly increased this percentage!

The answer to the second question is no, not all computers operate with an operating system. All can, but not all do. Most do, probably 90 percent or more. We'll see later that in real time use, standard systems software is sometimes just too slow to use!

Clearly now the systems software is beginning to do things that before had been done by individual application programmers in applica-

TABLE 4-4   Functions Performed by System Software

System Function	Used to be Done By
1. Tape switching	Operators
2. Scheduling, prioritization resource allocation	Operators and machine room manager
3. Error recovery	Operators; programmers
4. I/O work	Application programmer
5. Data or file work	Application programmer
6. Communications work	Application programmer
7. Display work	Application programmer
8. Interactive work	Application programmer

tion programs. And both systems programs and applications programs run at use time. (See Table 4-4.) How then do we tell the difference between them?

Two criteria help us distinguish between application software and system software:

1. Where it came from. Was it developed by the application programmer, or a separate group charged with supporting the programs; or from the hardware manufacturer? Who supports the program?
2. Is it general, useable by many application programmers?

In use at use time, the programs done by applications programmers and by a separate systems programming group do not look different to an outside observer than if the entire job were done by the application programmer. But the differences at development time and continued-development time are very, very significant.

A Plethora of Operating Systems.   One of the confusing things about operating systems is that the use of them has evolved to the point that we now have operating system specialization.

There are operating systems to be used at use time, and there are those to be used at development time — for the same hardware. There are batch operating systems and transaction driven operating systems; there are real time operating systems; there are user-oriented operating systems, and there are mixtures of all of them in some installations.

Cost of Operating System.   Operating systems cost manufacturers millions, sometimes billions, to create and support. But they are often not priced separately from the computer hardware.

They "cost" at use time too; they eat up machine time and memory. Operating systems are used by thousands of users, so a very wide range of functions must be done. If I don't use some features, I can delete some of them from the operating system, but some I cannot. Therefore, the computer is doing things for me that are unnecessary, but it is usually still easier than my writing my own operating system or putting its functions into my application code.

Source of Systems Software.   More and more systems software is now being written by software companies or users, but the hardware manufacturers are still delivering most of it. Most data base management systems are separate from the operating system; they are used with an operating system, but developed separately, and often by a different vendor than the one who did the operating system.

Systems Software and Applications Software at Use Time.   The programs that actually calculate the payroll, guide the missile, track the airplane, write the check — these are the application programs.

Most applications programs are written to run with systems programs that will be controlling the machine and the use time environment, and providing common functions; e.g., printing. Look at the use time memory map of Fig. 4-16 — it shows the programs in the memory when the computer is executing the production jobs, doing the work that it was bought to do.

As we see, in Fig. 4-16 much of the memory space is occupied by systems programs that are managing the machine and external environment.

In most computer installations, the programs are written to fit with the operating system, work with it, run with it. The programmers and analysts employed by the ABC Manufacturing Company design and write the programs to do the company's payroll. When the computer runs the payroll job, the operating system software, other systems software, *and* the payroll program are operating at the same time.

As the job gets started, the operating system is the program being executed, setting up the job, telling the operators what tapes to mount on what tape drives, etc. Then the sequence is shifted and the payroll program is executed. If there is an interrupt (e.g., an error), the control unit switches the sequence back to the operating system and *it* handles the error, then passes control back to the payroll program.

But this is a simple use. In most installations, several or dozens of application jobs are in the memory at the same time.

In multiprogramming, the operating system manages dozens of applications programs simultaneously, allowing them to share the computer resources, maximizing the amount of work done in a given period of time. We'll see more about this in Chap. 7.

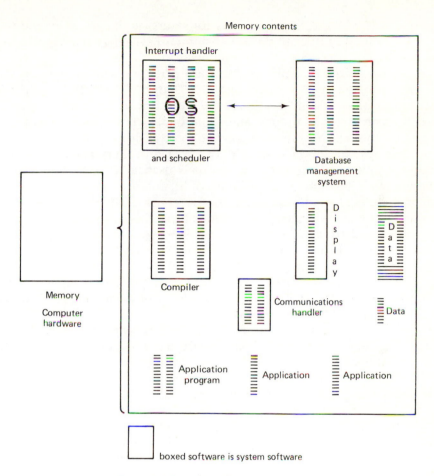

Interrupt handler

OS

and scheduler

Database
management
system

Compiler

Display

Data

Communications
handler

Data

Application
program

Application

Application

Memory

Computer
hardware

boxed software is system software

Figure 4-16. Use time memory map.

*A bad operating system can hobble good hardware, and a good
one can save poor hardware.* Systems programs are often slow simply
because there are thousands, even millions, of instructions in there to
handle a universe of possible users, data, etc. Sometimes they are slow
because they are poorly designed or poorly constructed.

Standard and Nonstandard Systems Software. *There are two
worlds — one uses standard systems software and one does not.* So
much effort and money has gone into operating systems and data base
management systems that they should be used if at all possible. To
write programs to perform these functions is very expensive.

Yet there is a portion of computer users that must write their own
systems programs -- the large real-time type V users. The need to finish
the cycle of processing in a given time frame -- milliseconds for defense,

FAA, and NASA users, and seconds for reservations systems — and the need for reliability rule out the use of standard systems software. Hence, many real time users must do it themselves.

Individualized systems programs are often written. Sometimes the systems programs can be used by more than one user. The PARS (or ACP) operating system developed by IBM for airline reservations is used by over a dozen airlines, and some banks. The PARS system had to be built because OS/360 was too big and too slow.

The system for helping Air Traffic Controllers manage the en-route air traffic was written once — but is used in 20 U.S. sites and at one United Kingdom site. OS/360 could not perform the reliability and scheduling functions required; FAA (via IBM Federal Systems Division) had to write their own systems programs.

This need to write a special systems program is one of the reasons large type V programs cost so much and take so long.

Recently, in two different books, I read the clear statement that said that computers do not fail. That is an absurd statement; of course computers fail. All electronic devices fail.

One author was attempting to show that when the excuse "the computer failed" is offered, it is usually a dodge; error is usually in the procedures or instructions.

Although I agree that "the computer did it" is one of the world's greatest cop-outs, to state that computers do not fail is very mischievous, especially in an introductory book.

Since management knows that computers will fail, it must put in place procedures to check for proper function. Anytime "the computer did it," poor management is at play, as *they* failed to properly protect the system through software and manual checks.

Management must use either standard or tailored systems software to assure correct, timely and fail-safe operation. It is being done regularly today.

From Batch to Real Time.   The transition from a batch system to a real time system does not require too much change in the application coding and logic. Ballistic trajectories are ballistic trajectories. What it does necessitate is a major revamping of the systems software.

So often this major effort is not foreseen, usually with disastrous consequences. People think that since they are running batch programs, it will be easy to move to the real time systems. Schedules are not met; cost targets are not met.

In real time use, time itself must be managed. In the batch en-vironment, data (e.g., radar data collected on magnetic tape) is read into the computer and processed. As long as all the data is processed in 24 hours — or in a week — then the computer has done its job. Time is not a factor.

But in real time, the radar *must* be processed in, say, 6 seconds or the system rejects vital data. So the operating system *must* schedule so as to process *all* the data in 6 seconds. Period. And of course reliability functions (back-up and recovery) must be programmed.

The move from a fine batch systems to a real time system is a *major* undertaking.

Benefits of Systems Software

1. Systems software increases modularity and information hiding, making changes to software far, far easier.
2. Systems software eliminates the need for a large amount of application programming by supplying standard programs.
3. Systems software maximizes the use of the hardware, by reducing idle time.
4. Systems software maximizes storage space by avoiding file duplication.

Disadvantages of Systems Software

1. Speed of execution of systems software is slower than tailored software, as it is general-purpose software.
2. Systems software is large, complex, and often difficult to use properly.
3. Systems software does not always have the flexibility to meet particular needs.

Summary of System Software.   We lose speed, storage space, and flexibility in order to gain schedule, avoid generating new code, avoid introducing more errors with new code, and ease of making changes. Systems software has been a great boon to users, greatly enhancing the utility of the computer. (See Table 4-5.)

In many systems there is a development site, an operational site and a continued development site. Some people call all the software sent to the operational site by the term "operational software." This is confusing, as operational software is a synonym for use time software. For example, a ship at sea is an operational site, but it is sent many programs that do not run at use time. Diagnostic programs to help

TABLE 4-5   The Evolution of Systems Software

Problem	Response
The computer was sitting idle as the operators raced furiously about mounting tapes; etc.	A program was written that kept track of the mounted tapes, switched the tapes logically instead of physically. Meant a lot more tape drives. Kept more than one program on the computer at a time.
The machine room manager was beset with decisions regarding which programs to put on the computer. How much memory did this program require? Tapes? etc.	A program was written that kept track of what computer resources were free and what programs were waiting to be run. The computer itself then determined the scheduling of the jobs and the allocation of the machine units.
The programmers were putting into their applications programs details about the physical arrangement of the data and the disks. New disks, cheaper and faster, could not be introduced unless the old applications programs were rewritten — which was tough because the programmers were either gone or busy with something else.	Data management programs were written that performed the getting and putting of data to and from the disks. The programmers then wrote instructions to the data management software which then did the data management for them. The names that were used to identify these standard systems programs were more mysterious than explanatory. "Access Methods" was one name, and of course one thinks of methods and arrangements, and not of the programs that implement those arrangements.
Programmers wanted the same data as all the other programmers, but in different sequences and in different order. So they made up their own files from the master file and used their own files. Two things were wrong with this: First the space for file storage got bigger and bigger, but worse, the data in one file did not agree with the data in the next.	Data base management programs were written that accepted complex logical queries of files even if the files were not stored by the key items that the programmer wanted to search for. These systems were called data base management systems; they freed the programmer from doing the logical design of how to store or retrieve the data; all that work was done by the DBMS.

maintenance engineers fix the machines are sent to the ship, but they run off-line, not at use time. They are a variety of support programs, and to call them "operational" merely because they run at the operational site is confusing. Table 4-6 shows but some of the software that runs *by site* by time, and Table 4-7 shows what runs off-line at various sites.

TABLE 4-6.   When Software Types are Used

	Executes at Development Time	Executes at Use Time	Runs at Continued Development Time
Support software	Compilers Librarian Dumps	None	Compilers Librarian Dumps
Systems software	Operating systems Data base management systems	On-Line Operating systems DBMS On-line diagnostics On-line accounting	Operating systems DBMS
Application software	None	Payroll (periodic) Monitor or control (continual) Date reduction (once)	None

TABLE 4-7.   What Software Runs Off-Line at Various Sites

	What runs off-line at the *development* site	What runs off-line at the *use time* site	What runs off-line at the continued development site
Support	Diagnostics	Diagnostics Accounting items	Diagnostics
Systems	O/S	Operating systems	O/S
Application	For *testing* purposes Accounting	None	For *testing* purposes Accounting

Support Software

The third major division of the body of all programs is support software. Support software is used at development time. Support software is the body of programs that are used to help programmers program, and to help software development managers control the development process and product.

The best known body of programs that fit into this classification are the language translators that help programmers produce instructions. The FORTRAN, COBOL, JOVIAL, BASIC, APL, and Pascal translators are support programs, in that they support the effort to create new object programs.

But language translators are only the most well known of the support programs; there are many more varieties. The fastest way to get an overview of just how many and how varied the support program world is is to simply look at a list of support programs that would be in use in a large programming project during development time. See Table 4-8.

TABLE 4-8.   Some Support Programs

General	Requirements/Specification
Text Editors	PSL/PSA
Document Formatters	Relational DB Systems
Library Systems	Consistency Checkers
Disk to Tape	CARA/CLARA
Models	SADT
	IA

Design	Writing
Graphics Package	Compiler
Structured Flow Charter	Cross-compiler
Design Analyzer	Pre-compiler
APLGOL	Library

Construction	Verification
PERT	Static Analyzers
Link-Editor	Symbolic Execution
Standards Checker	Simulation
Librarian	Test Case Generators
	Statistics Gathering

This use of the computer to run programs to help in the creation of new programs is not obvious to those outside the computer profession. Yet the computer professional talks about support (development time) and systems (use time) software in the same breath, assuming that the uninitiated know about the role of support software. Just as at use time (for applications programs) there is systems software running, system software runs with support software at development time.

The cost for the development environment to be well stocked with tools for program development can easily run into the many dozens and even hundreds of millions of dollars. There must of course be a computer to run the support programs. We'll see the details for this environment in the section coming up on *development facilities*.

Not so obvious is the fact that the support software often has errors in it just like all other programs, and so we must have tool support people to make sure that our support tools are sharp and in good working order, to catalog them, to help the production programmers learn to use them, and to fix them when they are not giving the right results. This team of support software programmers is a most valuable asset (Who wants to work with bad tools?) and worth the cost in the results of increased productivity on the part of the development programming team. It is also an often ignored resource, with no budget allocated for it.

In addition to the "normal" development tools we find there are some ancillary areas of support as:

Development Test Software
Drivers; simulators; stimulators

Maintenance Test Software
Diagnostics, tests, maintenance aids

Training Software
Learning aids; programmed instructions; exercisers

Cost of Support Software

Support tools can cost hundreds of millions of dollars. It is U. S. Navy policy to use only two different computers, in different performance ranges, aboard ships. Maintenance and spare parts at sea place such demands on the system that having the same computer on every ship greatly eases the logistics problem.

A side benefit of this standardization is that the instructions sets are the same *and* therefore the vast body of support software that has been developed over the years can be used for all shipboard application development.

By mid-1979, the Navy estimated it had spent $300,000,000 on the support software for these computers. This figure is not that unusual. For a computer to be well supported, there must be a great variety of software tools.

The U.S. Navy, in a bold and successful move, avoided the creation of an entire set of new support software when it procured an airborne computer with the specification that it execute the same instruction set as one of the shipboard computers. Many thought the effort beyond the state of the art; it worked beautifully, saving the taxpayer millions of dollars.

SCALE, COMPLEXITY, CLARITY

All software development efforts should be characterized according to the attributes of scale, complexity, and clarity.

Software is too broad a word. It is generic, like the word "animal," which can be a pet cat or an 800-pound polar bear. Yet people talk about software as though it were *a* thing, or *a* uniform body of things. It is anything but.

I can sit alone and in 20 minutes write a 100-instruction program to calculate my monthly payments on a loan. I have developed a program. In 20 minutes.

Or I can be one of hundreds of programmers and supervisors creating the program to track and guide a spacecraft to the Moon. I will contribute a portion — over several years time — to a 1,000,000+ instruction set of programs.

In both cases, I am a development programmer. But the efforts are quite different. And to be the manager of the team responsible for all 1,000,000+ instructions is vastly different again.

There is "programming in the small," and "programming in the large." The 100 instructions are a program; the 1 million instructions are software.

Let us look at the physical world to learn some of the lessons about technological understanding. A bridge builder may be a person who builds 5-foot structures over tiny streams in back yards, or a person who builds the suspension bridges across our rivers and bays. There is really no comparing these two bridges; they are at the opposite end of the scale. But both are bridges!

Let us just look at the planning, staging, and controlling of efforts of large size. The requirements of the large bridge, its load capacity, its location, its access roads, and a score of other things that are not obvious must be studied. Then a rough estimate of cost is arrived at. Then another pass at requirements and possible bridges is made.

After the location and rough outline of the bridge is accepted, then the planning phase gets underway in depth. The detailed design of the bridge is laid out, its moorings, its supports, its towers, its sway factors, its cables — the myriad of technical detail that makes a bridge. Warehouses for the drawings are needed. A system is needed just to keep track of the drawings so that they are available when needed.

A "work plan" is drawn up. Detailed flows of what and when and by whom and the interdependence of each on others is detailed and documented. Then concurrency is specified (what jobs can be done concurrently).

All this is laid out and understood in advance. Only then are construction people hired, orders for materials placed, tools and equipment procured.

Payroll systems and clerks are employed to pay the workers.

Figure 4-17.   Verrazano Narrows Bridge.
(Courtesy of Triboro Bridge and Tunnel Authority)

Filing room upon filing room is added as the immense flow of paper needed to control and create this huge edifice proceeds.

Years go by. The bridge is a reality, a work of wonder. Millions of people see it, see it in the building phase, then use it. A triumph. (See Fig. 4-17.)

No one sees the years of planning, the tons of documents, the intricate and marvelous work plan. They are invisible as you cross the bridge but absolutely necessary to the final product.

The lesson in Table 4-9 is obvious — there is a great deal of "infrastructure" needed to build a $300,000,000 bridge. And the same thing is true in building $100,000,000 software with 500,000 to 2,000,000 lines of code.

This scale effect is true in almost all endeavors. Donald Douglas, the airplane pioneer, stated that "when the weight of the paper equals the weight of the plane, the plane will fly." (See Fig. 4-18.)

James Martin states that "the paper for the 747 weighs more than the plane." So too with large software. At this point the question may arise as to how many one million lines-of-code systems there are, or will be. I'll list just a few in Table 4-10 but the point is that there are more and more of them every day. The decrease in cost of the hardware along with its increase in power have encouraged large systems. There are many more; the list grows and grows. I know of many other Defense programs that have expended over $50,000,000 on the soft-

TABLE 4-9.   Scale Effects on Effort

	Footbridge in a Park	Verrazano Narrows Bridge
Requirements	1 day	1,825 days
Design	1 sheet of paper	Warehouse of paper
Material Plan	1 hour	1,460 days
Flow/staging	1 hour	182 days
Materials	½ day	182 days
Procurement	½ day	182 days
Store/inventory	1 day	182 days
Staging	1 day	182 days
Use	2 days	36,500 days
Plan for People		
Number of people	2	5,000
Hire people	1 day	365 days
Use people	3 days	3,650 days
Pay people	1 day	3,650 days
Accounting for all this	1 day	3,650 days
Build	3 days	1,825 days
Documentation	1 day	555 days
Number of pieces of paper	5 sheets	500,000 sheets
TOTAL COST	$1,000	$300,000,000

Figure 4-18.   Boeing 747- "... the weight of the paper...." (Courtesy of Aer Lingus)

TABLE 4-10.   Large Software Projects

	Life Cycle Contract Value	No. of Instructions	Effort (Man-Yr)*
Houston (Apollo/Skylab)	$209M	23.00M	6,000+
NASA range monitoring	30M	1.25M	1,000+
FAA air traffic control	103M	1.48M	5,000+
SAFEGUARD anti-ballistic missile	120M	1.87M	3,500+
SATELLITE real time data reduction	23M	.55M	1,300+

*Note that one can not get any consistency if one divides any column by either of the others. We cover productivity in Chap. 6.

ware development. Industry is now entering this arena. The big communications network of ATT, Satellite Business Systems, RCA, W.U., and others will be in this range. The operating systems of the major manufacturers are more costly and much larger.

Airlines, we have seen, have programs this large. Banks (especially foreign banks) are moving to systems of this magnitude.

One of the programs that cost far more than $100,000,000, was the ground control for the Apollo launches at the Manned Space Center in Houston. I visited there in 1970, shortly after entering my position as General Manager of the Federal System Center, to review the efforts of the 700 people that reported up the line to me.

They showed me how they controlled the development of a million lines of code. I was appalled! "It is sheer bureaucracy," I thought, as they showed me planning and control and configuration control and test and more documents than can be imagined.

I shortly thereafter visited some other locations reporting to me. They did not have a vast control system — and they were out of control. The Houston approach was sound — to control the development of something that large, more than 50 percent of the cost is involved in planning, checking, scheduling, management, and control. It is simply the infrastructure that we see in all large endeavors. They showed me the chart in Fig. 4-19 back then. It is still valid.

Perhaps the clearest example of the effects of scale falls out of the interesting and puzzling fact that I found when I arrived in the Federal System Division in 1968 to be the assistant to the president, Bob Evans. There were 10 or so people from the Houston space team assigned to a bank in London. What's this? Space people in London helping a bank get its data processing going?

Did we just happen to have a group of people in the space effort that had come from the banking area? No, not so. The reason they were there stems from the fact that IBM's largest overseas customers are

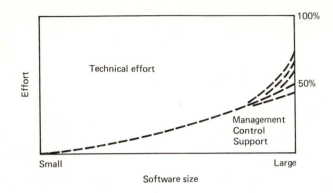

Figure 4-19.   Technical vs. support effort percent by scale.

the banks, and these European, Japanese, and other foreign banks are not constrained the way the U.S. banks are by state boundaries and laws. They are installing $100,000,000 equipment systems, linking up thousands of branches.

The banks loved the Federal Systems people from Houston. Even though the space people know nothing about banking, they knew a great deal about installing systems *on the scale* that these banks were undertaking — and they were some of the few people in the world at that time who did. There are ways of managing scale that are not just linear progressions of managing small efforts. There are subtleties of making large bodies of code work.

Complexity

One of the last discoveries of basic mathematics was the digit zero. It came along late, because at first it was not recognized that it was needed.

So it is with the idea of complexity. Complexity is easy to envision but hard to describe. We have few tools to work with complexity. There are no metrics of complexity, to measure that a job is twice as complex as the next. There are no definitive adjectives. We are reduced to saying "more complex" and "very complex," which may be true, but this is not very helpful when we have millions of dollars and great consequences riding on the outcome of our efforts to do the thing that is "more complex" than something else. However, we can recognize two "types" of complexity:

1. Technical complexity of the application.
2. Logical complexity of the application and/or of the system software.

Technical Complexity. I have two programs, each of 50,000 instructions. One may "do" payroll, and the other may "do" missile safety calculations. The missile program will be more complex; it will require the calculation of some complex equations.

Weather forecasting, nuclear equations, orbital calculations, gravity effects, ballistics — all of these require special mathematical, engineering, or scientific skills and knowledge. This knowledge must be used *and* communicated throughout all phases of the development of the software. Knowing it is difficult enough; communicating it is tougher.

Logical Complexity. There is a second type of complexity, logical complexity, and it is usually even more difficult to handle than the mathematical or engineering complexity. This is the complexity encountered in having many possible choices at each succeeding step. How does one keep track of the possible or desirable paths that large programs can proceed through? Programs can have very few conditional branches — or they can have a great many! Let us look at why people have difficulty coping with programs with lots of conditional branches.

In how many different arrangements could we connect 5 of 7 wires to five posts? 2520.

How many batting orders can I list with 12 — only 12 — kids on a Little League baseball team? Ready? 79,833,600! With only 12 kids!

The program for the En-Route Air Traffic Control in the United States and U.K is a very "logically intensive" program. It cost over $100,000,000, is in use in 20 En-Route Traffic Control Centers in the United States and in one outside London. It has been in use for over 5 years now and works very well. The United Kingdom picked it up — and paid $10 million for the IBM 9020 computer to run it in the teeth of a fierce "Buy British" policy. (The fact that a foreign country would select and use the U.S. system was a fact that the U.S. Federal Aviation Agency would throw back at their many critics who were claiming the U.S. system was "no good," "obsolete," etc.)

In negotiating for the follow-on air traffic control contract, we looked at the then 600,000 plus lines of code in the Use Time Central Computer Complex and counted the number of conditional branches. There were 39,203 such branches, one every 15.3 lines of code. This is a very decision-intensive program, representing the involved logic of control, of conflict prediction, and the myriad of choices needed to allow up to 97 controllers to enter data, query the system, call up new formats and displays. How many possible ways or paths are there to execute this many instructions? 39,203 factorial! The number is astronomical — it is 10^{11801} or 10 followed by over eleven thousand eight hundred zeros! If we could test one path through the programs per second, it would take us thousands of years to test every path. We could not set up a test system to present all the variations of the real world we will encounter.

People who state they want 100 percent error-free software are talking about *very* small programs — or do not know what they are talking about.

Large systems software is very logic-intensive. There are many conditional branches. Systems software, Brooks states in his *The Mythical Man-Month**, is nine times more difficult to develop than application software. The basic reason is this logical intensity.

Applications programs, standing alone, are not very complex. But when we try to join a number of applications programs into an integrated, smoothly running system, we begin to discover complexity. Figure 4-20 is from James Martin's *Computer Data Base Organization*.

Unfortunately, there have been too few studies of logical complexity to date. As computers move deeper into the large operations and process applications, we'll have to understand this area much more clearly.

The Problems of Complexity.   Complexity has troubled people throughout history, and still does. That it bedevils us in developing large software should come as no surprise to anyone — yet it does. We tend to forget how troubled we are by complexity elsewhere.

People have long had problems with the complexity of bridges. In the decade of the 1870s, 40 bridges *per year* fell down in the United States alone. Citizens crossed bridges at their peril. The "sociology" of that period is very similar to our experiences today:

> Highway bridge failures were far more frequent than railroad. Most local highway bridges were contracted for by county officials who combined a lack of technical knowledge with a pressing commitment to economy. Bridge-promoters and salesmen sold low cost virtually to the exclusion of other considerations. Fly-by-night operators sold wherever and however they could, threw together a bridge, and moved in a hurry. The more established firms were pressured into dangerous economies by the competition.**

How these words would fit so many situations in the software area today! And the 1870s were not the first years of disasters. Harmonic vibrations had wrecked bridges for centuries. One marched soldiers *in step* across a bridge only with great peril. In the 1940s came the wind problem. In 1940, the bridge across the Tacoma Narrows

---

*Frederick P. Brooks, Jr., *Mythical Man-Month* (Reading, Mass.: Addison-Wesley, 1975).

**Joseph Gies, *Bridges and Men* (New York: Grosset & Dunlap, Inc., 1963).

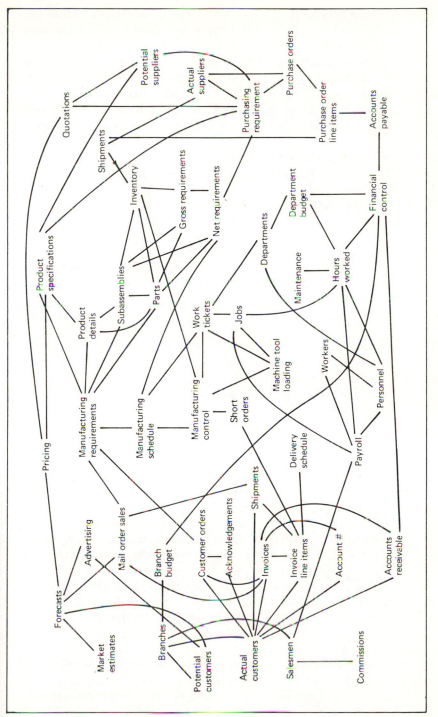

Figure 4-20. Interrelated functions. James Martin, *Computer Data-Base Organization*, 2nd ed. (Englewood Cliffs, N.J.: Prentice-Hall, Inc., 1977), p. 227. Reprinted with permission of the publisher.

blew down. In the 1970s the Bronx Whitestone, "stiffened" after the Tacoma loss, galloped so wildly that people left their cars in panic and fled on foot off the span.

Not only suspension bridges had problems. In 1944, a double truss bridge over the Mississippi River at Chester, Illinois was pulled out of its insufficient anchorage by the wind. In 1905, 87 workmen were killed when the great cantilever bridge across the St. Lawrence in Quebec collapsed. The physics of this kind of structure were just not understood.

Newer phenomena bring complexity to plague us. The Lockheed Electra had its engines fall off due to a "design insufficiency." The DC-10 is under a cloud.

Glass windows would not stay in the John Hancock Building in Boston in the mid-1970s. Ten thousand 400-pound windows had to be replaced.

People have yet to cope with the complexities of nuclear power. The cost of the Three Mile Island accident continues to rise, and is already estimated to be over 4 billion dollars!

Clarity

The clarity of a program once it is created and running relates to its design and implementation. At development time, we are often in trouble with the clarity of its purpose. What is the program to do? To some degree the five basic uses of the computer reflect the attribute of clarity.

The job of the computer in a type I (accounting) is very clear. The accounting task to be programmed in most cases is already being done. All we need do is understand the present procedures, and write the program to do it. On the opposite end of the scale we have the operations/process use of the computer, the type Vs.

Here we often find the process is being done by the "old master," by some bright, ingenious, perceptive individual who has in his or her head all the parameters, trade-offs, traps, inconsistencies, incongruities and discontinuities. This individual "sees" how things are going, and "can tell" when something is askew, and "knows" what to do.

Try to write down the rules, the algorithms, to do what this person can do in his or her head, and you find judgment, pattern recognition, intuition, and "feel." It is very hard to define these, and one finally gets a usable program only after several failures and misdesigns, and much, much money.

IBM lost over 10 million dollars automating the Exxon refineries at Edmonton, Canada and Antwerp, Belguim. Two hundred of my Houston people were doing the job. At one point, one of the software designers asked an Exxon engineer how he knew which way to turn a control handle. "Easy" was the answer. "I put my finger in the flow and *taste* it." Try programming that!

In the large operations/process type systems with many operators interacting, the real use of the computer is usually understood only *after* it is placed in the *hands of its users* — that is *after* the development is theoretically complete. Users always find new ways to use tools.

By now the reader may have protested that these are *systems* problems, not software problems. And the reader is correct.

> ## Software Inherits the System Problems

In the case of large type V systems, as the other pieces of the system solidify, the last piece that can be modified is the software. What do we mean, "solidify"? In large type V systems, there are often *many* elements that are under development, being improved. The communications/display/radar/sonar/IR/telemetry/missile/satellite/propulsion/control/whatever — some of these will be the newest, most advanced in the world when they work in our system, or they will be in new connections. Therefore, they will surprise us in the way they work, and we will have to adapt to reality.

The burden for adapting to the differences falls on two pieces of our system — the software and the human operators. We try to push as much into the software as we can, and then let the rest fall onto the operators. The software is "soft," *if* we designed it right and controlled it right. *If* we documented it and modularized it. Then, indeed, it is soft. If we did not, it can be a block of solid concrete!

Great planning and wise expenditure of funds often can save millions upon millions of dollars at a later time. The George Washington Bridge for vehicular traffic from New York City to New Jersey was built in 1931, with one roadway, but with structural strength adequate to add a second level with a six-lane roadway 30 years later. Sure enough in 1962 the second roadway was added to the George Washington Bridge. (See Fig. 4-21.)

The bridge had been originally designed to carry a railroad on a second level. The railroad was never built, and the bridge structure, unchanged, was sufficient to support the second deck.

Contrast adding a second level to having to put up a whole second twin bridge, next to the old one! Look at the bridges across the Chesapeake Bay. (See Fig. 4-22.)

Although there is a sizeable number of programs that do not need to evolve, *most* programs for large businesses and to control complex operational activities must either continue to evolve or be scrapped.

Large programs that are used for 20 or more years have the over-

Figure 4-21. George Washington Bridge, New York/New Jersey, adds a second deck. (Courtesy of The Port Authority of NY & NJ)

Figure 4-22. William Preston Lane, Jr., Bridge. (Courtesy of the Maryland Transportation Authority)

whelming percentage of total dollars expended in the continued development phase.

TABLE 4-11.   What Requirements are Going to Change

Products	Marketing structure
Product numbers	Divisions
Plants, location	Customers
Organization	Payroll laws
Key people	Privacy laws
Number of plants	Product mix by plant
Networks	Hardware
Procedures	Therefore, application programs
Required data	Therefore, data base

The lack of clear requirements is *the* single most difficult problem in developing large type V systems. The project manager does not know where he or she is going.

> The first requirement of a large system of software is that it be built so that it is easy to change.
>
> The first job of the manager of a large software effort is that he or she budget for many releases of the software.

Summary

Scale, complexity, and clarity must be estimated in advance and planned for. A million-lines-of-code system is as much of a triumph as a great bridge, and often costs as much. But the software is invisible. No one sees it; only a few insiders understand the whole thing. In a way, it is sad. When something that complex is created, there ought to be a way of showing it off. Even when such a program runs, only the tip of the iceberg is being seen. There is just no way to *show* the vast complexity and achievement that has occurred. One must study or experience the complexity and scale in the creation to appreciate it.

PROJECT SOFTWARE AND PRODUCT SOFTWARE

It is useful to categorize software into *project* and *product* software. The development process is quite different for one versus the other.

A software product is designed to be used in many different installations, for many different and diverse users. A software project is software developed for one, or a few, users. And within product software, we have three subtypes.

1. Product software packages	Software that happens to run on a computer, any computer; e.g., a COBOL compiler.
2. System product with software the distinguishing component	Software differentiates the resulting system; e.g., a word processing system.
3. Hardware product with a minimal program	A product with minimal software; e.g., a copier that uses a computer to regulate its operations.

Products versus Projects

There are two major differences (also see Table 4-12) between developing product software versus project software:

1. The process of defining requirements.
2. The breadth of the effort in terms of diversity of the functions being developed.

When we put experienced and successful project people into product jobs, we had disasters. The same thing happened when we had product people manage project software development.

TABLE 4-12. Differences Between Product and Project Software

	Product	Project
Number of users	Hundreds	One or few
Competition	After use starts	To do the development only
Continued development	Critical	Not so critical
Control over use	Very little	Great deal

A software product is a program that is intended to be sold to a widespread market — thousands of users, or at least hundreds. Project software has a far more restrictive user set. A standard payroll program, a standard graphics display package, a COBOL compiler, a standard general ledger program, or a report generator package are examples of software products. The development of a set of programs to control a satellite is an example of a software project.

Software products are designed and intended to be used by as many users as possible. This affects the entire life cycle, but most significantly the requirements portion of development.

The easiest way to see the utility of this categorization is to look at the extremes, not at the boundaries. Apollo, the space project and the lunar landing, had *one* user, and the developer and the user lived and worked side by side. A tight and efficient communication channel was established and maintained between them. But generalized payroll is aimed at hundreds of users, most of whom the developers have never talked to or met. These prospective users are also being offered other payroll programs from other developers. Therefore the question is not whether our payroll program is adequate but whether or not it is saleable. The difference is all encompassing; it will make the difference between success and failure.

Table 4-13 represents a range of software environments. It includes products and projects, and it includes products with software. Perusal of the chart has yielded surprising insights in some cases where the developer thought he or she was developing one sort of system, and then decided he or she had mislabeled — no, misunderstood — the effort on which he or she was embarked.

Project versus Product Requirements. It is much easier to get the requirements for an Apollo than it is to get the requirements for a word processing system. The process is more forgiving, as the Apollo management has close contact with and control over all the people who are going to use the software. This tight communication means slight errors can be better tolerated. Should 100 or more users need to be told of slight errors or changes, the very job of telling them is obviously much greater.

To get good requirements for a product we must exhaustively research the needs and desires of many many potential users, and then understand what the competition has. We must not only satisfy a wide variety of users; we must beat the competition.

In a project, all competition is settled when the software development team is assigned. A large number of people, a long period of time, and a rigorous process is required to define requirements for a product.

Project versus Product Breadth. Many projects must develop unique systems software to handle extreme reliability or speed of processing requirements. Many projects must create their own development tools. On the other hand most product environments are much

TABLE 4-13. Product and Project Software Characteristics

Example	Payroll	Houston	Defense Support Program	FAA Air Traffic Control	Shipboard Systems Navigation	Wizard of Avis	Rocket Guidance	Television Circuit	COBOL Compiler (370)	Text Processor
Number of users	1 User	1 user	1 user	Dozens	100's	100's	1000's	1000's of users	1000's of users	1000's
Number of development organizations	1	1	1	1	Several	1	1	1	1	1
Intermediary between user and developer	No	No	Yes	Yes	Yes	Yes	Yes	Yes	Yes	Yes
Concurrent hardware development	No	Yes	Yes	Yes	Yes	No	Yes	Yes	No	Yes; then no
User requirements or market requirements	User	User	User	User	User	User	User	Market	Market	Market
Software competition after building	No	No	No	No	No	No	No	No	Yes	Yes
Risk money	No	No	No	No	No	No	No	No	Yes	Yes
Maintenance of software	Hi	Hi	Hi	Hi	Hi	Hi	Lo	Lo hardware intensive	Hi software intensive	Hi Software intensive
									Hardware product with software	Software product	

Project ————→

Product ————→

more constrained. The product is circumscribed, with clear interfaces defined for use with other parts of the software. For example, if I am developing a COBOL compiler or a payroll, I do not need to develop an operating system. I write instructions to interface to an operating system but I do not develop it. If on the other hand I am writing a navigation program chances are very good I'm also developing an operating system. (See Fig. 4-23.)

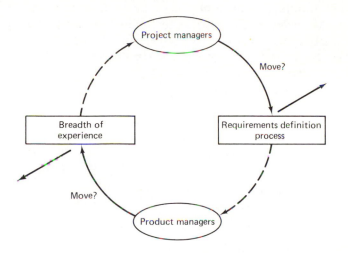

Figure 4-23. Barriers to software management movement.

"Productizing" a Program

There are several processes that are performed to take a piece of software that is working in one location and prepare it to be sold into hundreds of locations. This is sometimes called "productizing" a program. To take a program that is running and make it a product is similar to the support engineering effort of hardware development.

The apocryphal story about the group of three geniuses who in the garage one night wrote a program and got it to work and then the big company asked $300,000 to do the same thing is an oft-told piece of irony, but it is superficial. The end results of the two efforts are markedly different. To see just how different, let's assume that some- one approaches us — a big company — with a working program and wants us to market and supply the program to thousands of customers. Assuming we believed we could make money on it, here is a list, not exhaustive, of what we would have to do to that program.

- *Review the existing documentation, if any*
  We would review not only the "back-end" documentation (of

the code) but the front-end sales documentation — what is the program to do, not do, its limitations, user instructions.

- *Create product documentation*
  Create sales literature to describe the product succinctly.

- *Thoroughly test the existing code*
  Test boundary conditions. The fact that a program is at work for me in one installation does not mean the program is being stressed. All my inputs, for example, may be in a certain number range. When it is used in a large number of installations, the inputs may vary widely. We must test the system for the boundary conditions, if they are stated. If they are not stated we must test to *find* the boundary conditions.

  Example of Boundary Conditions

	Input Value	Limit
Payroll	Salary per week	$9,999.99 — zero, no negative
Radar	Range	1,000 feet to 99,432 feet

- *Clear user documentation*
  It is very unlikely that a program to be used in one installation has much user documentation. Instructions for use are likely to be informal and verbal from the builder to the user. But to have the program used by hundreds of users, I need crisp, clear instructions, written in clear text, or else I will encounter user rejection of the product.

- *Clean the code up*
  Inspect the program; make sure there are no loose ends, dead ends, etc; add defensive code — e.g., editing for out of bounds input parameters.

- *Modularization/compartmentalization*
  To ensure efficient and the least expensive modification and update, it is essential to do a review of the program and modify it to make it as modular and tightly compartmentalized as possible.

- *Good documentation for the continued development programmers*
  Crisp and clear documentation is essential to reduce costs and increase the productivity of continued development programmers. It is rare that such documentation exists for a one-user program.

- *Test with all systems software it will run with*

The product software will probably run with several different software systems. The product must be tested with each before it is let out.

- *Budget for and identify the continuing development programmers, equipment, etc.*
  Far too often the planning for the continuing development is *not* done. "We'll get to it" is the attitude. By the time they get to it, the damage is done. The budget should be in place to change and fix the program as it is stressed in actual use.
- *Establish a "trouble reporting" system*
  This sounds simple but it is not. People *and* procedures are required to perform this function. A well planned and well executed system here can make the product appear better in the users' eyes.
- *Establish a distribution system for changes*
  A trouble system feeds *in* to the continuing development effort. Now we need a system to get the changed software *out* to the user. Again, *not* a simple effort.

These efforts are not usually done in a project; they should always be done for a software product. "Garage Programs" are not products!

Software Products versus Products Differentiated by Software

The effort to develop software that will sell because and only because it is software (and it happens to run on a computer) should involve a very different process than developing software that is to be the distinguishing factor between system products. A payroll program is an example of the first. A word processing program is an example of the second; here the hardware doesn't distinguish between products as much as the software does. The user of the software may not care which computer does the payroll — runs the program — as long as it is reliable, etc. Should the computer be remotely located, the user may never even know which computer make and model is running the payroll.

In a word processing system, the hardware becomes important because the user interacts directly with it. The features and their location and their ease of use become differentiating items, that distinguish between products. But most vendor's hardware is almost identical and the software is much more of a differentiation item than the hardware.

The developer of the product differentiated by software has a far more complex integration of hardware and software, in every part of the development process, than the software product manager.

Products that Have Minimal Software in Them

Yet another category has entered our everyday world, as a result of the microelectronic circuits. The digital general-purpose computer is more economical in many systems than *ad hoc* circuits. Yet the memory of this computer must have instructions, and the instructions are programs.

We wish to put this kind of program into our taxonomy because it is useful to do so. There is also a question that bedevils the policy makers as to how to treat these devices and this software.

An example of such a computer used as a circuit is one used *in* a television set to lock on to the signal coming in. The computer is programmed with only a "few" instructions, e.g., 200, then the program is loaded on to 500,000 or so chips, and they are put into the TV sets. We call this a *hardware-intensive application* of software, of a program.

The one overriding consideration here is that of correctness of the program. It must be correct, or we must go and get 500,000 TV sets *in user's homes* and fix the program. The economics of doing that are overwhelming. Such disasters have occurred in consumer products. What happens as our chip begins to be able to hold more and more instructions at no increase in the cost of the chip? The engineers using it begin to put more programs into it, of course. Where we can be sure that our 200-step program is 100 percent correct, we cannot usually be sure that our 1000- or 10,000-step program is.

The policy maker sees this danger and wants to cut the world of software into two pieces — hardware-intensive programs where we expect *no* changes and no errors, and software-intensive software, where we fully expect to have to fix or modify the software.

With the latter, he or she will insist on standards — language standards, development process standards, testing, and documentation standards which we will enumerate later. But in the hardware intensive programs such standards do not make economic sense. To saddle that kind of development and use with such strict standards will multiply the development cost by 5 or 10.

So the desire to make a separation is clear. And if a knowledgeable manager sees and understands the development effort, the control is easy. But how does a corporate manager *set guidelines for* hundreds or thousands of developers to ensure modest risk in the development process? There are computers with faulty programs being used in scores of thousands of products with no plan or budget to modify or fix them.

The cleanest way to draw a line between these very different types of software is to arbitrarily state that all program development must use software intensive development standards *if* the use phase computer has 2,000 instruction-sized units of memory or more!

This is arbitrary. There are many examples where 3000 instructions are simple as there are few conditional branches. But the point is that we are trying to prevent unsuspecting hardware builders from falling into *the ease of interconnection pit*. The marvelous new electronic chips are like siren calls to engineers. The power is so great, so cheap. But so is the cost of an error.

Whether the limit should be 2000 or 1000 or 4000 units of memory, we do not know. Some arbitrary limit should be imposed by corporate policy makers. The builders can ask for an exception if they are sure of the clarity and stability of their application, and of their ability to write an error-free program.

Should we *think* we have correct software and field the product only to find that there is an error in our small, say 1000 lines-of-code, program, we may be forced to rip out or recall thousands of microwave ovens, or send thousands of service men out to replace chips in copiers or TV sets. The stability of the program is absolutely essential to the economics of the product. A mistake in either requirements or implementation *can be fatal to a career here*, despite the fact that we are talking about "small" programs!

If one has management responsibility for software, one wants to be very sure whether or not the application is hardware intensive. A different, lesser, set of standards should apply to software development for hardware intensive applications.

USING THE TAXONOMY — DIFFERENT JOBS

I was once asked to name the ten top people in software in the United States. I had to break my list into the three parts. On the first list I put the people who really know and have built large systems software.

On the second list I put the people who are really knowledgeable about languages and libraries — support software. Here I put many university people.

The third list was not applications software people, but the project software people. The application area is just not that hard. The project software people use the products of my first two groups, merge in applications, and come up with the final working system. They are total integrators of software, building the biggest, the fastest, the most complex systems. They did the air traffic control system, the satellite systems, the airline reservations systems, the military's command and control systems. They have built systems programs and merged in applications programs, relying on a host of support programs. They have managed the $100,000,000 efforts.

A most important fact springs from this categorization — each of the three areas calls for different talents and skills! I would *never* put a language person in charge of a large real time system development; he or she would have no credibility in this area. And vice versa. Nor would I put even a proven systems person in charge of an air defense control system! And I would not put the real time, complex system person on either of the first two tasks. *They are all very different jobs.*

A Project with Software Products

A nationwide communication system that also provides services is a major project software effort, with software products to be developed as well. A message switching system can connect offices of subscribers and move data from a device (e.g., a copier) in one office to a second one elsewhere.

To make such a system work, a network of transmission facilities (microwave, satellite, etc.), storage units, and switching units must be built and operated. The system controllers would be a small group of people who would control the back-up facilities of the various nodes and balance the system if overloads occur.

Much of the network would be controlled with computers. The programs that must be written and interconnected are *project software*. Yet the services to be offered to users would include a *broadcast* facility. The operator of a copier that is hooked into the network could send a copy to a dozen different locations. If there was a regular set of locations that frequently got the same copy, the operator could avoid dialing in all the addresses each time and dial in a *group identification*. The network — by means of a program — would translate from the ID number entered to the actual addresses. This program would be a *product*, not a project, piece of software.

This product program:

- Must satisfy a wide range of users; thousands of them, in different businesses and fields.
- Must be easy to use, hard to get stuck in, easy to add or delete from.
- Must be extremely well documented.
- Must perform a large number of functions so that it satisfies the wide range of users.
- It must be backed up by people *ready* to fix or add to it.
- Its rich function must be carefully defined and selected *before* it is offered for use.
- It will be in competition for the customers' use *after* it is in field, the competitor being other networks.

Therefore, to develop such a network service business, both project *and* product software must be developed.

Table 4-14 shows examples of several programs and how they are categorized by the taxonomy. In addition, a rough indication of difficulty of each program for each of the three phases of the life cycle is given.

TABLE 4-14.   Examples of Programs and How They Fit the Taxonomy

	Payroll	Orbit calculation	Management information system	Air line reservation system	COBOL compiler	Sort routine square root	Office automation	Office copier diagnostics	TV set tuner	Data base management system	Air traffic control
Development time	LO	LO	HI	HI	HI	MOD	HI	MOD	MOD	HI	VHI
Use or run time	LO	LO	HI	HI	LO	LO	HI	LO	LO	HI	VHI
Continued development time	LO	LO	HI	HI	LO	LO	HI	LO	LO	HI	VHI
Application	✓	✓	✓	✓		*	✓	✓	✓		✓
Support					✓						
Systems						*				✓	
Scale	SM	SM	MOD	LG	SM	SM	MOD	SM	SM	MOD	LG
Complexity Scientific	LO	HI	LO	LO	LO	MOD	LO	LO	LO	LO	LO
Logical	LO-M	MOD	HI	VHI	HI	MOD	HI	MOD	LO	HI	HI
Software project	*	✓	✓	✓		*					✓
Software product	*				✓	*	✓	✓		✓	
Product with software-hardware intensive								✓	✓		
Product with software-software intensive					✓		✓			✓	

✓ — usually here

* — can be in more than one

THE COST OF SOFTWARE

We mentioned in Chap. 2 that the cost of large software may indeed be 90 percent of the cost of the total project.

There are many uses of software where the cost of the software is trivial compared to the cost of the hardware. The developers of these types of efforts may have no software crisis at all.

If we are going to develop a major program for use on one and only one computer, for example a Management Information Systems for XYZ company, then we cannot divide the cost of the program by the number of users. The number of users is 1, and the full cost is applied to that one. If on the other hand we are going to embed our little computer in the innards of a TV set, then we divide the cost of *the* program for that computer by the number of sets we will put it in. If the program has cost us $200,000 to develop, then when we divide it by, say, 500,000 sets, then the cost of the program per set is $.40 Trivial! What is all the fuss about? As long as the program is correct, there is no problem. Table 4-15 is a representation of the numerical diversity of the use-time computer.

TABLE 4-15. Examples of the Numbers of Copies of a Program in Use

The Product in Which the Program is to be Used	Number of Copies of the Product Used
Television set	500,000
Automobile	20,000
Missile control (on board)	15,000
Navigation (shipboard)	500
Airline reservations	20
Payroll	1
Management information system	1
Satellite control	1

If we are developing system software and application software for a major project, say the control center for a nationwide communication network, the cost of such software can easily be 30 to 60 million dollars for one site. And the cost of the TV chip software we mentioned earlier is in the $.40 range per set for the software.

VOCABULARY OF SOFTWARE

If we are to talk about software without an adjective in front of it, we should do so only with the clear knowledge that there are gross oversimplifications being made. Few statements made about hardware-intensive software will hold for software-intensive software, and vice versa.

$$\left.\begin{array}{l} \text{Systems} \\ \text{Product} \\ \text{Project} \\ \text{Support} \\ \text{Test} \\ \text{Large} \\ \text{Real Time} \\ \text{Batch} \\ \text{Application} \\ \text{Interactive} \\ \text{etc.} \end{array}\right\} \text{Software}$$

We should not tolerate statements such as "70 percent of the cost of software is in the continued development." In many instances this is right; in many wrong. It is too gross a statement. We should insist on more specificity, or qualifying adjectives. Noncomputer people are not only mystified by computers and software, but resentful of the jargon and sloppiness of the field. If the professionals do not demand precision, are they professionals?

5

SOFTWARE DEVELOPMENT

We have categorized the world of software, and will now look specifically at its development. This is the area that gives us the most trouble today.

The aspects common to every program give us insights into some of the more subtle but very important attributes of programs. There are at least 12 such aspects or attributes. See Table 5-1.

PROGRAM ATTRIBUTES

TABLE 5-1.

Attributes of Every Program	Usually Called
1. Causes the computer to do something	Function
2. Takes memory to reside in	Size
3. Needs the CPU to run	Efficiency
4. Ease of use	Useability
5. Ease of recovery	Robustness; recoverability
6. Contains errors	Correctness
7. Takes time to create	Schedule
8. Takes people to create	Human resources to develop
9. Takes tools to create	Nonhuman resources to develop
10. Takes money to create	Cost
11. Is modifiable	Architecture, structure
12. Exists in at least one form and should be two	Documentation

These 12 aspects compete with each other for their embodiment in the program. Programs written quickly (Aspect 7) are usually more wasteful of storage (2) and machine cycles (3) than those written more slowly. The quickly-written program often does not do 100 percent of the function it was supposed to do (1). It may do almost all the payroll, but we may have to keep two clerks to perform a function that the computer was supposed to do, and has the capacity to do, but which just didn't get programmed on time. This is a *very* common occurrence.

If we need a program to compute a payroll by June 1 of next year, we may add more people between now and then so that the extra man-months can shorten the duration of the development. Obviously if it takes 100 man-months to create a program, we might put 10 people on the job for 10 months. But we cannot put 100 people on it for one month and get a program.

Short schedules thwart the attempt to make the overall structure easy to modify (11). Low development cost, (10), is in opposition to *all* the other items. See Table 5-2.

Management must make the trade-offs, after the designers give their estimates of the possible choices that are open.

TABLE 5-2.   Twelve Aspects of Every Program

Development phase	Takes time to create	Schedule
	Takes people to create	Development team
	Takes tools to create	Development tools
	Takes money to create	Cost
Use phase	Causes the computer to do something	Function
	Takes memory to reside in	Size
	Uses the CPU to run	Efficiency
	Is easy to use	Useability
	Is easy to keep running	Recovery
	Contains errors	Correctness
Continued development phase	Is modifiable	Architecture
	Exists in at least one form and should be two	Documentation

Let's look at the use phase aspects

1. Every program performs a function; e.g., it calculates a payroll. At this point we have no metrics to quantify function, but by observation we can determine if the program is performing the functions we want done.

2. Every program requires storage space to reside in when it is running. If memory is scarce, we'll expend time and people to squeeze the program into a small version.

3. Every program uses machine resources as it is executed. Said differently, how quickly does the machine do the payroll *with this program*? If our CPU is slow, developers will pore over the program to design it so as to eke out the last ounces of CPU power.

4. Ease of use. Some programs thwart the attempts of people to use them. They are not "user-friendly." Such ease of use is not an accidental byproduct of development, but of careful design and of stating the requirement for it.

5. The larger a program, the more chance there is that there are errors in it, and even rigorous testing will not catch them all. Many of these errors will only show up with uncommon combinations of data and users.

6. Every program has to be kept running. Some are easy to restart; others are not. Again, this is a feature to be *designed* into the software.

Let's look at the development phase aspects:

7. Every program takes time (duration) to develop. This is almost always inadequate in large systems. And it often is *the* ruling criteria, dominating the other aspects.

8. Every program takes some number of people over time (man-months) to create.

9. Every program takes tools to create; e.g., a computer to compile from high order languages, to test with, and cards, tapes, space, programs to compile, programs to test with, and many more.

10. Every program requires money to develop.

And now the continued development time aspects:

11. When new requirements show up, they must be added to the program. A hastily developed program will be harder to modify than a carefully designed one. How well designed, how modular, is the software?

12. So many programs exist on only a magnetic tape that it is almost a cliche to mention it. And the poor people committed to fixing errors and adding features must go on archeological expeditions to try to understand what the original developer was *trying* to do. We need clear documentation!

Let's plot these aspects of every program against the life cycle of a program (Fig. 5-1).

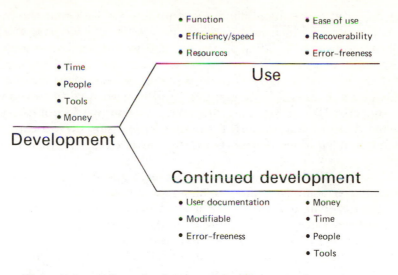

Figure 5-1. Life cycle phases and the 12 aspects of a program.

Note that the four development time aspects are also continued development time aspects!

Often modifiability *is never considered at all*, with the result that the team at continued development time is trying to modify a block of concrete! Often with no documentation.

There are many programs that do not need to be evolved. There are many that do not have to be user-friendly. And we should not burden the development of such programs with requirements that do not exist. But we should expect our development managers to consciously *decide* that these are not requirements, and to be able to defend that judgment.

The life of *any* product or tool is a multiphased one. All tools have at least two phases — development and use. Some, most, have a third, maintenance or improvement.

The simple wooden *tooth pick*, like the hammer in Chap. 4, is a two-phased tool. You make it, you use it, and you throw it away. There is no maintenance phase.

There are "toothpick programs" that I write once, get them to run, get a satisfactory answer, and then throw away.

Then there is a metal hammer. We make it and we use it. It requires no maintenance, but we use it over and over many times.

There are "hammer programs." We write them, and get them to work and then we run them over and over. They, like the hammer, need no updates, or changes, or fixes.

Then there are "building programs" which, like an office that we

work in, need to be maintained. Occasionally we find that the builder
did not quite put in a nail or screw just right, and we have to fix it.
Most programs are "building programs" and we often add a new "wing"
to the building.

Now we have looked at these three examples because they set the
stage for us to look at software quality. We need quality in the tooth
pick only for its use. With a tooth pick program, we do not care about
its construction — as long as it works for us — nor do we care about
documenting it, since we are going to use it once and then throw it
away.

The quality of the hammer we do care about since we are going
to use it over time. Not many hammers will break upon first use, but a
poor quality hammer will break a lot sooner than one that is made
from better material and in a more careful manner.

So too with *"hammer programs."* Since we will use them over and
over, we will put a little more care and effort ($$) into their construc-
tion, and will be content that this investment will pay off for us in the
use phase of the "hammer programs."

But note that we have no modification (maintenance) phase in
these programs. Therefore, we need *documentation* only for the use of
these programs. As long as we have a copy of the program in machine-
readable form, we have no need for any documentation about the
program. If it is correct and will never need to be changed, all we need
is user instructions.

Now we go to the "building program" and we see immediately
that if we wish to add an additional room to our building, then it is
of great help in estimating and planning and execution if we know
where the water pipes, joists, electrical junctions, wires, and a lot of
other things are. We need the documentation of the details of the
construction, not user documentation, so that we can more easily
change.

> The only reason that we need documentation for our "building programs" is
> because we know that we may have to change them and the documentation
> makes the changing easier.

This is a most interesting assertion; let us poke at it.

Stated negatively, if we know that we will never have to make a
change or fix to a program that is working for us, we never have to
have it in any human readable form.

If we were the possessors of such a program, and there are many
such possessors in our world today, we would simply load it onto the
computer, run it, get the results, and be happy with the answer.

Of course, we would be nervous at times that we might uncover
some latent deficiency or error in the program, or that the environment

might change and we might be forced to either try to understand the structure of the program or write a new one from scratch, but if those disasters never occurred during our turn at the helm, then we would say of our program that we were very well satisfied with it indeed. It did its job and we were content.

Now probably the majority of the programs in the world are "building programs," containing errors and omissions and needing updates to keep them in tune with the changing world out there. And therefore, just like the construction crew, the modifiers need the blueprints and documentation to get in there and fix the program.

If our builder followed good commercial practice, he or she put in a certain size of wire, wood, pipes, and he or she put them in in a certain manner. Knowing this, we can count on these things, and this makes our task easier again.

So too with the software. If our programmers and designers of the original software followed "good commercial practice," then our task is much, much easier. Even more so than with the building, as we are dealing with intangible things.

THE PROCESS OF SOFTWARE DEVELOPMENT

There are many ways of breaking the development of software into parts. Some breakdowns have more subpieces than others. Six steps seem to be adequate, and they are:

Software Development:
  Requirements definition
  Design
  Write the code — program
  Construction
  Test
  Documentation

The first activity, requirements definition, is the area of most difficulty in large type Vs, and we will look at it shortly in some detail.

Design here is the software design, not the system design of which the software is but a part. We will cover design in some depth, after requirements definition.

The writing of the instructions, the reduction of the design of the software or programs to actual machine usable instructions, is third. We also call this programming.

Construction means the process of combining, interconnecting, parts of programs written by different people or teams into *one* software system. If we have 700 programmers creating programs, then the task of "linking" them together can be formidable, time consuming, expensive, and error prone. We will see that there are separate development tools for construction apart from those tools for writing the instructions.

Testing, or verification as it is now frequently being called, is a critical and difficult activity.

Documentation, as we have seen, is critical to continued development.

The Path Through

When we list the process as we do in Fig. 5-2, we know it is never quite this crisp and clear.

Obviously only the simplest of tasks goes through the steps without iterating back to some of the earlier steps continuously. One learns in design that a specific requirement will double the cost of a

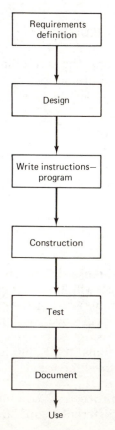

Figure 5-2.   Idealized path through software development.

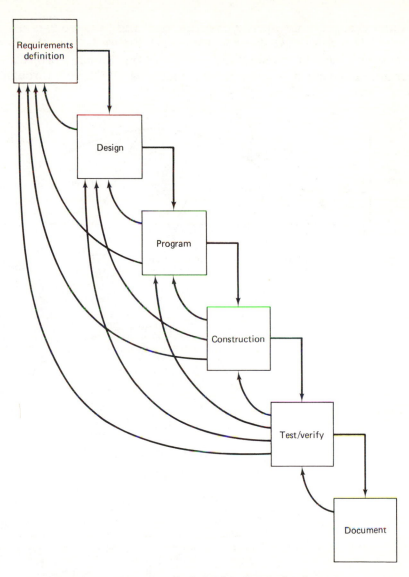

Figure 5-3. Real path through software development.

subsystem. The developer must reset and reevaluate the requirements. This process is incessant. As new information flows into the project team as it builds the software, the design must be modified. (See Fig. 5-3.)

In the late 1960s we conducted a course in IBM FSD Gaithersburg called the PPMC — the Project Programming Managers Course, designed to tell the new manager what to look out for in his or her effort, and how to manage the project to an optimum end. (See Fig. 5-4.) The material changed only slightly over the years and here are two manning diagrams that were used about 5 years apart. Figure 5-4 was finally seen as incorrect. Design would really never end on the large projects. The diagram was changed to show design occurring all the way through the entire development phase. (See Fig. 5-5.)

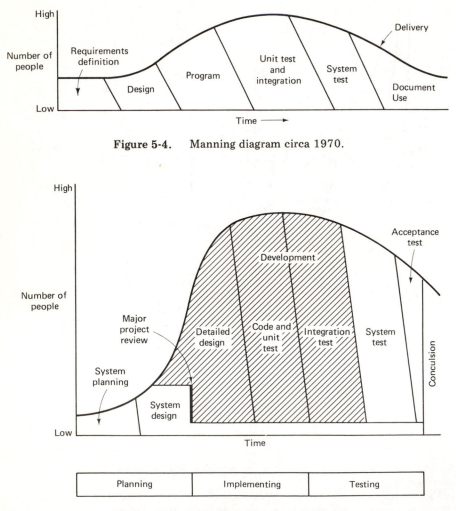

Figure 5-4.   Manning diagram circa 1970.

Figure 5-5.   Manning diagram circa 1975.

We never did catch up with the fact that the requirements activity, just like the design activity, had to continue through the entire effort.

The number of people is shown as falling off rapidly after the delivery date. It never did on large type Vs. The reason it did not fall off was that the "Law of Fixed Schedule" almost always applied — the schedule dictated that many functions promised and planned had to be abandoned in order to meet the schedule. Abandoned but temporarily, the project put the promised function in *after* the 'delivery.'

How much time must be spent in each of the six steps varies based on many factors, as we will see. But the size of the software, based on the functions to be done, is one of the key determinants. Writing the code shrinks as a percentage of time and effort as the size of the project grows.

These erroneous staffing diagrams have a long life. A diagram like Fig. 5-6 appeared in a leading magazine in the field in 1979.

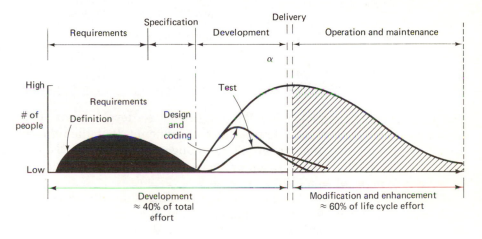

Figure 5-6.   A Manning diagram for types I and II.

There is nothing wrong with the diagram *for a small program* in a well-known, already automated application. But the diagram is *wrong* for large software systems and even small-sized operations/process applications! The requirements definition and design effort continue.

Figure 5-7, by Andrew Ferrentino, comes much closer to depicting what really happens, or better said, what should happen in large scale software development.

Look once again at the model of the development we used at IBM Federal Systems Division in the early 1970s (Fig. 5-5). It's depiction of design is correct, as we have seen, but it is incorrect for all developments in its depiction of testing. It shows testing starting well into coding.

As we can see from the correct model, testing should start soon after the requirements definition "first pass."

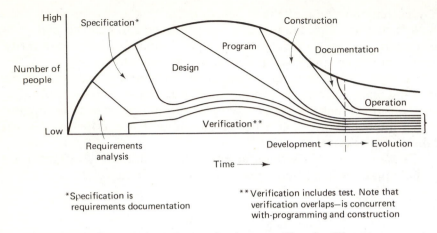

Figure 5-7. The software development Manning Diagram.

BIG BANG VERSUS EVOLUTION

The early diagrams depict a Big Bang approach to development. This presumes that the developers know the requirements, that the requirements are stable, and that an efficient enough approach to satisfying them can be designed. This situation occurs only in simple programs, type I and type II, of small to medium size.

What occurs in type III, IV, and V situations is that the developer does not understand the requirements. When the *user* gets the *first version* of the system and says, "Ah Ha—Look at what we can do with this," a flood of new requirements flows from the use of the initial version! No one can predict how the user will use a *really* new tool. How fast the developer now responds with a second system depends on a great variety of things, and a very important one is the amount of *control* the developer has over the user! In other words, are we in a project or product situation?

And as we have mentioned, the initial delivery rarely contains all the functions promised. The missing functions are created *after* the first delivery.

The key point is that the predicted staffing curve should *not* come down by 50 percent after initial delivery! It does not in the real world! What really happens is that several versions of the system are built, each with more function and fewer errors, and user experience is incorporated into the later versions.

This practice of planning and budgeting for a long-term development is lacking in many large organizations. The "sociology" of getting

98

approval for new systems, perhaps, explains some of this, but sheer inexperience is often the reason for this mistaken adoption of the Big Bang approach.

"Sociology?" Yes, to show the number of development personnel staying constant year after year may be so expensive that the project is rejected. So the Big Bang manning chart is used. Big Bang development works just fine for small type I and type II computer application software development. Big Bang anywhere else is nothing but a gamble, and usually a senseless one! (See Fig. 5-8).

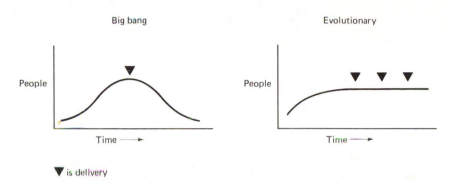

▼ is delivery

Figure 5-8. Staffing plans — Big Bang versus evolutionary development.

Nothing we have seen so far in any way describes the vast human effort to *create* a large body of instructions — software. Let us now look at the process of creating and developing a million-lines-of-code system.

First, we will look at the end result — what does the million lines of code look like? No one has ever seen a million lines of code. If we listed the 1,000,000 lines on a paper, 10 instructions to the inch, we would have 100,000 in. of paper. That is more than 8000 ft of paper.

The way we visualize the 1,000,000 lines of code is to visualize sub pieces of the program *and* their interrelationships. We will look at ways to depict such software shortly on page 120.

The scale of the development effort must sometimes be seen to be believed. Dozens, even scores, of people can be involved in the effort to define the requirements, to state *what* the system is to do!

Fewer should be involved in the initial design, but hundreds and even thousands may be involved in the writing, the programming. Dozens again in the construction, and scores or even hundreds in the testing, and scores in the documentation. (See Fig. 5-9.)

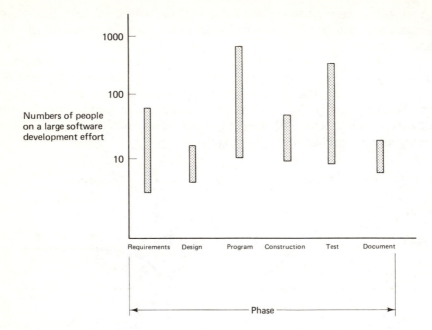

Figure 5-9. People per development phase.

REQUIREMENTS DEFINITION

This step is the most important of the six in the development process. It affects and colors all the rest. Alas, it is the least studied and the least understood.

There are at least two pieces to this effort; first, to understand what is to be done and second, to document it. Without the second part, the large project is not under control. *If it is not written down and available, it does not exist.* That it may exist in the mind of a brilliant person leaves the large project open to the disaster of sudden disappearance.

Systems Level Requirements

Requirements definition is a system level problem that evolves down to the software level. If we look at the typical large operations/ process type V system we can see something like Fig. 5-10.

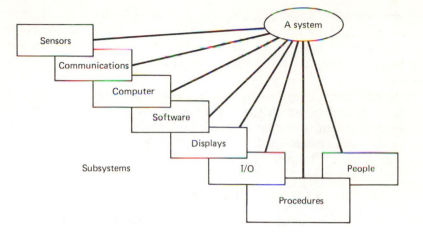

Figure 5-10. A system/subsystems.

CHANGE IS INEVITABLE

From the system level requirements come the requirements for the sub-systems. As effort proceeds, changes, limitations or breakthroughs in the subsystems will affect the system level requirements and design, and the process is iterative.

The software requirements are the most affected by this in-process adjustment as the software becomes the last adjustment possible with which the project manager may fix the discontinuities. The hardware — computers, radars, displays, banking units, modems — all take years to change. Hopefully the software can be wrenched around to meet the new situation in a few months!

I had 500 people in the Los Angeles area doing a real time effort involving a satellite. The satellite went into the wrong orbit, an irregular orbit. The instruments did not work the way they were designed, and some did not work at all. With great effort, my people modified the software so that it got the job done.

Then we found that the customer was upset because we had exceeded our budget! We patiently pointed out that our $3 million extra had saved years of time. And avoided the expenditure of $50,000,000 for a new satellite. We were reluctantly judged to be OK!

Software is always last; it naturally takes up the slack for the failures of other subsystems. It inherits their slips and errors.

The requirements definition for a type I accounting use, or for a type II, is simple, and it is almost always well done. The opposite is true for the large types III, IV, and V. The newness of the computer compounds the requirements definition of never-done-before large systems. People have never used mechanized systems in these areas, and therefore they do not understand what is possible with these new systems.

In addition to this unknown, two other factors are at play. First, the environment in which the system is to work will change, probably before the system is in operation. Second, the system itself will change. Its various components will not be as they are expected to be by the time the system is fielded.

TABLE 5-3.   Real Time Systems Changes

Outside the System Changes	System Changes
The number of users	The satellite
The strategy	The radar
The tactics	The sensors
The structure of the user organization	The displays
	The navigation
The user regimen	The platform
The priorities	The missile
The communication network	The intelligence inputs
The decision strategy	
The threat	

Indeed, the better question is "What will not change"? This sets up the first requirement for all large software systems, as we saw on page 75.

> The *first requirement of large software systems* is that the software be designed to be changed easily!

How this is to be done will be discussed in the next section on design.

WHO STATES SOFTWARE REQUIREMENTS?

How do we arrive at the first statement of requirements? I say the first because we know that the process will be done several times, as the development moves from requirements to design and back to requirements.

Who is available to state requirements? The user, of course, and the systems designer. *Both* of these groups should be charged with stating requirements. Neither one alone can do an adequate job in this area.

The user knows the application and the many nuances present in any complex endeavor. The user must be sure that the requirements state accurately *and* completely the operational problem.

The user does *not* know the state of the technology and what is easy. When the user alone states the requirements, we often see technologically naive statements of requirements, demanding far too much or way too little.

The designer usually never knows the intricacies of the application. Were we to allow the designers to state the needs, we'd likely get a statement which *missed* subtle but critical functions. When the user receives such a system, they are sure that it was conceived and built in an ivory tower. The designer must state the infrastructure needs, which are usually not visible to the user. Both user and designer must state the requirements, in order to have an adequate statement of needs. (See Table 5-4.)

TABLE 5-4.	User and Designer versus Requirement Definition	
Statement of Requirements		
	Can Do	Will Miss
User {	Get important needs clear	Technological advances
	Priorities in right order	Infrastructure needs
Designer {	Technological state of the art	Sizing what the user can absorb
	Assess the completeness of the need statement	Subtleties of application

Requirements Documentation Language

The language in which the requirements are stated should be comprehensible to the user. The user must be kept in the evolving statement of the requirements. The requirements statement will tend to slip into technical design vocabulary. This kind of statement belongs in the design document, not the requirements document.

OVERRIDING IMPORTANCE OF REQUIREMENTS

Since the requirements come first, they affect the rest of the effort. If this process is not done carefully, precisely, and adequately, all remaining parts of the development process suffer. The following development efforts may be superb, but they are not creating the right system.

Errors, distortions, and ambiguities will be treated by the implementers as valid requirements, not only wasting the effort to implement them, but creating additional effort to *get them out again*! A bad requirement is like a warped microscope lens — it distorts all.

A Department of Defense study was conducted in August, 1977 of nine major automated systems. Most were communications systems. They were:

1. TRI-TAC
2. LDMX/NAVCOMPARS and AMMC/SRT
3. SATIN IV
4. WMMCCS NORAD/COC
5. WWMCCS ADP-LANTCOM
6. Pentagon Telecommunications Center
7. WWMCCS ADP — CCTC
8. Automated Tech Control
9. CUDIX/NAVMASC

The study summarized:

- All had unstable and changing requirements; the bigger the system, the worse the rate of change.
- Most lacked any formal mechanism to track/manage requirements.
- Some did not even perceive the need to validate requirements.
- Most were plagued by "wish lists."

The study summary accurately describes my experiences in the commercial realm of computers.

An experienced home builder can get into deep difficulty if he or she is working for a rich and relaxed buyer. Such a buyer may be guilty of introducing constant changes into the den, the living room, the porch, and to all and any rooms in the house. The builder may be experienced, proficient, efficient, resourceful, and competent — and yet he or she will not be able to finish the house within the assigned time and dollars. Nor may he or she be able to deliver a decent looking house. Changes made midway in projects of any kind have a way of looking out of place when the job is done.

Even if one perceives the need and applies the talent, the requirements can still resist being tamed. Once again, we need to:

1. State the requirement as accurately as possible.
2. Plan to change the system.

IN A PROJECT, WHO IS THE REAL USER?

Often systems are developed by the research and development division of an organization. Its task is to understand what is required by the eventual user.

We were feeling very satisfied when in the early 1970s we had successfully completed the first delivery of the system for the new En-Route Air Traffic Control System. The R&D Service of the FAA had signed the certificate of completion. It had been a long haul.

The system was sent to the Jacksonville, Florida En-Route Air Traffic Control Center for a live use test on the 12 midnight to 8 AM shift. The controllers in Jacksonville refused to use the system — it was "unsafe," they said.

"Unsafe" in Air Traffic Control gets attention. We solved this problem by ripping out — disabling — a sizeable percentage of the functions that the software was capable of doing. We then delivered to Jacksonville much less system function. The controllers loved it. And we gradually — slowly — added back the functions already programmed and tested.

This was corroboration of what the Houston people had told me. You cannot give people 40 pounds of icing and expect them to accept it in one lump. It doesn't work.

It cost us more to do it this way! It took longer to get all the functions brought on-line. But there was no alternative.

This is another reason for the need for the evolutionary approach to systems development. The users cannot swallow all the function at once, even if the developers can deliver it.

But we had learned our lesson. Starting then, the FAA assigned full-time line controllers to the requirements definition team. Over the years, these invaluable people were rotated to the project and back to the field. In this fashion, the real user needs were the ones the development team were working on.

The bigger the system, the more prone it is to be built too complex to be used, or to solve some problem that went away years ago.

I am personally aware of two major systems, developed over several years for several millions of dollars, where the user threw out half of the delivered function *after* it went through the whole development cycle. The operators could not accept it.

CONFLICTING REQUIREMENTS OF MULTIPLE USERS

My development team lost 2 million dollars automating the two largest newspapers in Japan — and later received the Japanese Ishikawa Medal for Achievement in Technology and Industry. We had signed up with one newspaper to go from text entry in Kanji (Japanese ideogram characters) characters, to manipulation by editors and page layout people on a TV display, to a film that went right to the presses. We could have done that job within budget. But IBM Japan had signed up a second newspaper, a competitor of the first, to use the system. And the two newspapers disagreed regularly on what functions were to be done and how they were to be done.

Such a conflicting set of requirements stresses the development process and the design of the system. It must have a "backbone," an infrastructure, on which to hang the different software pieces that do different things for different newspapers. Building it that way and changing requirements constantly made the effort larger than simply automating one newspaper.

A few years later we lost 10 million dollars automating two new Exxon refineries, one in Edmonton, Canada and one in Antwerp, Belgium. The same problem again, trying to *understand* the functions to be done, and then trying to satisfy two *different* users. Just because they were both Exxon didn't mean they agreed on the way to control a refinery. Again, the system worked! And worked well. It is just that it could not be estimated with any accuracy in advance.

The other underlying reason that requirements can not be "frozen" is that the users of such systems are about to use a new tool. And our tool law applies. As the understanding of the power of the new tool dawns, the users see new functions that will be far more effective if they are put into the system. They *can not* forsee all, or sometimes even most, of these functions in advance.

One lesson that comes out of these efforts again and again is that of the difference between a product and a project. A project is working for *one* customer; a product must satisfy a great many customers. Time and time again — on both the refineries and the newspapers — we had to reset and restart because, after *one* refinery/newspaper agreed to the process to be automated, the second one wanted something different. "Just a little different."

PRODUCT VERSUS PROJECT REQUIREMENTS

One fundamental difference between building software for a product and building software for a project is in the *process* of coming up with the requirements that the software is to satisfy.

With a product, one has multiple customers to satisfy, and a process of requirement definition and *compromise* is needed to avoid overburdening the effort. Yet the product will run into competition when it gets announced. And if it works but doesn't sell, what good is it?

For software products as for hardware products, a sizeable and knowledgeable team of product requirements personnel should be applied full time — before the development goes forward into its other phases.

Users Change

The seasoned systems manager knows that to design a system to fit the idiosyncracies of one or a group of powerful users is to doom the system to a short life. Systems that are this personalized never survive the departure of the user they were designed for. This problem is encountered far more often in the military systems than anywhere else.

Adaptability Invites Unceasing Change

No one seriously suggests major changes to the Golden Gate Bridge. And the lower deck on the George Washington Bridge was possible because the bridge was designed to carry that lower deck *from the beginning*.

Bricks, iron, and steel take years to prepare and construct, and are not easily reconfigured. One does not *bend* steel into new shapes. One does not rebuild into a new architecture the tens of thousands of transistors in a computer. Ah, but software!

Its very name indicts it; it is soft. It exists on *paper*, in electrons! We can change it easily, if we build it properly. And we want *it* to be easily changed!

Requirements Definition is a Continuous Task

Unless there are people assigned full time to requirements definition, then the design and implementation team will produce a "wrong" — and perhaps unuseable — system.

In the normal course of events a document is produced, signed by all parties, and labeled Requirements — and it is then promptly forgotten and allowed to become obsolete. It is an archival piece of junk, useful only for fault finding. On a 1 million line of code DoD system, the Requirements document was not changed in 8 years! The software was! Requirements documents are essential to a good development effort and *must* be kept current. And this means money and *good* people must be applied to the task throughout the life of the project.

So many projects do not even see a need for a requirements group. They usually assume that the development and/or the design group will do that function. But they do not! They've enough on their plates as it is; they are too busy with designing and developing to worry about the requirements, and they will deflate needs in order to meet their cost and delivery targets.

If asked, they'll state confidently that they "know the requirements." Nine out of ten times they do not!

The Requirement Specification

English is full of ambiguities and therefore mischief. We found that the English language is not up to the task of doing these specifications. With NSDG (the U.S. Newspaper System Development Group) nine newspapers around the U.S. were going to automate their newspaper production even beyond the Japanese accomplishment.

We anticipated the problem of specifying user requirements and spent great effort and years coming up with a precise document, 2400 pages in length, that covered *everything*. Except that when we went to the document to settle questions, we found that we and they read it differently. In good faith, in good faith. Indeed an editor from one newspaper could not agree with editors from a second newspaper as to what the document specified in the editing areas. The language is just too ambiguous for precision.

We had the same problem on a Navy real-time system. We were only a few months from delivery, and we had a 1500 page User Requirement Specification — the development manager told me he would make the delivery date and cost targets — and "the requirements keep changing." "What about the Requirements Spec?" I asked. "Oh, no one pays any attention to it. It's been out of date for months." Yet he was going to meet delivery and cost. For what?

The Requirement to Define the Use-Time Environment

Up till now we've been talking about the need to define the *user* requirements. But one other thing must be clearly defined, the use-time environment requirements. *The need to satisfy the use-time environment requirements can multiply the effort required to create the software by a factor of 10.*

The *major* use-time factors are:

1. Reliability requirements
2. Response requirements

3. Real-time requirements

4. Interactive (with people) requirements

These requirements must be satisfied by software and hardware, yet are seen by the user only in their absence. If they are done correctly, the user never sees them.

We'll discuss each of these in this chapter, and other use-time requirements and development-time factors, and see why these factors have such a pervasive effect.

The developer often has the opportunity to state the use-time environment to the user! But the opportunity to do so must be seen and seized! I have seen large type IIIs that were evolving into Vs *because* no one told the users — executive management — that there would be periods of downtime of several hours duration. This should have been an acceptable condition. There was plenty of data to keep the users busy. The system need not be fail safe! But someone has to state that before the user demands — unreasonably — that the system never be down.

To get a fail-safe system costs a lot of money — a lot of redundant hardware *and* a lot of very logically complex software.

Managing the Requirements

The requirements cannot just be "gathered" and documented. They must be managed! This is especially true in the software product. So many software products die — after expenditures of tens of millions of dollars — because the development manager has said OK to too many requirements. Some call this "creeping elegance." The better is the enemy of the good. It is usually fatal. Salesmen will always fight for the nth function; development managers must refuse to add to the requirements.

The same is true for projects in the type III, IV, and V categories. One cannot simply *list* all the items the user (we assume we have found the real user) desires. To do so is to overburden the system. The user often doesn't know what is needed, nor the cost of what is desired.

The software development manager must assign someone to be the requirements manager, and this job goes in both directions at once. First, the requirements manager must force the real user requirements into the statement of need. And second, he or she must keep the user under control and not allow a ridiculous specification of requirements.

In a project, the user should be a codeveloper with the software developer. And the communication between the two should be continuous and intensive. Co-location is essential in getting the right facts! The software developer's job is to satisfy the user. If that is done, the project is a success.

There are new techniques, too few at present, that are helping make this first phase of software development more manageable. Similar to the concept of languages and compilers, the underlying principle of these new techniques is the concept of abstraction. The techniques are a combination of notational rules and process rules.

The process rules force abstraction to occur; the notation rules allow for ease of communication and review. The process forces the systems people to spend *long* periods of time in the requirements definition phase — sometimes to the dismay of management. But it pays off.

The desired characteristics of the methodologies are:

- Decomposition into levels of abstraction. (Fundamental for analyzing complex systems.)
- A limited number of elements per level of abstraction — essential to success — usually 7 or less.
- A bounded context: *all* items that belong to a process must be included; all that do not must be excluded.
- Both data and activities must be included.

The new techniques for improving the process of defining requirements are promising and complex. They are usually a combination of documentation techniques *and* process rules.

Several of the new techniques are:

SADT	Structured Analysis/Design Technology
IA	Information Analysis
HIPO	Hierarchical Input Process Output Charts
PSL/PSA	Problem Statement Language, Problem Statement Analyzer
RSL/REVS	Requirements Statement Language/Requirements Evaluation and Validation Systems
CARA	Computer Aided Requirements Analysis

Most of these have the formal and rigid notation, and the stepwise refinement process.

These techniques hold great promise, and some day we will look back and wonder that we didn't always do it that way. These techniques can't be summarized in a page or even a chapter. They require books and a 2-week course to understand.

Experience

We failed at first trying to really understand the FAA Air Traffic Controllers' needs. The R&D group needed the constant input from the "person on the line." We did fine when our developers sat side by side with the users — at Houston.

We failed — with the Houston group — when we tried to understand the needs of the power companies. We failed — with the Houston group — when we tried to understand the needs of the oil refineries. We failed — at first — when we tried to understand the Japanese newspaper requirements. The requirements process is still the major stumbling block in the new and large software systems.

Summary: Requirements for Large Software Systems

1. The first requirement is for a system that can be changed easily, as the requirements will change constantly. The software must be planned to evolve; the budget and plan must allow for this.
2. There should be a permanent requirements manager through the life of the effort.
3. Requirements should be controlled.
4. If the requirement is not written down and available, it does not exist. Requirements in people's heads are mischievous and perishable.
5. The real users must be sought and involved, not their surrogates.
6. The personality of the users must be kept out of the requirement.
7. A requirements definition methodology should be used.

DESIGN

What is Design?

The word is a noun *and* a verb, and a transitive and intransitive verb. Design, as a transitive verb is (1) "to prepare the preliminary sketch or the plan for (a work to be executed); especially to plan the form and structure of; for example, to design a new bridge, and (2) to plan and fashion artistically or skillfully."

This area is difficult because it is to a large extent art. Design involves choice. One chooses the form, shape, sequence, color interconnection scheme, or other variables, and makes an arrangement.

There is very good design and there is very bad design. In architecture, design has a functional *and* aesthetic quality. In the functional sense, it either makes "good use" of space or it does not. In the aesthetic sense it either "looks nice" or it doesn't. In the functional sense, there are some "metrics" one can apply, some rules of thumb. How much did it cost per square foot to build? To heat? To cool? How many "living units" (or working units) were achieved? How long did it take to construct? There are numerous measures one can apply here.

In the artistic sense, what is beautiful to one is not to another. Only if something is very good or bad do we find some kind of unanimity of opinion.

With software, what is it that we are even designing? This is not a trivial question! What parts or pieces, shapes or colors, interfaces or shapes can we select?

In *"Notes on the Synthesis of Form,"** Christopher Alexander makes several significant points about design. One of the most interesting is that there is no way to measure design positively, but one can only look to the *absence* of negative features to see how well the design fits (his word) the situation. This idea of "fit" is one he dwells on, and he means by it the applicability of the design to the situation, to the circumstance.

Alexander differentiates between "self-conscious" and "non self-conscious" design. Non self-conscious design evolves over centuries, so that the houses and huts of all native people fit the environment in which they are used. All changes are slow and gradual, each being evaluated carefully and over decades before it is generally accepted. Design is the adaptation of the dwelling to the needs.

Self-conscious design is the type of design we do now. With change rushing at us rapidly from all directions, with new tools and technologies and businesses arriving every day, design is ad hoc and immediate. One sees if it is good or not by looking at fit, and by comparing it with a competing design, if any; by seeing if it works.

SOFTWARE IS A SUBSYSTEM

System, subsystem, software, program and even code are the levels of design we must go through in order to get the system we desire.

The system as a whole is composed of subsystems, and the very choice of subsystems is a design in itself. For a nationwide satellite system we could have many different sets of subsystems.

---

*Christopher Alexander, *Notes on the Synthesis of Form* (Cambridge, Mass.: Harvard University Press, 1964).

Arrangement I	Satellite; space to ground system; terrestrial system, etc.
Arrangement II	Satellite; microwave system; computer system, etc.
Arrangement III	Satellite; communication system; message system; control system, etc.

This top level decision is a very critical one; it will set to a major extent the way the system is built, run, and maintained.

The software subsystem fits within the data processing subsystem, which can be a subsystem of one, two, or even all of the major subsystems. There are certainly computers in the satellite and therefore, there is software in the satellite. There is probably software in every major subsystem.

Computer hardware and software together make a DP subsystem. The software *must* "fit" the hardware and be designed so as to enhance its performance and the performance of the system.

This sounds so simple; yet often the manager of the DP hardware has no knowledge of software, and selects the computer based on price and speed alone. Software development is ignored. I have seen this mistake made even when software development is acknowledged to be *the* pacing item in the development schedule.

Systems design should make trade-off choices between hardware and software, and software designers must contribute to the information used to make the choice.

Multiple and Concurrent Design

There are scores and even hundreds of designs under way concurrently. Figures 5-11 through 5-17 depict this.

Requirements

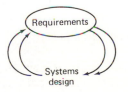

Figure 5-11. A requirement.

Figure 5-12. Iteration between requirement and design.

As designs progress, the developers return again and again to the requirements, revalidate them, or modify them based on specific conclusions of the design effort.

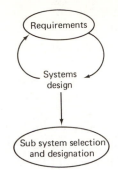

Figure 5-13. Into subsystems.

One of the most important outputs of the systems design effort is the compartmentalization of the entire system into subsystems. The selection of subsystems sets the nature of the system and its development to a major extent. Requirements for each subsystem are produced, and each is to be compatible with the top level requirements.

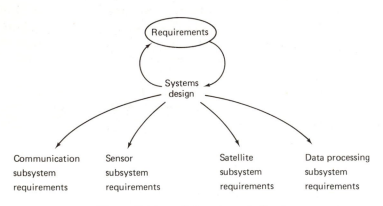

Figure 5-14. Subsystems defined.

Parallel Development

At the point shown in Fig. 5-15 each of the subsystems is developed concurrently. Obviously different people are doing the individual designs, and all of this must be checked and controlled by the systems designer (or systems engineering group).

This process of adding more and more detail to the higher level designs continues. From here on we will show only one subsystem. Since we wish to go into software to some depth, we'll follow the data processing subsystem (Fig. 5-16), which should have most of the soft-

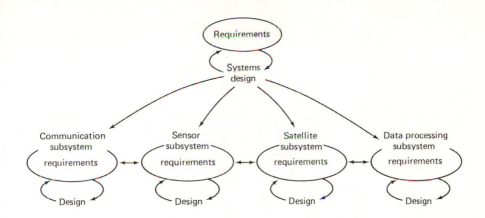

Figure 5-15.   Subsystems design — more iteration.

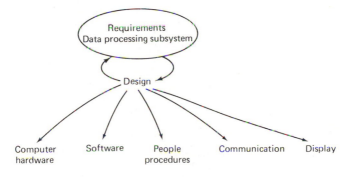

Figure 5-16.   The DP subsystem and its parts.

ware. But every subsystem may have some software. The data processing subsystem design must be partitioned into further parts.

And of course each of these subsubsystems can be further divided. If we were to depict the "final" breakdown into sub pieces, we would see a rich "tree" of designs, as shown in Fig. 5-17. We quickly run out of means to depict the system in one diagram. There are scores of designs under way at once! And the interconnection of those sub pieces that must interact with each other is a part of the system design. The selection of subsystems is in the first place based on minimizing the interplay between subsystems — *and* the design of each of the subsystems must itself state the means of satisfying the input required from each of the other subsystems, and the items that must be sent from the subsystems being designed to the other subsystems.

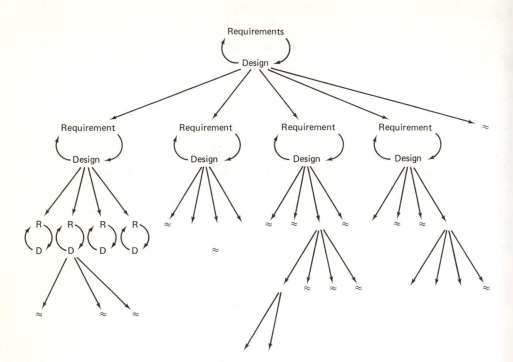

Figure 5-17. A 'tree' of designs.

Iteration of Design and Requirements

Another way to show iteration is Fig. 5-18. The dotted line areas depict the yet-to-be defined activities that stem from the defined, solid lined areas. The month of the activity shown is a gross depiction of the passage of time. The months could have been numbered weeks and would be on a smaller system, and even days on a simple system.

Note the restart in March. As the detailing in February progressed, the designers found either a major flaw or a far more optimum approach. Therefore, they have backed off to the start, redefined the old start, A, to a new one, B. Obviously all or most of the subsequent subdivisions must be changed also. Parts of the earlier 1, 2, and 3 may be used in the new C, P, and L.

The iteration of design occurs constantly. It is the nature of design to encounter surprises. If one could see the path through perfectly, it would not be design but depiction. The iteration occurs at all levels, even the micro design level. The events and discoveries that cause change are not always hierarchical; some are lateral or peer design efforts. The February depiction shows that four activities are being detailed and

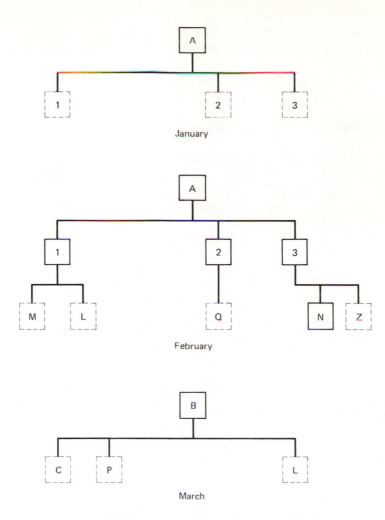

Figure 5-18. A changing design.

defined simultaneously — *and they do not exist* independently of each other; they often interact. The interactions must be examined, detailed, and sometimes designed. The interaction and the detail of one or more of the activities or functions may need to be changed depending on *how* a designer chooses to do something. As Z is defined, we may have to make modifications in Q, for example.

Obviously, this example is inadequate to describe what is happening in a large development effort. Dozens, scores or hundreds of designs are being done simultaneously. A beehive of design activity is under way, and it *must* all be coordinated.

A logical conclusion of all the above is that the statement "90 percent designed" is not a fact, but an estimate, as no one really knows if some surprise will not force us to iterate back and redo supposedly finished design.

Yet we hear over and over that "design is 90 percent complete."

THE DESIGN OF USE-TIME SOFTWARE

Let us hold hardware constant for the moment, and assume that it's a perfect fit for the task. What then do we design in the software?

We design, choose, first the major partitions of the programs. Are we to have separate systems software? A separate operating system? A data base management system?

How do we judge whether we want these functions separate or integrated with the application programs? We judge that by looking at two things; the requirements stated in the Requirements Statement (both functional and environmental requirements) *and* the 12 aspects of programs, broken into the life cycle pieces.

Design should consider all 12 aspects of a program and software, and all three of the parts of the total life of a program, even if it rejects some aspects!

For a team of commandoes forging through a swamp at night, *any* route that gets to the objective is an acceptable route. Does it seem to work? To get us there? Yes? Then that's it! No time to study, to optimize. Run for it!

This is fine for toothpick programs, or when no one ever has to go through the swamp again.

If long-lived software is being designed, then the effort should be expended in the design phase to make the continued development phase as easy as possible.

In some cases, we will not be concerned about use-time aspects of programs. The program may be run very infrequently. In some cases, the development-time aspect will swamp the effort, and in other cases the needs of continued development will, or should, prevail. We'll see more of this shortly.

But *if* the use time computer has the power *and* the memory, and we can afford the extra overhead that is usually associated with general-purpose, already-written and available systems programs, then we should select that approach. Next we should decide which are the best available programs. This is design, this choice of what to have *as separate programs*, and indeed, it is critical design. It forms the system in a definitive sense. It is compartmentalization; it is akin to defining sub-assemblies in hardware.

The designer makes trade-offs between costs and speed, between ease of inquiry and speed of retrieval, between the size of memory needed, the packing scheme and the response time, the schedule versus the richness of function, the environment management versus the function to be done, and on and on.

WHO SHOULD DESIGN

Design is not something that just any one can do. Dijkstra in his paper *"The Structure of 'THE' Multiprogramming System,"** makes two points:

> Taking care of the "pathology" took more energy than we had expected, and some of our troubles were a direct consequence of our earlier ingenuity. . . . Had we paid attention to the pathology at an earlier stage of the design, our management rules would certainly have been less refined.

and

> . . . at least in my country (The Netherlands) the intellectual level needed for system design is generally grossly underestimated . . . . this type of work is very difficult and . . . . . every effort to do it with other than the best people is doomed to either failure or moderate success at enormous expense.

Note the words: "the very best people."

In selecting a designer: find one who has done it before! Someone who has taken a system from start to finish! and then stick with him or her. If you do not have someone who has designed *this type* of software before, create a "design team." Watch it in operation. From the design team will emerge the one or two persons who will design the software.

The *one* individual who is *the* designer on the large systems is usually a quiet, bright, and stubborn individual. He or she is usually too quiet to be a good manager, but bright enough to assimilate the myriad of conflicting goals, stresses, approaches and conflicts and make sense out of them.

Too many people on a design, too much democracy, or too rapid a turnover of *the designer*, and the development effort is in deep trouble.

*Edsger W. Dijkstra, "The Structure of 'THE' Multiprogramming System," *Communication of the ACM*, Vol. II*, 5 (1968). Reprinted with permission of the Association for Computing Machinery Inc.

THE END PRODUCT — WHAT ARE WE CREATING?

It is so difficult to visualize software. Static representations of it are pale representations, but often the best we can do. Let us look at the Apollo ground control software that ran for many years in Houston to see an example of what it is that we are setting out to create.

We had a large (over 1 million instructions) software system that was well documented and tested. These instructions were "packaged" in programs, subprograms, and modules. Subsections were built separately and molded into or onto the overall structure.

Our software "came" in several forms. There was a "listing," a machine printout of every instruction listed in sequence. There was a deck of punched cards, and a magnetic tape on which the program was written. None of these embodiments is very easy for a human to look at — not even the listing. None show the structure or flow of the program. We needed such as those shown in Figs. 5-19 and 5-20 to get the idea of the software. The overall software was broken into eight major pieces, shown in Fig. 5-19.

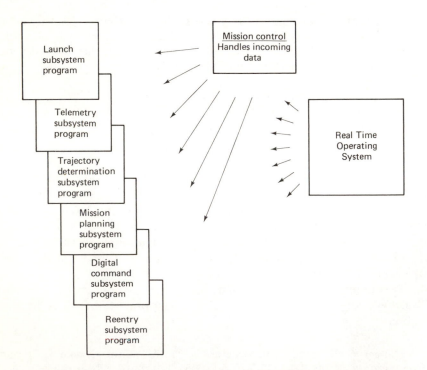

Figure 5-19. The software structure for the Apollo ground control.

Launch subsystem program

| Go/No Go | No abort | Abort | Track |

Towers jettisoned | Tower not jettisoned | Mode 3 abort orbital velocity

Figure 5-20. The Apollo launch subsystem software structure.

What each major subsystem did is fairly clear from its title. The real-time operating system was in overall control, scheduling which program was to run.

Let us just follow the Launch Subprogram down to further detail, as shown in Fig. 5-20. Each box shown is a lengthy program that will be executed when needed. The operating system decides *when*. If we were to continue to decompose these blocks of software, showing more and more detail, we would get a rich tree like Fig. 5-21. Each box represents the act of design. It is a choice of how to combine functions into separate, definable programs.

When we see a static representation of a program that looks like Fig. 5-21 we must remember that every box is a program, ready to be called into play at any time and in a vast variety of sequences.

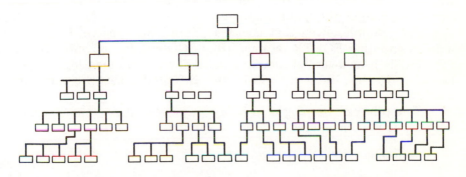

Figure 5-21. A typical depiction of a large software system.

For the ground control of Apollo, there were over 400 modules of programs. But we still cannot "experience" the program. The diagram is a stale representation of a program. The running program is a very different thing.

It is akin to comparing a movie to a reel of movie film. Seeing the reel — without the motorized projection — is not to see the movie! Here we even have two different words! "Film" to connote the idea of the medium; "movie" to connote the idea of the result — the object of the films being projected. Alas, we do not yet have such a distinction in the software field.

THE PARTS AND THE PROCESS OF DESIGN

Design can be split into three parts. Solution, structure, and representation/exposition. (See Fig. 5-22.)

Solution

Are we going to search based on a sequential-look-and-then-add-1 basis or on a binary search basis — go into the midpoint of the file, determine if too high or too low — go to the midpoint of the correct half — repeat till find?

This is the solution, the algorithm, the process. It is usually a creative act to come up with the approach, especially on new, complicated, or very large efforts.

Structure

Once we have come up with the approach, we "detail" it out in a "structure." On any sizeable job, there can be dozens of different structures that will yield the same result. The differences in structure can be substantial, the result the same.

For example, given that I wish to do a binary search, I can now write it in either FORTRAN or COBOL. COBOL has no subscripting; FORTRAN is awkward at handling data. The two source programs will be very different; the result will be two different object programs that both do a binary search.

Structure can be judged in many ways. Modularity and interface crispness are two measures that can be applied.

Representation/Exposition

The representation of the program can be in one of many forms. It can be flow charts plus narrative; it can be HIPO diagrams; Warnier-Orr charts, etc.

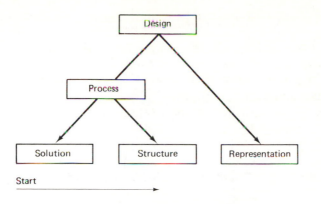

Figure 5-22.   Parts of design.

The purpose of the representation is to explain to a reviewer/newcomer what is being done and how by the program. Therefore, the representation is judged by how well it transmits these facts. "Well" here means clearly, unambiguously, and expeditiously.

A book by Lawrence Halprin called *The RSVP Cycles, The Creative Process in the Human Environment** explores the process by which humans attempt to depict, to document in hard copy, the activities or forms in various fields of art. The word "score" is used to mean a depiction, "a synthesization of processes over time. The most familiar kind of 'score' is a musical one, but I have extended this meaning to include scores in all fields of human endeavor."

Halprin goes on to discuss dance and how it is scored. Then city planning, astronomy, architecture, a play, the lunar landing — and a dozen others. He shows people's remarkable ability to invent notations to depict what is to happen.

He also points out that the score and the performance, although inextricably linked, are quite distinct from each other. A superb violinist does Brahms so much better than the student using the same score. Software developers know that the depiction of the large program is static and that *in process* many things happen that are not depicted! We can not depict a running program. As we saw on page 69, the possible number of different sequences the program can "choose" to execute is astronomically high and impossible to test. When our large software systems begin to run, it is a performance, an instance, of this software running.

Many of the new "design techniques" that are being introduced today are really exposition techniques. That is not to demean them. We

*Lawrence Halprin, *The RSVP Cycles* (New York: George Braziller, Inc., 1969).

desperately need better ways to communicate complex ideas to each other.

Very little is to be found in most books, including this one, about the first part of design or creation. We simply are not in a position to say much about this area. The books that do deal with this area are far broader than computer or software books. They usually deal with free association, or brainstorming, or examine the process in solving real problems.

THE FLOW OF THE PROCESS OF DESIGN OF A SOFTWARE SYSTEM

The process, the flow of designing is not well understood, even by good software managers. Some just do it right instinctively, and without some of the steps that are necessary to good development techniques. Some do it very badly.

The flow of activities shown in Fig. 5-23 takes us from requirements definition through several stages of ever more detailed design.

We saw in the previous section the function of requirements definition. Here in the flow diagram we show it again — and its outputs, the resulting documents that it produces, are step 1. Note that we separate the action from the product of the action and label both. We do this because there is so much confusion in the software (and systems) development field as to the meaning of some of these terms.

The second step, design, arrives at an approach to the problem by conceiving approaches to see if they are leading us towards a solution. This step is characterized by a trial and error approach, iterating back to the preceding step. As we progress, we often have to move far forward in the design to test that indeed we can make it all the way through to the end that we desire. When we have done this enough times and progressed into enough detail, we have an approach — and often this approach becomes *the* approach, and it usually works — more or less.

Unfortunately, most *design* stops at this point and the rest of the project is devoted to fleshing out the steps that have been selected.

But note that the output of step 2 is a very voluminous set of documents and reports. *A* workable approach has been arrived at! In many cases the resulting stack of documents is 6 feet high or higher.

Is this a design? Yes, but clearly not a finished one, and in all likelihood a poorly understood and difficult to communicate one!! Even if it works!

It is step 3 that makes the design tighter, crisper, easier to understand, to communicate, and, therefore, to implement.

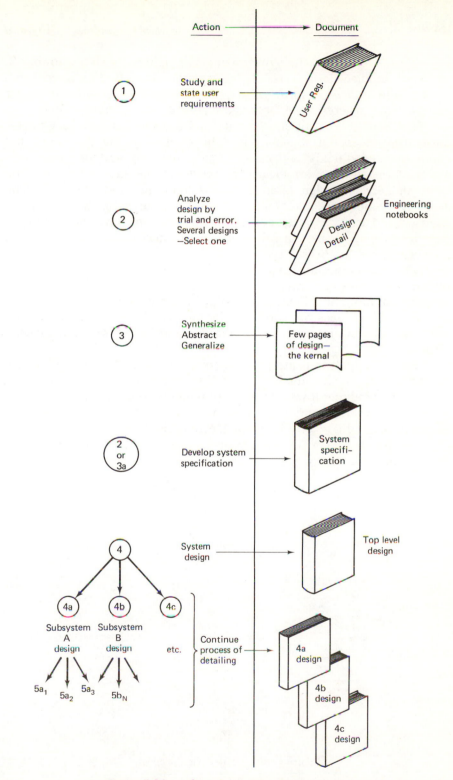

Figure 5-23. Overview of the design process.

Most efforts *skip* the synthesizing and tightening step, number 3, and start detailed design, step 4, immediately after finding a workable design, step 2. *The benefits of step 3 are significant, and the loss of these benefits severely hampers large software development efforts.*

The benefits of this step, clarity and succinctness, are easy to see, once the process has been done. The design can be described and communicated quickly and easily. The underlying and unifying principles of the solution are clear. The results at the end of the heuristic (trial and error) design (step 2) are voluminous and not clear. The design may be workable, but it is not communicable without great exertion and time. It is usually understood by an individual, or hopefully a few individuals. All other project workers understand pieces of the system, not the overall system.

The taut design after step 3 can be shown to all, with the benefit that the designers and implementers of the subsystems will execute the subpieces in more beneficial relationship to the whole.

Step 4 produces the top level design. It is a specification that will serve as the requirement statement for another, lower level design effort.

By continually repeating step 4 for the next lower levels of design, successive designs are created, until the lowest level is reached. Each level may produce lower level requirements specification, and the design of a module, until the implementing (writing) level is reached, or until a level of triviality is reached. More on this later.

Let us look at a different representation of this third step: the distillation step. Figure 5-24 shows the flow of design from the left to

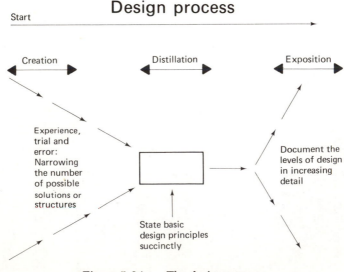

Figure 5-24.   The design process.

the right. On the left side, as design begins, the process is *creation*. The design, forming, is loose and in the mind of the designer. The small, middle box represents the distillation that should occur. The distillation is critical. It removes redundancies, ambiguities, and trivia. It focuses on the essential parts of the solution. The process of distilling boils out accidentals and allows the underlying principles to be seen and followed. The tight, concise definition of the solution makes the whole remainder of the software development incomparably easier to control.

To repeat, this distillation is often not done. It is hard to do; it takes talent and much effort. It should always be done.

The widening of the space after the distillation process represents the expanding amount of design and of the documentation of the design as time progresses. The succinct statement we have generated shows the fundamental backbone of the design, and we now begin to add level after level of detail as we move towards implementing the design.

John Livingston Lowes (1867-1945) in *The Road to Xanadu** writes about creativity and cites examples of great discoveries. He states there are three parts to creativity, to discovery, and he names them "The WELL, the VISION, and the WILL. The WELL where all the facts lie, waiting to be used. . .

> Where indeed at any instant are all the countless facts we know and all the million scenes we have experienced? Wherever that shadowy limbo may be. . . The WELL is only a convenient symbol for a mystery. And there they had lain, "absorbed by some unknown abyss," to all intents and purposes in utter non-existence — asleep. Some for weeks, some for months, and some for a period of years. Then, all at once, they awoke. . . .

> The panorama was set in motion and unrolled without my will. For the moment I simply allowed the images to stream. Then I deliberately assumed control. . . .

> Without the Vision the chaos of the elements remains a chaos. And the FORM sleeps forever in the vast chamber of unborn designs. Yet in *that* chaos only could creative Vision ever see *this* Form. Nor without the co-operant WILL, obedient to this VISION, may the pattern perceived in the huddle attain objective reality.

What Lowes cites as the three main ingredients is very close to the three parts of design that we just described. His "will" is not quite the distillation phase, but close.

*John L. Lowes, The Road to Xanadu (Boston: Houghton Mifflin Co., 1927). Reprinted with permission of the publisher. © 1927 John Livingston Lowes, © renewed 1955 John Wilbur Lowes.

LEVELS OF DESIGN

The design of a car is an interactive effort. Figure 5-25 depicts a top down, level by level approach to designing the auto. At the highest level, we have a representation of the car. At the next level, we have a

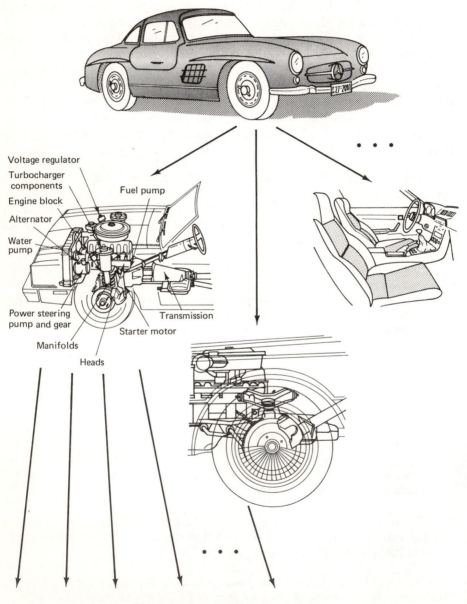

Figure 5-25.   Level by level design.

requirement for the engine, the steering mechanism, the dashboard, and of course there would be many more subassemblies at this level.

Then we take each subassembly and break it down further. We begin to see a tree-like breakdown, with more and more details until we finally reach a level of triviality, which is the point at which there is nothing to be gained by adding further detail. When we get to a windowpane, or a headlight, or a handle for a door, we have probably reached a point at which we can simply state "here is the X we want" and *be confident* it will get done correctly.

The choice of which subassemblies to break an object into is an act of designing, and it has profound impact on our work to create the system, and on its resulting operation.

This level-by-level detailing is found in almost all fields, and the more mature the technology, the more stable and safe is the passage of information from one level to the next. The *information* needed at each level is fairly well understood, and the *representation mechanism* (format, language, etc.) is also well established and understood.

In software, neither of these level-mechanisms is stabilized. The content needed at each level is murky, and the mechanisms to pass information from one level to another are shaky or nonexistent. Therefore, the lower level implementers or designers often accept fragmentary or obscure requirements/design *because there are no standards* against which to measure the specifications! With the best of will and intentions, the lower levels can stray from the desired approach.

Because of this lack of "technological infrastructure" the process (or system) of providing software is error-prone. *It must therefore be far more tightly managed than more mature technological development.*

High Level Design

For landing on the moon, the ground control program had about 400 modules. In the IBM operating system — OS — for the 370 systems, there were over 3000 modules in 1975.

Obviously, the number of possible ways to connect are very, very large. When we start interconnecting things, our possibilities get astronomical.

With large software systems, we break functions to be done into smaller and smaller units, until we get to a "module" which should be short, 30 to 50 high order language statements. Then we interconnect the modules. Then partition into subsystems.

Hardware engineers at this point recognize that all we are talking about is the principle in hardware systems that states that the cleaner and more well-defined the interfaces are between the various pieces of the system, the easier it will be to apportion the work and get the subsystems tested and working. The more self-contained each piece is, the easier it will be to make the whole work. In the software we do the same things, and we call the result of this process "information hiding." More on this in a moment.

In software development, selfcontainment is more important because it is easy for programmers to jump over the "boundaries" of the software modules and get into the modules that belong to someone else. We must plot the component interactions and make a determination of what to make subprograms.

We interconnect and partition based on compartmentalization. The subsystems should have neat, clean interactions between one another. This greatly simplifies testing as we can test subsystems alone, then together and concentrate on the interface among them.

Compartmentalization

"Divide and conquer" is one of the basic paradigms of all complex undertakings, and it is true in software. Compartmentalization will ease the task of reassembly of the building blocks when changes are introduced into some of them. This principle is very old. It exists in most human organizations and in engineering. Indeed, it is a major tenet of good engineering.

Macro Compartmentalization

Although we normally do not think of the operating system and data base management system as compartmentalization, they are precisely that. We deliver certain functions with each of them and restrict the delivery of those functions to one compartment.

Time Constraints

Systems must be designed for peak loads — loads that usually will not occur. But if they do, it is usually the point at which the system is most needed. (The sheer weight of effort to generate a peak load to test the system is an interesting challenge. We'll cover it under Testing.) Peak input and output and user messages and "traffic" must all be identified, analyzed, and studied for their interactions. And then the system must be designed to handle *that* case!

Middle Level Design

A software design issue at the middle level might be the following: How do we separate an inquiry program into pieces that will result in efficient use?

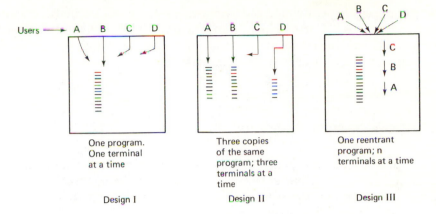

Figure 5-26. Three designs for an inquiry server.

The first design in Fig. 5-26 has a "single server" module that puts all tasks that need it into a queue and "serves" them one at a time.

Design 1 will cause delays in response time if the queue is lengthy; i.e., there are many inquiries occurring simultaneously. The second approach is to put several copies of the same module of code into memory at the time, so that several queries are being processed simultaneously. This eats up memory.

The third design shows *one* query handling program handling several query entries simultaneously. The program is reentrant. It can be executed by several users simultaneously. Which way the software team decides to design this function will have a profound effect on the performance.

Micro Compartmentalization

Within the module that is to handle communications, we may have 100 micro modules of say 30 statements of high order language each — or 30 modules of 100 statements. Each of the micro modules should be compartmentalized as much as possible. By this we mean, specifically:

1. No module depends on another module, except in a series fashion, for input; each module should be self sufficient except for input-output.
2. Each module should be as small as possible, preferably about 30 HOL statements. This gives micro modularity.
3. Each module should do one and only one function.

The key to easily-changed software is to create it in tight, seg-
mentable pieces.   Fortunately there are now fairly standard ways of
doing this. The technical methods are described in numerous publica-
tions, and we will list only some highlights.

Module Design

We continue to divide software modules into smaller and smaller
units, until we get to pieces that can be "written" in instructions. Each
group of instructions that can be "called" to run we call a *module*.
Module design involves:

- Size of the module
- Data coupling
- Information content
- Type of interconnection
- Type of communication

Low coupling is desired; this means independent modules. A module
that performs a single, well defined function has *functional strength*.
Modules that have informational strength can be implemented in
a fashion that yields information hiding. The various states of data as
it passes through the several functions of the module are known only
to that module and therefore the designers and writers of other modules
should not know the internal workings of this module. And they will
not count on things that they might count on if they knew *how* we
were going to write *this* module. Which, of course, cuts off short cuts!
Good!

Information Hiding

The following example shows the principle of *information hiding*.
The instruction in BASIC to print with the "at" sign (@) followed by a
number, e.g. PRINT @ 482, counts the number of print positions *line
by line* starting at the top left-most point and prints the values at 482.
If I programmed assuming a screen with 32 characters, then PRINT @

69 would leave two blank 32 position lines and a 4 space border before writing on the screen. To print:

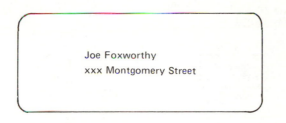

I would write: Print @ 69, N (for name)
                  Print @ 69, A (for address)
But if the TV screen we were using were changed to 79 characters across, the program is now wrong. I will get something that looks like the following:

```
                                          Joe Foxwor
      thy

                                          xxx Montgo
      mery Street
```

The program must be changed to fit the new device.

Now this example is trivial, but assume that we had hundreds of programs that have been working for years that we now have to change. What a problem! Many of our programmers have left; and all the rest are on critical projects. The answer is simple — no new display is installed! Even though it costs less, is more reliable, etc!

The way around this is to have the programmer write the program *independent* of the number of positions on the screen. The programmer follows a convention that states he or she wishes the text to start: (1) at the beginning; or (2) 1/8 of the way across, etc.

A *systems program* takes the designation of where, converts it to an actual number based on the actual display, and then the program is executed. Now if the physical display unit changes, the only thing that must be changed is the systems program. With hundreds of application programs, the savings are clear. The ability to actually change is preserved. (See Fig. 5-27.)

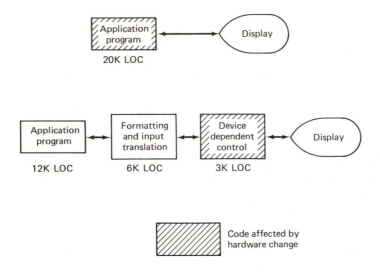

Figure 5-27.   Device independence, software information hiding.

Why use information hiding? It probably costs you in the development cycle — it lengthens time to design and implement, and it costs you at use time — it takes more memory, not much more, but more.

Where does it help? At continued-development time, in that it is now easier to modify the software. We have built the system with pieces that are more easily pulled out and changed, and any change will ripple less into other modules.

I can construct an office building with permanent interior walls, or with moveable walls. It makes quite a difference. Quite a difference when I build it in the first place, *and* quite a difference when it comes time to rearrange the offices.

If we *know* that the software is going to be changed very infrequently, and that the program is fairly free of errors then there may not be reason to go to the trouble of imposing the discipline of information hiding on the development process and team.

This example of information hiding could be an example of middle level design, or low level design, depending on how much information is to be displayed.

If the display of name and address is the whole display, I would call this low level design. Were there 40 variables to be displayed and 8 different formats possible, it is easily middle level design. Again, we have no metric for complexity with which to measure these concepts.

Design at Lowest Level

The act of designing — choosing the parts to break the program into and the arrangement of the various parts — continues to even the smallest of programs. The process of requirements definition, design, writing instructions, testing and running is present for the smallest program. There are a few, very few, development organizations that separate the writing of the code at the simplest level from the design. Rarely does a design group do the design *all the way* to the point that the person writing the instructions is doing nothing but translating on a very trivial level. When we reach this level, the person writing the instructions is doing *no* design at all and is indeed a coder. This is a definition loaded with economic consequences.

A programmer is a professional; a coder is a clerical employee. This is my assertion; there is still debate on the issue. The Department of Labor is in the middle of this. A Department of Labor guideline seems to imply that programmers are clerical employees and are not called upon to exercise judgment in their duties. Therefore, they *must* be paid overtime!

A court decision in Florida found that three programmers who sued their former employer for overtime pay for a period of several years were not only entitled to the back pay, but to treble damages as well!

One can imagine the chaos that could be caused if 10,000 programmers in IBM suddenly wanted to get several years of overtime pay and treble damages!

The Department of Labor guideline only *seems* to say that programmers are not professionals; the guideline is very ambiguous, and obviously written by someone who did not understand what a computer is or what programmers do!

The key distinction between clerical and professional in the DOL rules rests on the requirement to exercise judgment in one's duties. Designing is exercising judgment.

To be an engineer, one needs to attend a university, and pass some tests. There is no such corollary in the programming world. And since the act of design is barely describable, it is difficult to teach. One need not be a computer science graduate to be a programmer. But programmers do exercise judgment, as they *do* design. Coders do not.

The flow of process and data at the lowest level, at the writing code level, still constitutes design. If one writes a 100 instruction program, one must *design* the flow and pieces of it.

How I arrange my flow, where I put my constants, whether I test after the body of the function is done or before, these are the decisions, at low level. How should I break up, let's say 3000 statements of higher order language, into modules? It is judgment!

Inter-Level Mechanisms and the Level of Triviality

Every field has these layers of design — medicine, aeronautical engineering, the building trades, bridge construction, and so on — and each field has a point of triviality that is peculiar to that field.

That is the point at which it becomes inefficient to continue to specify in more and more detail, as the field is perfectly capable of taking it from here and not messing up the implementation.

The point of triviality usually is a combination of the maturity of the field (how long have how many people been doing this) and the complexity (how hard is it to specify clearly all that I need to specify). Obviously, these two affect each other, with complexity delaying the maturation of the field.

Software development is on the short end of this learning curve. It is very complex, as we have seen, and it is a very young field. There have not been that many years or that many people doing it.

As a field matures, the practices and content that must flow from level to level are arrived at by experience and study. With time, they become established. When ignored or done poorly, the recipient at the lower level knows immediately that the specification is seriously deficient. He or she will react to a poor design with a "You are not serious!" comment.

But in software the experience and practice do not exist. Faced with a similar lack of specificity, clarity or content, the recipient at the lower level almost always *accepts* the specification and charges off with great energy to implement it. The results of this should be no surprise — delay, departure from goals, confusion, failure.

The lack of standards for these inter-level hand-offs is *the* main reason that software development must be managed with excruciating exactness. Each hand-off, each level, is too often freedom to go in some random direction.

When we design in areas that we are fmiliar with and where we are confident of success, we pursue the design down to a certain level and then stop, leaving the remaining design to a lesser skilled designer. When we get to a level where the remaining effort is so easy that nothing could go wrong, we can call this the level of triviality.

We hit the level of triviality at different levels of detail in different endeavors simply because some are more mature, and because the infrastructure of available and competent designers and techniques to finish the design beyond the point of triviality is present and mature.

Thus for example, in designing a new sports car today, the chief designer would no doubt leave the structure of the door to a "detailer." He or she could do this with complete confidence that the result would be workable and acceptable.

He or she is confident of this outcome for one other reason beyond the fact that there are competent "detailers." That reason is that over the years there has also been developed a stable and rich mechanism to state the requirements of the door and be sure that the "detailer" will fit the constraints and objectives that are specified in the specification.

In the software field, there are not yet a suitable number of detailers available. There are such demands for designers that any one who can design *at all* is quickly elevated to the role of chief designer on some other project, too often too quickly, and we have the Peter Principle at work. In addition, the procedures and rules for stating the constraints and the objectives are not in being yet. This double lack creates great confusion, as designers do not realize that they are not communicating with each other, and are amazed and furious when they find that programs that they have thought to be clearly and completely defined come back unrecognizable.

The recognition of the shortcomings that we are describing is the first step in avoiding the problems that result. Forewarned is forearmed here; it should result in far more care and more control than we might otherwise put forth.

The coupling mechanisms that exist between levels of design in other disciplines do not exist in software. Therefore, the design of a large software system must be more detailed than we might ordinarily think necessary. When one asks to see the design of the system, the response should be "At what level?"

Now there is a level at which the point of triviality is passed in software as well. It is simply far lower than in most other technical fields. The fact that the coupling mechanisms are faulty requires that the designs at adjoining levels be scrutinized to assure that they fit together and have integrity. If this is not done we find that the design often does not work, or is jerky or has holes.

Variations in the Level of Triviality and Inter-Level Mechanisms

With a job to be done, I will have a very different level of triviality if I am given novices to implement my effort as opposed to being given experts. What will be adequate in one situation will be totally disastrous in the other. Also, if my team has developed much software together in the past, I can be more confident and less concerned about interlevel mechanisms.

STRUCTURED PROGRAMMING

Structured programming belongs in the design portion of the development process. It is used to control the interconnections, to structure both large and small programs. There is widespread confusion over what structured programming is and what it is not. Many confuse top-down implementation (see p. 178) with structured programming. Some confuse the Chief Programmer concept (see p. 168) and walkthrough reviews with structured programming.

Harlan Mills, Rick Linger, and Bennie Witt have written a book called *Structured Programming*,* that has a very precise definition:

A *structured program* is a compound program constructed from a fixed basis set of prime programs.

A *prime program* is a proper program that has no proper subprogram of more than one node.

A *proper program* is a program with a control structure that:

1. Has a single entry and exit line, and
2. For each node, has a path through that node from the entry line to the exit line.

This is a good definition as it allows the basic set of structures to be stated at a separate time. (See Fig. 5-28.) The point is that *if* all software is constructed with only Prime and Proper programs then the flow and logic of the process is considerably cleaned up by the discipline enforced by use of the structure. The use of the structure forces a discipline on the program developer, which results in more understandable programs and therefore less error. Also, it is much easier to read the program. The complexity of the program is *structured*.

The unbridled freedom available to programmers is constrained — with the result of clarity, standards and crispness — and to the dismay of some old time programmers.

That structured programming is done top down is an accident. That it is more adaptable to top-down and stepwise refinement is an added benefit of structured programming, but top down development is not an essence of structured programming.

*Richard C. Linger, Harlan D. Mills, and Bernard I. Witt, *Structured Programming: Theory and Practice* (Reading, Mass.: Addison-Wesley, 1979).

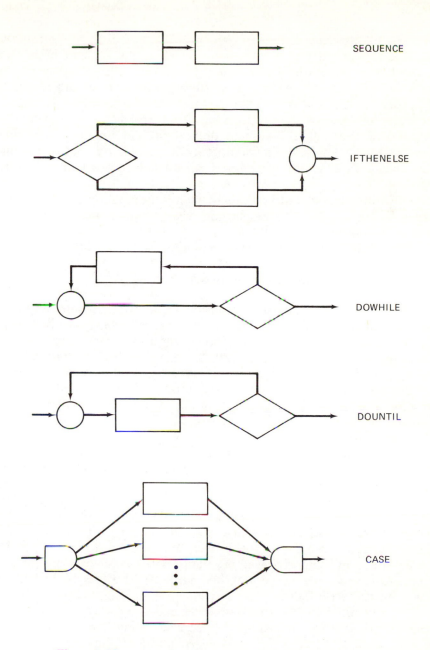

SEQUENCE

IFTHENELSE

DOWHILE

DOUNTIL

CASE

Figure 5-28.   Structured programming's basic structures.

We are covering structured programming here in the design section and not in the writing section, because when the flow of program is laid out in a structured fashion, *and* the people who are to write the code are told it must be done in a structured fashion, we are designing, not programming. The writers also do some designing, and they *structure* the lower level programs into the basic structures, as we have seen.

But if the higher levels are done first and are not structured, structuring the lower levels is not going to yield the benefits possible. The *overall* flow of the program is back to the "bowl of spaghetti" shape.

This may not sound like much, sitting here coldly on a page, but structure makes programs much more visible and understandable than they are when they are not structured.

Structured programming is reshaping the software field.

Introduction of Structured Programming

The *New York Times* automation of its morgue (clippings) has become a landmark software implementation, and rightly so. Performed by Terry Baker of IBM Federal System Division under the guidance of Harlan Mills, it changed the course of software engineering. It is still widely reported in the literature. It set new productivity records. It *proved* the worth of structured programming. We demanded the use of structured programming, and the training of our 2600 professionals in it, based on the spectacular *Times* results.

The story behind this effort is not well known. It is worth reporting, as it shows many items that are of interest to management. The *New York Times* fixed-price contract was won by IBM in 1969 after competitive bids. To the dismay of our people in Gaithersburg, the IBM bid was about $200,000 compared to the others at about $1,000,000. My predecessor was then running the IBM Federal System Center. Henry J. White was and is a fine, capable executive. He called for an audit, which showed that the approach bid would not work. (It was to merge some existing retrieval programs with some existing systems programs — and they could not be merged!) The loss looked like it was going to be $800,000.

White called in Harlan Mills. Mills had only a year or so earlier joined IBM after a distinguished career as a mathematician and executive. He had been at GE, and RCA, and Mathematica. He was on White's technical staff. White gave him the *New York Times* contract to perform.

Mills accepted readily, picked Terry Baker to be the chief programmer and Bob Meier to be the back-up programmer. A librarian was assigned to do all record keeping and clerical support.

The team worked in Gaithersburg, traveling to N.Y. very often.

They did the job — 83,000 high level instructions — beautifully, in 22 months for about $300,000. There were almost no errors, it was on time, and the system came up and ran! Like that! We had saved about $700,000!

When I (I had come in in December 1969) gave Mills, Baker, and others outstanding contribution awards, I discovered that no one in IBM had any statistics on productivity! How many lines of code was normal per man-month? No one knew. No one even had a definition of a "line of code." All agreed to the award, but was the productivity improvement 5 to 1 (as I believed) or 3 to 1? As a result of this we installed in Federal System Center a programming measurement system that has been in continual operation for over 8 years. Collecting statistics and data on all aspects of the projects, the data base now contains voluminous data on over 100 projects. It is the only one of its kind I've encountered! We'll see it later in Chap. 5.

We decreed that *all* new projects would use structured programming. To my amazement, we got a *very* negative reaction from competent programmers! "What does Mills know about programming?" "The *Times* is a fluke!" "Baker did it." "Mills and Baker are not average people." I had to agree to that! But we persisted, and it was the correct thing to do. We spent a great deal of money and effort training over 2600 people. Two weeks of training for 2600 professionals is 100 man years of training! There is no question it was the correct thing to do.

The reason that the *New York Times* job was done with such great productivity was that Mills and Baker implemented many advanced software engineering techniques, back there in 1970-71. They used:

Structured Programming
The Chief-Programmer Team
Top-Down Implementation
The Librarian
Walk-Throughs
Formal Grammars

The very success of the *Times* effort sowed the seeds of confusion as many writers carelessly lumped *all* of the techniques used into one category under the heading of Structured Programming.

Benefits of Structured Programming

Structured programming gives structure where anarchy could dominate. To the manager and reviewer it yields reliability! Visibility. Visibility begins to make software manageable! Reviewable! Walkthroughs became possible! It gives standards and communicability. It gives clarity in a field troubled by complexity. Software development entered a new era.

Acceptance of Structured Programming

There are many programming shops pledging allegiance to structured programming — and not using it. Some still confuse other good practices with structured programming. Most have no definition.

Any sizeable software development group that is not using crisply defined structured programming is not at an acceptable level of competence. We'll go into this and further discuss the resistance to structured programming in Chap. 6.

GOOD DESIGN

Good design is clean design; it has unity. Brooks* in his book, *The Mythical Man-Month* cites the cathedrals in Europe that took hundreds of years to build. The ones that are spectacular are those where the ideas of the origniator were preserved. The ones that are "bad" are the ones where each century added a little of its own. Many programming languages have failed because they try to embrace too many different ideas. Brooks mentions that this is a problem in PL/1.

Mills, Witt, and Linger agree and Jensen and Tonies** agree with the unity of design concept. And my experience is that there is usually *one* designer on large systems. And he or she sets the direction.

Beauty is often in the eye of the reviewer. The FAA En-Route Air Traffic Control System took 10 years to field (it will never be finished), and FAA had many audits over that span. One audit by a group of independent software experts stated that the design of the control (systems) program was "archaic and wrong." Yet the program worked beautifully when it was finished. (But what furor that comment set loose!)

Some software managers push their programmers to be innovative and "cute" in their approaches. They are trying to find new ways of doing old things, or to find new things to do. The tools provided to these programmers are designed to enhance the flow of creativity. Indeed, we should call this research, and not software development.

---

*Frederick P. Brooks, Jr., *The Mythical Man-Month* (Reading, Mass.: Addison-Wesley, 1975).

**Randall W. Jensen and Charles C. Tonies, *Software Engineering* (Englewood Cliffs, N.J.: Prentice-Hall, Inc., 1979).

On the other hand we find managers who have arrived at a design and now need 400,000 or so lines of code written. And after it is written and sent to users, they will have to support it. These managers want no cuteness or invention. They want dependability, clarity, reproducibility. They want plain vanilla programs.

DESIGN IS . . .

Design is still an art and something we do not quite understand. Stravinski called art "creativity requiring a leap of the imagination." Perhaps there is a design that is not art, merely following a pattern — for bridges, buildings, clothes, etc. — but would we call that design?

Iterative

We find what doesn't work and correct it. The first time we made the multiprocessor work in the En-Route Air Traffic Control system we found that the "lock out" procedure (ensuring that a second or third or fourth CPU could not update the same record that was in the process of being updated and thus destroy the validity of the data) worked too well. We were causing CPUs to sit by idly waiting for the unlock. In the second pass we shortened the procedures to be performed in "lock out" mode.

Compromise

A design involves many compromises, trading-off one for another — memory used less efficiently versus CPU cycles saved, for example. Just as an airplane designer trades weight against speed against fuel economy, so does the software designer trade off the 12 aspects of every program against themselves, and many more aspects that go beyond the program and into the functions that are to be automated. What is happening in the rest of the system? What is changing in the radar? In the environment? Has our bank merged? Or pulled out of territory or service area?

The Design of a Large Type V Program is a Multidisciplined Effort

We have seen the effort to create a program to run a large type V application is much less an effort to *write* the instructions than it is to understand the problem or opportunity, to state the requirements, to understand and communicate these requirements to the designers and coders. And understanding these requirements usually takes experienced, professional people who have either worked in the area to be automated before, or who have the background needed to absorb the information from the people who do the job now.

For example, if we are to automate the control for a lunar landing, we must have on our team some people who understand the physics of the lunar landing event, who understand the gravity of the moon, the effects of thrust of the lander's engine, etc.

This knowledge is needed continuously. It is not something that we plug in at the beginning and use from then on. It is the mirror in which we see what we are doing. We cannot simply *write* the requirements, once and for all. We will iterate constantly from requirements to design and back again and to coding and back again. The design must be run against the functional experts and verified *before* programming starts.

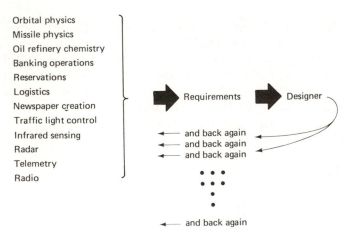

Figure 5-29.   Functional knowledge in design effort.

The process in Fig. 5-29 looks so nice and neat but the arrows cannot possibly show the intense mental effort and work and design that must occur for the process to be successful. Nor can it show the heated exchanges, the intense emotions that erupt when the functional expert (requirements) rejects an approach (design) as "risky" or "confused" or "wrong."

Detailing is Design but Mediocre Design

We had one project that was already 3 million dollars into the red. It was a real time data reduction effort for NASA — fixed price. Harlan Mills kept telling me they had no design; the project kept telling me they did.

I called for a full day review and the project people presented for *10 hours*! They had reams of graphs, logic, paper, and data.

At the end of the 10 hours the question was answered! They had a design, an approach that seemed feasible — it was somewhere in that 6-foot high stack of view graphs and inside the brains of two of the key people. It was *not* visible to us, the audience. We got glimpses of it during those 10 hours. We were persuaded it was there, but we hadn't seen it nor could any of us have articulated it.

Mills, Linger, and Witt call this "detailing." It satisfies the need for design but is a pale shadow of it. Detailing is often "satisficing" — the picking of the first solution and not looking for the better one.

ROBUST OR USER-FRIENDLY PROGRAMS

So many programs have been developed by the R&D group, shipped to the field (the 'user') and never used. They are too difficult to use or do the wrong functions. We have already related the incident when the software that had too much function was rejected at the En-Route Air Control Center in Jacksonville. What we want to focus on here briefly is the people-interaction portion of the program.

The moment we add people in an interactive role with the computer (types III, and IV and V) we have greatly increased the task to be done. We must write programs to enable the person to interact — to converse — with the system.

I once had a small programming group — 7 people — producing interactive Multiple-Attribute Decision Analysis programs. There were programs in the APL language; they were about 10,000 APL statements in size — and 9,000 of those statements were to handle the people interface. Nine out of ten. We had to keep the user from becoming frustrated — or he/she would not use the system.

If the input called for the letter O and the user hit the number zero, or vice versa — we did not just print "invalid input." We put out prompting messages to help get the process under way again. "Did you mean to hit zero or O?" would be displayed.

The design of this part of the program is critical and difficult. It usually involves iterative changes once the user has had a chance to use the system. Yet it is essential to user acceptance of the system.

DOCUMENTING DESIGN

If there is not a document, available, at several levels of detail, then the project is in trouble. By several levels of detail, I mean that a design can be described in 30 minutes, in 2 hours, in 8 hours, or in 16 hours. If there is only a 30-minute overview and the 16-hour version and nothing in between, watch out. Why?

Because the design now exists only in the head of one or two designers. We cannot grasp and follow the evolution of a good design at the level of detail of the 16-hour briefing variety unless we spend *full* time on the project and know it intimately.

Our United States Newspaper System Development Group effort had a 30-minute and a 16-hour level of design. I knew the manager and the designer — Bernie Witt and Terry Baker, respectively. They had never failed, had done fantastic work in the past. And I trusted them! But what if one or both got sick or left? The whole project — millions of dollars — was at stake.

The design of these large systems should be documented and reviewable at all levels of design. This takes money and talent, but if you don't have this, you are flirting with disaster.

A Specification is a Design and a Requirement at the Same Time

Design is HOW; a requirement is WHAT.

If I write the simple word "car" on a sheet of paper, and ask you to get me one, the content of the paper is a what *and* a how. To you it is a what; it is a car and you have to go and get one. To me it is a how, a design, in that it is not a motorcycle, truck, bike, or other mechanical means of transportation. I will travel how? By car.

Looked at from one vantage point the same thing is a design; from another vantage point it is a requirement. (See Fig. 5-30.)

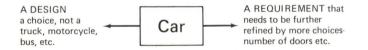

Figure 5-30.   A specification is a requirement and a design.

If "car" can be both a requirement and a design, how much easier it is for a 100 or so page document to be both.

I cannot describe the hours of intense, high level warfare I have been through over the turf problem of whether or not such and such was a design or requirement. It is both!

NEW DESIGN TECHNIQUES

A glut of new design techniques seems to be upon us. Many of these techniques are primarily techniques of notation and not of process. They are valuable, as any help in design is most welcome. They go by many names: Warnier-Orr, Jackson Method, HIPO, SADT, IA, Structured Design — and all are better than no formalism in design. All of them have to do more with documenting and showing the design than doing it, more with the last two parts, structure and representation, than with the first, creation.

Data versus Process

Most methods emphasize starting with the process and then moving on to the data. A few advocate starting with the data and then moving to the process.

It depends on the application or system software being designed as to whether one starts with data or process: Which is the predominant activity? In a large type III, it is the data, and design should start with it. In large types IV and V it is probably the process.

Structured Design

This name is given to so many very different techniques for documenting design that the words are almost useless. What is structured? Structured here has no connection to structured programming!

The fact that there are many new techniques emerging in the design area, even if only for documenting, is encouraging. Almost all have fairly strict rules about how to mark down the *what* and the *how* and the sequence. Almost all have rules to govern the levels of detail encountered, and to restrict the user from clobbering up the notation with too much detail.

Since the communicating of complex ideas and concepts is one of the key difficulties of managing complexity, we must be grateful for any help in this area that is available. Most of the new design techniques are very helpful in this area, and are therefore recommended.

Difficulty of Introduction

Like all new human efforts, the new design techniques are very hard to introduce to a group of people. Change is resisted; the rules chafe; the rigors seem useless. At first. Like many new techniques that are useful, they are finally accepted as "the only way to do this" and the old way is viewed with amusement and self-consciousness.

This happens with all new techniques — and structured programming was, as we saw, no exception. One needs at least one week, and usually two, of formal schooling *and* then coaching for some months to absorb the new techniques. And auditing and enforcement. All our information systems personnel — programmers and analysts, etc. — need this indoctrination.

If the information systems group consists of hundreds of people, we are looking at a very expensive learning cycle. Yet it *must* be undertaken. The results are too significant to not move to the new techniques.

WRITING THE PROGRAM — PROGRAMMING

We now get to the activity that so many people erroneously think of as software development — the writing of the program. It is but a part of software development. In large projects it is the easiest of the six parts of the software development process. It is the most time consuming on small projects.

At some point, design gets to a low enough level that one can write the instructions to make the computer do what the designer has laid out!

With very small programs, written by one or two programmers, the only real issue is which tool, which language, to write in. And with large programs, this is still one of the key questions.

We will break our look at the writing of the instructions into three parts — the language to be used, the process of getting the code to run, and the management of these activities. And we'll restrict ourselves to *just* the activities for a small program. The writing of a small program (10,000 lines of object code) is not much different than the writing of a million lines; the difference between the two are mostly in the other parts of software development. Since very few of the differences are in the writing, we'll discuss the writing here as though the writer did not have the extra duty he or she does for the million lines of code effort. This is not accurate, and we will outline those added tasks in the next section, construction. The added burden on the writer of the instructions is usually in the form of restrictions and set definitions of data, constants, and interfaces.

After the programmer has laid out the flow and structure of the program, he or she writes the instructions.

Writing the program is usually just that, the act of writing instructions on a piece of paper that will eventually go into the machine.

After they are written, they'll be typed into some storage medium that can be read by a machine and then loaded into a computer to see if they make it do what they are supposed to make it do. Hundreds of thousands of programmers put pencil to paper and *write* the instructions. They "code." Today there are more and more programmers sitting at terminals and typing in the instructions — but more on this form of writing the code later.

The important things about writing code are:

1. The clarity of what is to be done — which we have already discussed.
2. The language to be used, and the standards to be followed.
3. The process of managing the conversion of the programs from a language to the machine language.
4. The tools to do 2 and 3.

Languages

Semanticists and linguists are still discovering things about language. There is still some debate as to whether the spoken language or the written language is more important. In *Introduction to Theoretical Linguistics*,* John Lyons notes that language is not just a body of rules, *langue*, nor just the collection of all possible spoken or written collections of words, *parole*, but that language is both. Even the mispronounced, syntactically incorrect expression can be understood. But this is because the listener fills in and corrects. Unfortunately, the computer with its translator program (an assembler or compiler) does *only* what it is told to do. Even the more advanced translators only have limited intelligence. In the computer language, the rules of syntax are critical.

Perhaps it is not so obvious that the process of giving instructions rests on three main supports:

1. You must understand the process you are about to give the instructions for doing.
2. You must be able to articulate (put into words) the sequence of instructions.
3. You must choose words that your audience can understand.

---

*John Lyons, *Introduction to Theoretical Linguistics* (London: Cambridge University Press, 1972).

We often assume that number 1 is present; that it is not we have seen in the section on requirements definition.

We also assume that the person who can "do the process" can put it into words — and this is not always so.

Now we wish to look at the third part — writing the instructions for *the* executor. In our case, the executor is going to be the computer, but I wish to explore an analogy before getting to the instructions for the computer.

If I were a great brain surgeon, and I could articulate the instructions for doing new surgical techniques, I should have no difficulty giving such instructions to other brain surgeons. Change my audience to general surgeons, my task is more difficult. Change to first-year medical students, and I am not sure I can do it. And so on.

So it is with the computer. The computer has the equivalent of a first grade vocabulary. And it is exceedingly difficult to instruct it in its native language, called machine language. Yet we must construct great edifices of logic *in this vocabulary* as it is the only language the computer hardware reacts to.

The early computer users quickly saw that this state of affairs would not do, so they "hired translators."

Sticking with the brain surgeon analogy for the moment, the eminent surgeon now gives the instructions to an intermediary, who translates them *down* to the first-year medical school level.

So too with computers. We no longer force programmers to use the computer's language, but allow them to use a higher order language. And we hire, as our translator, *the same* computer that will *do* the process *after* it has translated it, *and* we put in the computer a program to cause it to do the translation, either a compiler or an assembler, both of which are translators. (See Fig. 5-31.)

To cause the machine to do the translation, we put in the machine, to *do* the translation, a *compiler* or an *assembler* program.

The compiler accepts statements in a higher order language, e.g., FORTRAN, COBOL, Pascal, BASIC — and directs the computer to convert statements into machine language instructions that can then be put on the computer and run to do the real job — the application, say, the payroll.

This is a two-step process, at the least. There is a translation phase and then a use phase. We have *not yet* begun to build machines that execute the high order languages directly.

One can empathize immediately with the eminent brain surgeon — he or she should not be importuned to struggle with the vocabularies of beginners. And so with the programmer. High order languages allow the programmers to write at close to their own level.

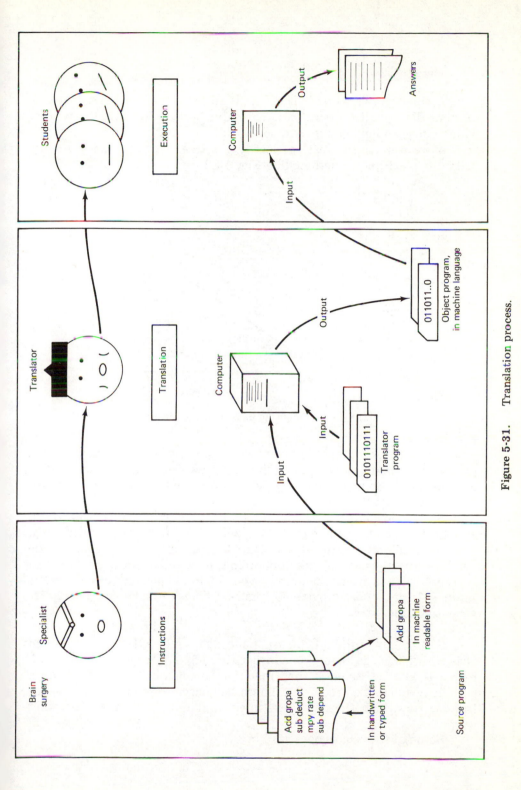

Figure 5-31. Translation process.

151

Language Power versus Difficulty

A language with power is difficult to learn just as the vocabulary of a medical doctor is difficult to learn, and as five syllable words, which convey so much, are hard to learn.

If we were to plot ease of learning with ease of producing quality software, we'd find something like Fig. 5-32.

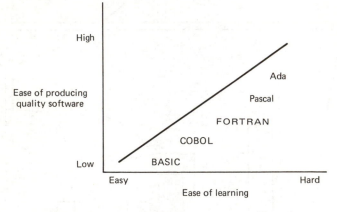

Figure 5-32.   Language power vs. ease of learning.

By quality software I mean well compartmented, easily traced, well documented software. Does this mean we should never use BASIC? No, not at all. Some programs we write do not have to be easy to modify, or easy to partition.

So the language we choose depends on what we are writing. APL and LISP are not on the chart. APL and LISP are for problem solving, not for building software structures. The machine language code produced by these languages and their translators is not important and in most cases is never seen nor saved. I cannot imagine using APL to build a large software system. Figure 5-33 shows POLS, Procedure Oriented Languages.

POLS — Another Type of Language A "POL" is a Problem Oriented Language or a Procedure Oriented Language. It too is at a higher level of abstraction than machine languages. It is designed for a certain problem or procedure. These languages, therefore, are fine for the use for which they are developed, and not good at all for other purposes.

Some of these languages are

APL   = Problem Solving
LISP   = List Processing
GPSS   = General Purpose Simulator
SIMSCRIPT = Text
ATLAS   = DoD Language for TEST Equipment

These languages are aimed at shortening the development of the program by making it easy for the creator of the program to "fit" the program to the job. In this sense these languages are less than general purpose. They are rarely used to develop software that will run regularly, as opposed to once or once in a while.

For these reasons we will not say more about POLS.

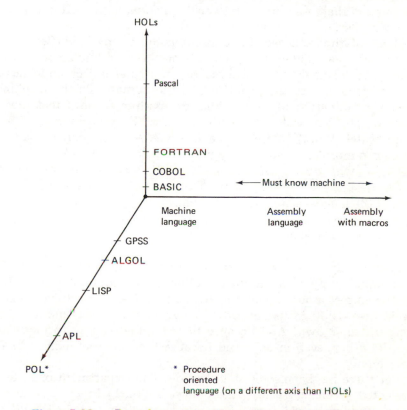

Figure 5-33.   Procedure oriented languages — a third dimension.

Each language is a collection of vocabulary and syntax. The vocabulary is the list of words that the translator will accept. The syntax is the list of rules of arrangement that the vocabulary must be structured into: the order, the punctuation, the allowable combinations.

There are many things happening when the computer plus a compiler program accepts statement in higher order language. A translation is taking place, *and* there is an *expansion* taking place. There is a lot unstated when I tell my aide to "go to the library and get me a copy of X."

He or she supplies the detail: what library, when, how to get there, where X is, how does he or she get it, etc.

He or she can do this *expansion* on the instruction because he or she is intelligent and knowledgeable. Had this person never been in this city before, he or she would have to go and get directions, but *I* need not tell him or her that. The same is true with computer languages and the compilers that translate them. Unstated variables are often supplied by the compiler.

Many of the languages for computers are trying for efficiency in one or more areas. They may make it easier for the human to express the big idea, or make the machine run the final object code faster. Tailor the language to the problem? To the human? To the machine? To some combination of these? What does a human need to know to define this problem, solve it, do the process? How do humans think? Communicate? Work? Write? Take breaks? What sequence makes a machine run more efficiently? Any machine? This machine?

This is why dozens of millions of dollars are spent annually on language design and development. This is why people spend whole careers in the language area of computing.

Language Proliferation

Fortunately for programmers, language development started almost immediately with the introduction of the computer. Unfortunately, languages abound. The Department of Defense estimates there are well over 1000 in use in DoD! Why? Because programmers keep making up their own! And because there's no good way to judge one versus the other, even in use. And because there is still much room for improvement.

Yet there has been some stabilization. The Department of Defense has selected seven languages (Instruction 5000.31) to be used for all *new* "embedded" (real time) DoD projects. (They are: FORTRAN, COBOL, JOVIAL, CMS-2, SPS, TACPOL, and TOS.)

DoD is introducing, after long and deep study, a new language called Ada, and based to some extent on Pascal originated by Nicholas Wirth. If Ada proves to be useful, it will be added to 5000.31. It is a very powerful, but very complex, language.

But Programmers Stay with the Old Languages.   The programmer population steadfastly refuses to move to the new languages. The overwhelming majority of programmers still write in COBOL and FORTRAN, even though those two languages are now considered antiques in terms of their capabilities.

Why do all the old languages persist, and remain so popular? They were the first learned! C.A.R. "Tony" Hoare, in a written report to the Navy in 1978, stated the following:

> The attachment of programmers to existing languages is in stark contrast to the enthusiasm of committees in condemning all such language as inadequate. The reason? . . .he spent a long time mastering it, a new language presents a severe threat . . . .or worse it may even be easier to learn and effectively use, which would wholly devalue the programmer's hard won professional expertise in his earlier language. . . .

In this way a complex language can keep out a simple one. An emigre from Russia tells a similar story. Apparently one of the first languages learned there was COBOL — *English* COBOL. Apparently the early computers there came from the United States and the programmers had to learn the English for *Print* and so on. And English COBOL has persisted! Because the old timers' attitude is against a Russian COBOL. "Let the new people pay their dues." English COBOL is still in use in Germany.

Once a large body of programs exists, it is hard to change to a new language. Possession is 9/10 of everything! The inertia to stay with what one has is very strong.

Language and Thought

The language we use determines much about the way we produce. Many argue that the language shapes the thoughts. In a book on writing style, called simply *Style**, F.L. Lucas writes:

> Hence, the pleasant story of the man who, entering a foreign cafe where there sat groups of English, French, and Germans, noted that the English were of course entrenched round their table in solid silence; the French all gabbling at once; but the Germans all listening to each other in turn with a tense concentration that for a moment astonished him. Then he realized — they were waiting for the verb.

The same is true of the programming languages. Which one is used shapes the process in many subtle and deep ways. Why did Nicholas

*F. L. Lucas, *Style* (New York: Collier Books, 1962).

Wirth come up with Pascal? Because he was tired of teaching languages to his students that "too often could not be explained logically."

Notation as an Aid to Thinking. Whitehead and Russell (*The Principles of Mathematics*, 1910) comment on the power of notation to free the mind from details and allow it to think of other things. Powerful languages, like APL, enable the individual programmer to cause the machine to do vast amounts of work with very few instructions.

Language Notation Binds the Mind. In his Turing Award acceptance speech, Edsger Dijkstra told the story about an experiment he ran. He sent a problem out to several of his peers and asked them to send him a design. They all missed the obvious and elegant solution, he said, because their idea of repetition was so closely connected to associated controlled variables to be stepped up.

Limitations of Languages

The perfect language will elude us for a long time. The following statements are from "The Logic of the Mind" by Jacob Bronowski in *A Sense of the Future**

> The *Entscheidungsproblem* . . . was a startling question which David Hilbert had posed: Whether it was evident . . . that all mathematical assertions that make sense can necessarily be proved to be either true or false. . . .

> In 1931 . . . Kurt Godel proved two remarkable and remarkably unwelcome theorems. The first . . . any logical system that is not excessively simple . . . can express true assertions which nevertheless cannot be deduced from its axioms. And the second . . . the axioms in such a system . . . cannot be shown in advance to be free from hidden contradictions. In short, a logical system that has any richness can never be complete, yet cannot be guaranteed to be consistent. . . .

> A.M. Turing in England and Alonzo Church in America showed that no mechanical procedure can be devised that could test every assertion in a logical system and in a finite number of steps demonstrate it to be either true or false. . . .

> Tarski showed that there can be no precise language which is universal; every formal language which is at least as rich as arithmetic contains meaningful sentences that cannot be asserted to be either true or false. . . .

---

*Jacob Bronowski, *A Sense of the Future: Essays in Natural Philosophy* (Cambridge, Mass. and London, England, The MIT Press, 1977). Selected and edited by Piero E. Ariotto in collaboration with Rita Bronowski.

An axiomatic system cannot be made to generate a description of the world which matches it fully, point for point; at some points there will be holes which cannot be filled in by deduction; and at other points two opposite deductions may turn up . . .

And finally, Tarski's theory demonstrates, I think conclusively, that there cannot be universal description of nature in a single, closed, consistent language. . . .

This is a cardinal point: it is the language that we use in describing nature that imposes (by its arrangement of definitions and axioms) both the form and the limitations of the laws that we find. . . .

It is characteristic of the human language that it is made up of past metaphors and analogies, and they are a fertile ground for the exploration of ambiguity and the discovery of hidden likenesses. . . .

Many logical problems grow from this common root, namely that the range of reference of any reasonably rich system necessarily includes reference to itself. This creates an endless regress, an infinite hall of mirrors of self reflection. And the regress comes sharply to a focus in all the paradoxes of logic, which are cousins of one sort or another to the classical contradictions that the Greeks knew: what they call the Cretan paradox. . . .

Bertrand Russell tried (with Alfred North Whitehead in the *Principia Mathematica*) to untie the knot in this kind of paradox, and to put an end to the infinite regress of assertions about assertions, by constructing a theory of types. This was intended to prevent us from using the same language to discuss our language as we use to discuss the things the language means. Human language is rich because we think about ourselves. We cannot eliminate self-reference from the human language without thereby turning it from a genuine language of information into a machine language of instructions. . . .

All thinking about thinking implies self-reference: the first statement of principle in the philosophy of Descartes, *Cogito, ergo sum*, refers to itself. . . . no logical machine can reach out of the difficulties and paradoxes created by self reference. . . .

A machine is not a natural object, it is a human artifact which mimics and exploits our own understanding of nature.

The 'STRANGE LOOPS' that Douglas Hofstadter writes about in *Gödel, Escher, Bach: An Eternal Golden Braid* are extensions of these ideas.**

And in the letter report to the U.S. Navy, Hoare wrote:

. . . and the implementers of newly designed high order languages discover hosts of incredibly complicated special cases and ambiguities and inconsist-

---

**Douglas Hofstadter, *Gödel, Escher, Bach: An Eternal Golden Braid* (New York: Basic Books, Inc., 1979).

encies. The standardization committees must be reconvened. . . this takes about 6 years. It is a "soul destroying" job because it is obvious that there is no "right" solution to the oversights of the original design. . . .

A language takes about 10 years from initiation to "successful standardization". . . .

This is true of FORTRAN, ALGOL, PL/1. Pascal is still not standardized.

Why? — because of the extraordinary, complex and unexpected interaction effects between all parts of the language.

Pascal is too high level to deal comfortably with a (say) binary input/output; and it is too low level to give full security checking on tagged records. It is a very serious problem to blend into one language both high and low level features.

Since it is the interaction effects that are crippling, the whole language should be studied to find out which features should be excised.

The main merit of a good high level language is the aid it gives the intellect in the design and documentation of a computer program; and the aid it gives in actually coding may be secondary.

In a recent report (1978) for the Navy, a researcher enumerated over 2,570 different capabilities or features that could be named and evaluated in a computer language. 2,570!!

How rich our minds and languages are!!

In addition to the natural complexities of a rich language as articulated by Bronowski, there is the inherent problem of what to optimize when we build our languages and their translators. When we optimize one of the 12 aspects of a program we penalize others.

To write a translator that translates rapidly, we slow down the execution speed of the resulting code. And vice versa.

Process of Writing a Program

The process of writing a program is an iteration of write, run, and correct. Correct because the program is rarely without errors the first time. Depending on the task and the programmer these three steps may be gone through a few or a great many times. The programmer writes instructions *to the translator*, which in turn writes them again in the language — more detailed — of the machine. But this translator is not human. It does not understand overtones, gestures, subtleties, pitch and tone, or facial expression and the myriad of symbols that are present in the interaction between the human translator and the speaker/writer. This *machine plus program* translator is quintessentially literal. And it demands that every comma, space, dash, and format be *correct* — as defined by the language.

When the programmer submits the source program to be translated, the first thing the translation program does is to check for syntax errors — and if any are found, the source program is rejected with a printed message that at such and such point in the source program, an error of such and such type exists. A missing parenthesis. A fixed integer to be multiplied by a floating point number (some languages accept that).

Gerald Weinberg* indicates that the "typical programmer" goes through two phases in getting the machine to run his or her program. First he or she works towards his [or her] first error-free compilation. Compilation is translation and expansion. "Error-free" means no *syntax* or obvious logical errors, as the first step is to achieve a "semantically correct" program. To achieve this, the programmer changes a few statements each time the program is to be rerun through the machine.

At some time the second step is taken. The machine language instructions are loaded into a computer *and executed*, usually with some data values that the programmer sends along with the instructions. The results are printed out and returned to the programmer. At this point the programmer studies the results to see if the program logic is correct and it usually isn't. He or she fixes the logic of the process of the program and reruns the program. When the program is right, it is either run, if it is a stand alone program, or it is given to a process or person who will merge it into a larger program. The process looks like Fig. 5-34. The syntax-checking of the translator is a very helpful process, assisting the programmer to find not only punctuation errors, but even some logical errors.

For example, if the programmer has written the program to transfer control to the subprogram called TRACK, but has not written the identifying letters TRACK on any subprogram, the translator will flag this logical omission.

Iteration of program submital

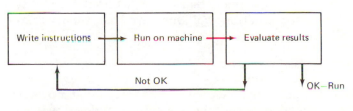

Figure 5-34.   Iteration of program submittal.

*Gerald Weinberg, *Psychology of Computer Programming* (New York: Van Nostrand Reinhold Company, 1971).

Hosting or Cross Compiling

A higher order language like FORTRAN can be used as input to different computers with their own translating (compiler) programs. The language is standardized, each computer has its own translation program, and generates object code for itself.

A logical step in the use of these translating programs is the use of one computer and a translator program, a host, to translate from a source language *to the object language of a different machine*.

This is called *hosting* or cross compiling. It is usually used when the machine that will run the object code is small (memory, I/O, or CPU limited). It is not very efficient to run translators on small slow machines.

Therefore, using a host goes like this: The program is written in a source language; it is run through a large machine with a translation program, which produces an object code for a second machine. The object code is then run on the second machine. The second, small machine usually has an entirely different instruction set (repertoire) than the large one.

This process is a logical extension of the machine independence benefit of HOLs. Machine independence allows us to submit a program written in a standard language to *any* machine type and model as long as it has a compiler program that will cause it to translate the HOL input to its machine language. A diagram of that process and of hosting is shown in Fig. 5-35.

Changes and updates to the program are usually written in the source code to be run again through the translator on the large machine. The small machine may not even have a translator program.

This process greatly speeds up programming. Obviously, a penalty of it is that a large machine is required.

Not so obvious is the fact that the translator must be available to the eventual continuing developer. Occasionally, a software developer will use a proprietary translator to create the program, deliver it, and the result is that the support team is left without the ability to compile changes! A nasty situation. Millions have been spent creating a "new" compiler!

Many Forms of One Program

An often confusing fact about software is that *a* program can exist in many forms at one and the same time. Indeed, we want it to. We want a "version" of it in object language (to run) and a version of it in source language (to modify). We'll see more of this later; for now let's just look at the various forms the program can take. Let us look at a simple business letter.

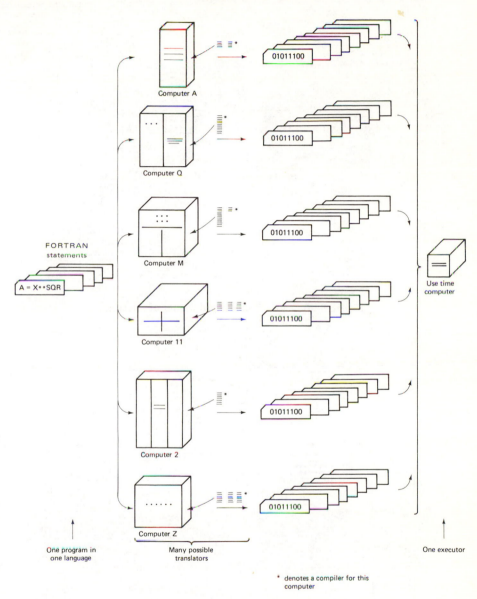

FORTRAN
statements

A = X**SQR

Computer A

Computer Q

Computer M

Computer 11

Computer 2

Computer Z

01011100

01011100

01011100

01011100

01011100

01011100

Use time
computer

One program in
one language

Many possible
translators

One executor

* denotes a compiler for this
computer

Figure 5-35. Hosting.

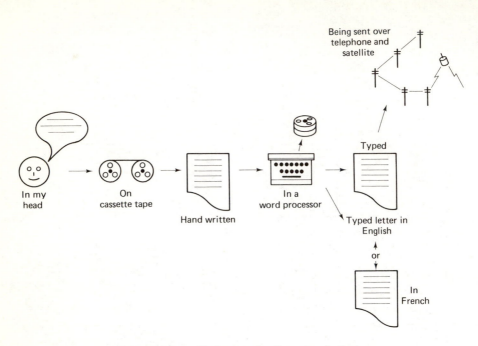

Figure 5-36. Various embodiments of a letter.

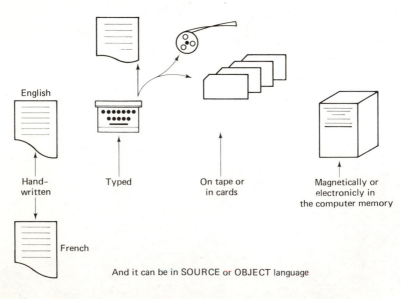

And it can be in SOURCE or OBJECT language

Figure 5-37. Various embodiments of a program.

"Where is my letter?"

"Your handwritten copy is on your desk; the typed copy is on the boss's desk; there is a stored version in the word processor and there is a copy en route via the telephone to Florida, and a copy is going over the satellite circuits to Germany." (See Fig. 5-36.) Some of the forms of the letter can be read by people; some can only be read by machine.

So too with a program. Figure 5-37 shows only five ways a payroll program can exist.

Computers to Compile

Often overlooked is the fact that in addition to the compiler, we need a computer to do the compiling. This seems so obvious, but in three large software development efforts in which I was involved the lack of a computer to compile with was an overriding factor in the software development effort.

For the development of the Skylab software, the computers that Houston normally used to compile and build on were in use supporting the control team on the final Apollo mission. The programmers wrote — but little compiling was done and no testing was possible. A million dollars was finally appropriated to rent a large scale IBM 360 Model 65 computer *just* to do the support processing.

On a Navy effort on the West Coast, my 40 programmers were producing very little, and one of the reasons was a poorly sized and poorly configured 370 host computer. The program was to run at use time on a Sperry UNIVAC UYK 20, but the computer that was to do the compiling was a System 370/138. Not only was this too small (not enough power) but there was only *one* channel on it, so it was I/O bound as well. We got a System 148 with more channels. My team had made a poor selection of the host computer.

In Europe a development effort of over 1 million COBOL statements that I was shown had some very large modules, far too large for good modularity. "Why so?" I asked. Because the computer to compile on was too heavily loaded with production, and therefore the design of the use time software was changed to reduce the number of hours required for compiling. It takes less compile time to compile one large module than to compile multiple small ones to do the same function.

Programming on Interactive Terminals

The advent of time sharing seemed to promise a revolution in programming. No longer would the turnaround time be a bottleneck; it would be instantaneous.

The jury is still out. It appears logical that giving every programmer a terminal would increase productivity, but there is as yet no hard evidence of this result. And the terminals cost money. The IBM Federal System Productivity data base "seems" to yield that conclusion, but the people who have studied it are not willing to state that.

On a large project with hundreds of programmers the number of terminals becomes expensive and there is a tendency to flail at the problem, to be slap-dash. If one sits at a terminal, one may feel compelled to *use* it. This is in stark contrast to a reasoned, careful approach. We'll see this again under productivity.

What Are We Interacting With?

Let us assume that I walk into the computer room and approach the computer. No one has informed me about the computer, but I am pleased to see that it is a DEC11/70, as I am familiar with that model and make. I see that the machine is on and that it is ready to be used.

Now comes the problem: Is the machine empty and waiting for its first instructions? Or does it contain a compiler? Or an operating system?

Depending on what is in there, I will instruct the computer in very different ways.

If there is nothing in there, I must start the loading sequence by using the switches on the console.

If there is an assembler in there and I wish to program, then I must feed it assembly language instructions.

If there is a compiler in there, then I must feed it compiler language instructions.

If there is an operating system in there, then I must know how to give commands to the operating system, as it has the control of the computer, and I must deal with it.

There are no physical outward signs of what is in there; and if there were no one there to tell me what was going on, then I would have to use trial and error to see what was in the machine. I would try one thing that should work if such and such were in there and see if that worked and so on.

There may or may not be in the computer memory the following software systems:

1. An operating system
2. A data base management system
3. A communications system
4. A display system
5. An assembler (translator)

6. An HOL compiler

7. Applications programs

When a person sits down to write a program, or type on a terminal attached to a computer, he or she may be engaging either the raw hardware (the *C* in Fig. 5-38) or a series of programs written to be used by the programmer or user. The person at (*A*) is interacting with six programs *and* the hardware. The person at B is interacting with one program and the hardware.

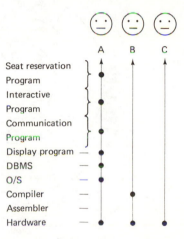

Figure 5-38.   Interacting with the computer program.

Obviously as we add different programs and interconnect them, we get a great number of different possible things we can interact with. Figure 5-39 shows but some of the paths from the programmer or the user to the hardware!

If I were "at" spot *A*, I am writing in machine code.

Spot *B*   I use assembler language.

Spot *C*   I use compiler language.

Spot *D*   I use commands to the Operating System.

Spot *E*   I use data base management language.

Spot *F*   I use a communications language.

The person programming at *E* need *never know anything* about the levels that are closer to the hardware. He or she can operate forever without going into any deeper level. He or she is dealing with an *abstract machine* that is made up of the hardware *and* the levels of software.

All of these people are programming. They are writing instructions for the machine to execute. The instructions will go through a translation, or many translations, as we have seen, but the end result will be a body of machine code that is executed by the hardware.

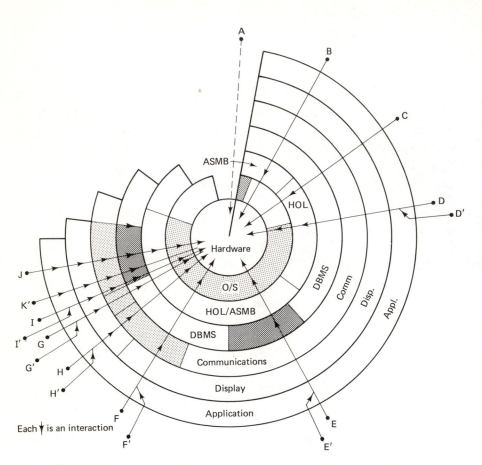

Figure 5-39. Possible interactions with a computer plus software.

The prime letters (*E'*, *F'*, etc.) represent *users*, not programmers. Note that what they put into the computer system (the hardware *plus* the software) first is acted upon by the applications programs. What the *user* enters is *data* to the applications programs, and the result is an answer or answers, *not* a machine language program.

This wealth of ways I can interact with the machine *plus* its software can be very confusing, as each way is quite different from the others. The number of ways I can interact with a computer system is almost unlimited. In our Figure 5-39, we have limited the applications level to one level of interaction, although it could be several levels, with each transaction going through several different applications programs. At the single level shown, there are 720 different combinations of hardware and software that a terminal can interact with. This wealth of choice is the blessing *and* the bane of the computer.

J represents a somewhat unusual but not rare example. All layers of the software are in use. If I were in one city using a terminal in an interactive way with the computer in another city and the compiler is interactive, I have a *J* use. The *K* use (skipping the HOL level) is very common.

MANAGING THE WRITING

The very flexibility of the stored program makes programming difficult; one problem can have 100 different programs that can be used to yield the same answer on a computer. All will work; all will get the same answer! Is one better than the other? Yes, in some ways. It runs faster. Or it takes less memory space. Or it took me a lot shorter time to write my program than it would have taken me to write yours. The fact that yours is a "faster running" solution is offset by the length of time it took you to write the program.

The possible instruction sequences are almost limitless, as a programmer strings together the steps by which he/she solves the problem. Who is to say the program is wrong or right or even workable, until it is tried? Until it is put on a computer and run?

It is very difficult to manage someone and be sure he/she is heading in the right direction when the paths that can be taken to get there are almost unlimited.

Managing the writing process is very difficult. The aspects of software that make it hard are abstractness and intangibility, lack of visibility, and variability.

Many fine new tools have entered the technology to assist in the control of this process.

Structured programming not only helps the design process but it makes the resulting program more readable. Other programs keep track of every developed program instruction (line-of-code) and are called *automated librarians*. These programs are also making the practice of programming more visible. They are taking it from a private art to a public practice.

Programmer Variability

Studies of programming "in the small," i.e., on small programs, show a fantastic range of productivity *and* resulting product among programmers. Lines of code per unit of time show a difference of 25 to 1. That is, some people write 25 times as many lines of code per day as others. Size of the resulting program covers a 20 to 1 range; some programs are one twentieth the size of others. The efficiency of the running program spans a 10 to 1 range; some programs run 10 times faster than others doing the same job.

It is not at all clear, however, that a programmer who writes 25 times as much code as his or her peer is necessarily a good programmer. Lines of code is a deceptive, inadequate measure of worth. Yet it is all we have. We'll study lines of code at some length in Chap. 6. For now we merely wish to point out that there is great diversity among programmers.

The message of these studies and the above numbers is that we must distinguish between our workers, recruit and keep *good* programmers, and assign the right person to the right job.

If your task is large enough, it will be foolish to estimate the output of hundreds of programmers based on the performance of the best.

The Chief Programmer

Perhaps we should ask the question: When do we break the program into two tasks to be done by two programmers? There is no good overall answer to this. There is an ideal, which is simply to avoid partitioning jobs whenever you can. The minute you break a job in two and give it to two people, they must communicate, and waste, confusion, and error have an opportunity to creep in.

So much depends on the job to be done, the programmer available to do it, the time before it is needed, and the tools to use to get it written. On the *N.Y. Times* project *one* programmer, Terry Baker, created a working software system of 83,000 high level language statements in 22 months. We used Harlan Mills's "Chief Programmer Team" approach with great success. Baker was supported in a way similar to a surgeon in an operating room. He was supported by a librarian, who handled all the clerical tasks, including the chore of getting the code to the computer to be compiled. Baker's tools were kept in shape by someone else. And a back-up programmer checked his code and made suggestions.

Clearly, the fact that *one* mind is executing yields a productivity increase.

The Chief Programmer approach worked well on the *Times* project — and on several other projects in the ensuing few years. But the approach has one major drawback, and that is the fact that one chief can only do so much, even if it is six or even ten times the average. The approach has not yet worked out for the large projects that have hundreds of thousands of lines of code.

The Chief Programmer worked well on jobs of less than 100,000 lines of code. We were not doing systems that "small" very often. We never did get the concept of a "team of teams" working well.

Because this technique was first used on the *N.Y. Times*, many people believe that it is part of structured programming. It is not!

Some maintain the *Times* effort was not a success. It was indeed. *We* (IBM) saved $700,000 and the system worked. At first the *Times* had very few people on board who were experienced in systems. As *Times* systems people came on board, the normal transition problems that occur when a development team passes responsibility to a continued development team were encountered. This normal difficulty has been incorrectly used to disparage the marvelous results of the structured programming *and* of the Chief Programmer techniques on the *N.Y. Times* Project.

Having begged the answer to how much to give to a programmer till now, I'll now avoid it altogether. There are at least 27 variables to be considered before we estimate the code produced per person unit of time. And first we must define what a line of code is. We will explore this in Productivity and Estimation in Chap. 6.

Librarian

A relatively new technique in software development is the use of the *librarian*. In the past, too much of the programmer's time was spent fooling with card punching, filing listings, and the like. These clerical tasks are now assigned to librarians. But a side benefit is that the code written by every programmer is now captured in a central and public place.

A subtle but profound difference is introduced into the development process. The code now is clearly in the possession of the organization, whereas before it was the property of the programmer until it was finished and handed over. The programmer often never showed anyone his or her many incorrect attempts to get the program to run. If it took nine tries, who knew? This looseness encouraged looseness in the programming process. It encouraged — or at least made very easy — a slap-dash, flail at the problem, approach.

Now the manager can scan the readable, structured programs that are entered into the computer to see how many attempts it has taken Programmer Jones to achieve a working routine. The practice of programming is becoming less private and more public.

A "library" has nothing to do with the librarian. A library is a collection of programs, usually support programs, to be used at any time.

Some incorrectly lump a librarian into structured programming. It is a separate concept or technique.

Figure 5-40 shows an automated librarian in an interactive programming environment, as well as a person assigned to be the librarian.

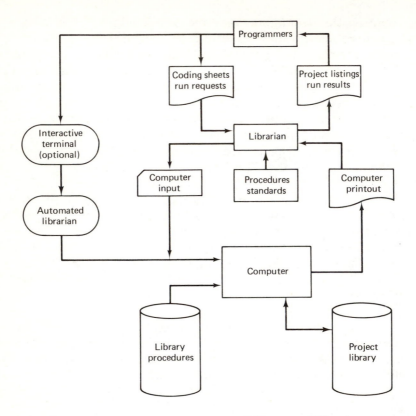

Figure 5-40.   Project operation with library and librarian.

CONSTRUCTION

Assembling Large Numbers of Modules into One Working Software System

This is the phase in which the developers take programs already written, *and tested* to some extent, by either individuals or teams, and connect them together so that the computer will run *through* dozens or hundreds of programs, from start to finish, end to end, achieving the desired result or service.

I choose the word *construction* because it signifies in the physical world interconnecting prefabricated pieces into a whole. This is precisely the process that we are engaged in when we create a large software system.

Our six phases of software development are:

Requirements definition

Design

Writing the instructions, programming

Construction

Test or verification

Document

If we have only a single stand-alone program there is *no* construction phase.

A compelling reason to view construction as a separate phase of software development is the abundance of new automated development tools for this activity. In the past this effort was largely manual and therefore slow. Today we see significant numbers of powerful programs to construct automatically hundreds of subprograms into a software system.

These tools dovetail with a selected language, and sometimes an operating system, but are separate from them.

Thus, the Ada language that DoD is moving to standardize on has associated with it a set of support programs that provide an "environment" that the software developers can use to construct large chains of programs. The environment is called an APSE — Ada Programming Support Environment — and there are specific constructs and verbs in the Ada language to use to call upon these tools.

There is a subtle difference here between the language and the environment, but it is a significant difference. If I do not need to enmesh my program in a large chain, I may wish to use only the language and not the environment. Therefore, I may want *only* the compiler to translate for me, and I may wish to run the compiler separately from the rest of the environment.

Construction Before Test?

We show test as the fifth step, after construction. But much testing of unit programs takes place *before* construction begins. Test here means system test and it does take place after construction.

Tools to Service Management

Just as operating systems helped the programmer and the management, so too the automated tools to be run at development time have a multiple function. They serve management as well as the programmer.

They aid the programmer in the fashion we have seen. Now let's look at the role of these tools for management.

When we have a large number of programmers creating a large number of programs, we have several activities that must be carried out:

1. Interfacing
2. Sharing data
3. Binding or builds
4. Running the collected pieces
5. Keeping track of versions and module numbers

Interfacing. The word "fungible" is an obscure word that describes a very well known phenomenon. If I buy staples for use in a stapler, I expect them to work. They always do. They do because the size, construction, shape, material, hardness and packaging are standardized. Many different manufacturers make staples. The complete interchangeability of the staples is stated by the words, "the staples are fungible." Interchangeable.

The same concept is coming into play in the software area. We want to *set* the manner, form, syntax, vocabulary, and necessary content for one program to work with a second. These interfaces are beginning to be defined, and the programs are able to be snapped together with less and less tailoring to make them work together.

Sharing Data. Programs must often work on the same data. We can share the data in two very different ways — common data or private. Private data is data that belongs to one module. Common data is passed to other modules. There are pros and cons to each of these techniques. Private data makes the modules more independent, but takes more effort to develop. Common data makes development easier, but can allow errors from one module to interfere or destroy the results of other modules.

Automated Construction — Binding or Builds. We design the modules so that we can connect them easily and cleanly. Then we replace people effort by computer effort by using programs that connect up the modules automatically. Once we have the rules clear, the connection is easier.

We call the connecting by many names:

Link-editing
Automated builds
Integration

Binding

Linking

and there are some slight differences between these, but the processes are very similar.

Running the Collected Pieces.   Here again we see the power of the new tools. In the past, and in too many installations today, the software team had to control the software system manually. If we have hundreds of modules, this is a most time consuming job.

Fortunately, many software packages exist (and are purchasable) that do this function automatically. They make the system (that results from the binding process) run on the computer.

Version Control.   We use the computer and programs to collect, catalog, and store all the pieces of the software, all the modules by name. We keep them separated into tested and ready-to-run systems, systems in test, modules in test, and modules in compilation. Again we use computer automation to make the task simpler, faster, and less error-prone. Figure 5-41 depicts a disk with the versions stored on it.

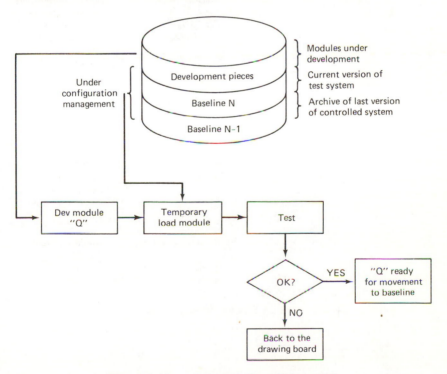

Figure 5-41.   Automated version control.

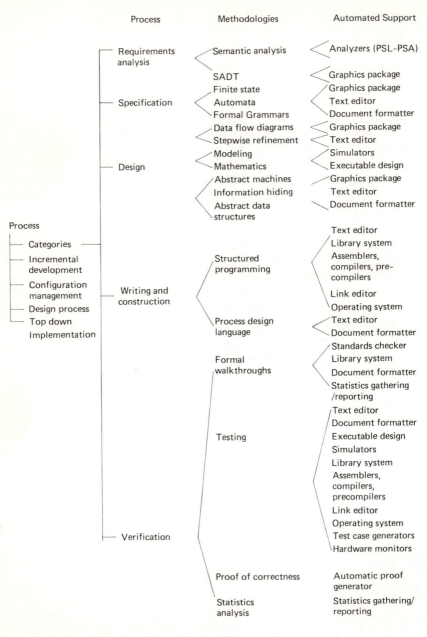

Figure 5-42.   Process, methodologies, tools.

Automated Application of the Tools

A collection of tools is one thing. An interrelated, automated set of tools is a quite different thing. In too many programming efforts today, the programmer must still *manually* apply the tools. He or she must put the software trace in with his or her program, or physically put the test decks with his or her program and send them in to run.

Today a programmer should write a *call* for these items and the software environment — running under an operating system — performs the tasks heretofore done manually.

Poor tools slow the process of development substantially. The newer the computer, the more erratic the tools that are available, and the fewer tools available at all.

Tool selection should follow the selection of methodology. If you pick a language first, you may preclude the use of structured programming. Some languages do not support structured programming.

Some languages give you no control over the modules produced. Some give you no ability to do information hiding. You must get to tool choice *after* you choose a methodology. And you select a methodology *after* you have selected a process. (See Fig. 5-42.)

Selection of Compilers and Languages

When we select a compiler we have a basic choice whether we want to optimize: (1) the *use* of the compiler (compile time), or (2) the *result* of the compiler (use time). The engineering program that will run once need not be optimized for use time.

A computer user who compiles once and then runs the resulting code daily does not care how fast the compilation is performed; that user wants "efficient code." (See Fig. 5-43.)

Language Selection.   The same kind of trade-offs go into the selection of a language. What language to use depends mainly on what you are doing, the people you have and the schedule. Language selection precedes compiler program selection, and language selection should be made by management, not by the programmers. (See Fig. 5-44.)

Language I (in Fig. 5-44) optimizes the developer's time; language II optimizes the continued-development time at the expense of the developer's time. Note that the choice of language is separate from the choice of compiler. Let's look at a diagram of the serial choice of language and the compiler program (Fig. 5-45.)

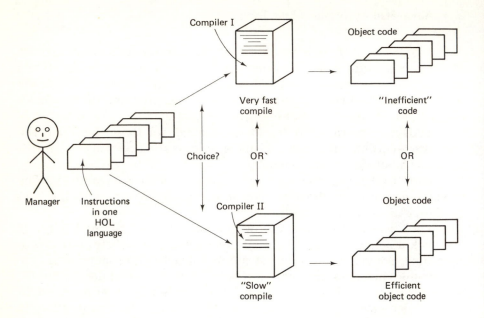

Figure 5-43. Compile to optimize use or development?

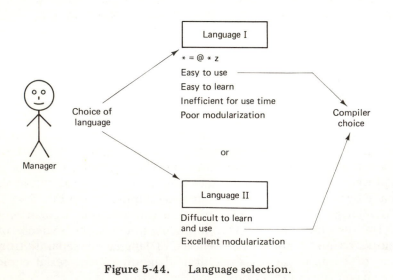

Figure 5-44. Language selection.

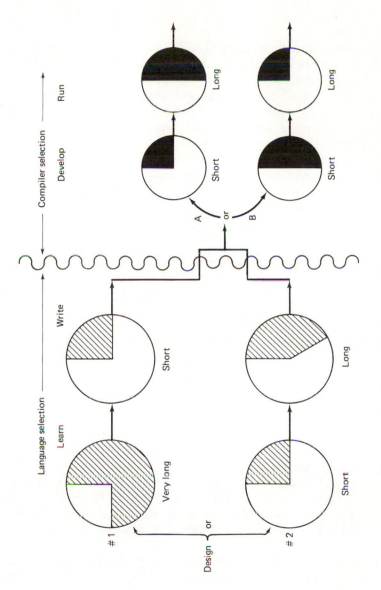

Figure 5-45. Language selection followed by compiler selection.

Top Down Implementation

We cover the Top Down techniques here and not under design. Top Down Implementation makes sense; Top Down design does not make total sense.

As we saw under the section on design, the first part of design is creative. By its nature it is filled with TOing and FROing. There may or may not be a top at all.

But if we can find the top during the design phase, then we can implement the software top down. We can create the top level programs and "fan out" from there, adding subordinate programs as we go deeper, level by level, into the creation of the software.

This is in marked contrast to bottoms-up implementation, where the most detailed sequences are implemented first. Is this top down design? Many argue it is not, that it is top down implementation. On many advanced systems, much bottoms up design must be done as the system often depends on one or two subsystem breakthroughs.

The Software Development Environment

The computer and a host of programs are the essential tools that help the individual programmer and the manager of the programmers produce a new set of programs. An effective development suite has:

1. A powerful computer to develop on.
2. A powerful and stable set of programs to aid the programmers.
3. A good team of people to set up and maintain the development programs.
4. A powerful set of programs to aid the management.

Development used to be a room, people, computers, and programs. Now development is automated and controlled more than ever by a development system — a set of programs called an environment. Such an environment — as described for Ada, by the Department of Defense — consists of: the user interface, the database, and the tools set.

The user interface should enable the program developer to handle any set of tools and to get information into or out of the system.

The data base may range from user manuals to a computerized library system.

The tools may range from paper and pencil to an automated test environment with problem-dependent generation of test data.

The user should be able to extract from the data base:

What tools are available.
How they work.
What application libraries are available.
Interrelationships between versions of tools and programs.

When illegal syntax or logic is detected by a translator, a translator will print an error message. The error message to the program developer should:

Be in plain language rather than code.
State the offending symbol, entity, or user action.
State the context in which the error occurred.

The data base should be up to today's standards for ease of use and should contain:

Information on itself, its structure, and context.
All versions of a program under development.
Training material on language and tools.

The system should capture data about:

Errors: frequency and type
Down times
Costs
Schedules
Test results
Usage reports: machines and programs

The system should include run-time modules (programs) similar to modules in normal operating systems. Standard I/O routines are an example.
Design support tools are called for:

Textbooks
Development standards
Cookbooks
Case studies
Computer-aided design both off-line and interactive

The tools should:

Aid in integrated design of hardware and software.
Support structured decomposition.
Include graphics.
Be interactive.
Use the data base if possible.
Integrate simulation and testing techniques.

Interface properties called for:

Standardized.
Use the link-load conventions.
Translation should provide interface with run-time modules.
Test and debug tools.

An initial set of tools and libraries are:

A compiler
A run-time support package, including I/O support
A file handling package
Library system for handling modules written in Ada
Link/loader
A set of debugging aids, working on symbolic level
Optimizer
Aids for glossary, indexing, cross referencing
Language oriented source editor
Program structure analyzer
Conversion aids

An IBM document describes a subset of such an environment in different terms, yet is so similar that it is worth showing. IBM calls them *Development Support Libraries*.

A development support library is a set of programs and procedures that:

1. Provides a constantly up-to-date representation of the product being built.
2. Provides management with a discipline for the control of the development of that product.

A development support library consists of four elements:

A machine-readable internal library,
A human-readable external library,
Machine procedures and programs,
Office procedures.

The machine-stored library contains all current project programming data, including source code, relocatable modules, linkage-editing statements, object modules, job control statements, test data, and information. The status of the internal library is printed out and kept in the human-readable external library. A history of previous versions is kept for reference. The machine procedures consist of standardized control statements to perform basic procedures:

Updating libraries.
Retrieving modules for compilations and storing results.
Linkage editing of jobs and test runs.
Backing up and restoring libraries.
Producing library status listings.

Office procedures are used by librarians to:

File updated status listings in the external library.
File and replace pages in the archives.

A programmer works only with the external library.

Forging Programs Together. If a process is to continue from person to person, or machine to machine, or program to program, there are two kinds of things that must be passed:

1. Data or raw materials. "Here is the stuff to do your thing to. Go to it; do it." *Data*
2. Process information. "Do your normal thing half as long." *Control Information*

Some of these transfers can become quite voluminous. Data transfer looks easy, but it can become burdensome and detailed. Control possibly could never be passed but *be* in the next process to begin with, but then the flexibility of the system is less.

There is one other critical question that is often *not* called out crisply, and that is "When is the control information passed?" There are four possible times to do this *coupling* from program to program.

1. At compile time. The resultant object code is *fused* if the control information is embedded here. To change, we must recompile.
2. At link-edit time. Separately compiled programs are fused with this part of the construction phase of software development. This allows more flexible change as no recompilation is necessary, only re-link-editing.
3. At execution time. This combining is done *in* the computer every time the programs are run. It takes memory and CPU time to redo the coupling every time, but the flexibility is very great. We can change, modify, adapt the nature or form of the program *every* execution. No recompiling nor re-link-editing is required. This is the most flexible approach.
4. At write time. Write one program that *only* compiles one larger program. This is the least flexible approach; the program must be rewritten if a change is to be made.

Summary

The point of all the foregoing is not to lay out the development-time system that should be used. It is to emphasize that well-stocked and well-run development systems are in use today. They are not simple, not naturally evolving accidents. It takes time and talent and money to design and install a system that will efficiently support a major development.

The construction of a bridge is obviously the result of the efforts of a multitude of laborers. Without the organization imposed on this labor by management the large bridges would never be built. The management funds, plans, designs, hires, pays, schedules, directs. The labor fits into this as but a piece of the whole effort.

So too with the development of software, especially large scale software. Management must perform the same functions; the laborers are mostly the programmers, those who write the instructions. Management's task is twofold; to maximize the output of the programmers' efforts and, second, to couple those outputs into a unified whole. This second part is greatly influenced by the design being followed, and by the practices used to connect the parts. The connection of the parts into a whole is what we mean by construction.

Figure 5-46 depicts the role of the computer and support software growing during the 1970's, and the manual effort expended diminishing. This is happening in well run software development activities.

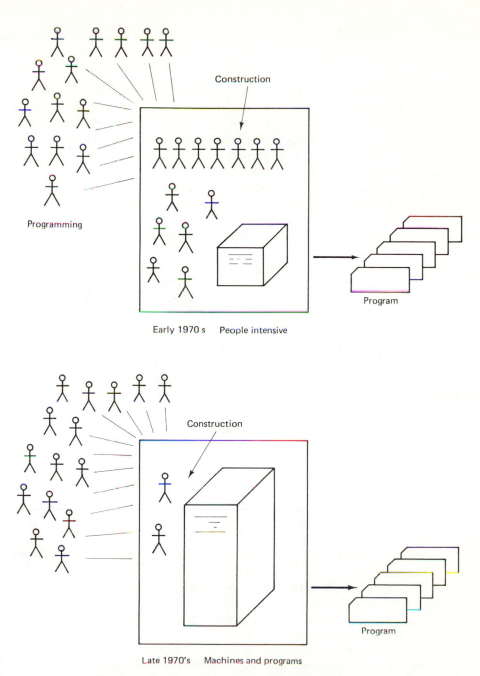

Programming

Construction

Program

Early 1970 s   People intensive

Construction

Program

Late 1970's   Machines and programs

State of the art in construction

Figure 5-46.   The growth of automated tools for development.

VERIFICATION AND TESTING

Verification

Testing tells us the state of what we have already built and shows us where to go in and fix a problem. Verification helps us to avoid having the error getting in there in the first place. An error in a program can be many things, from a miscoded statement that will cause the entire system to stop, to something as trivial as a column error on a printout that makes the report look a little less neat but which affects nothing else. An error can be caused by misstatements in requirements, in design, or in coding. It can stem from omission or commission. It can come from a mistake, an ambiguity, a void, or a confusion.

Verification is a new term, having come into the field in the last 5 years or so and it means the process of checking the requirements when they are documented, the design when it is documented, and the subpieces of the program when they come into being. Before the idea of verification, the whole process of determining whether or not the software "fit" the requirement was left till the end of the process when the software was tested. Verification moves the process of checking forward in time and catches mistakes and oversights early, preventing the programming team from implementing the wrong requirements. Testing refers usually to running the finished programs to see if they do what that requirement calls for.

Verification is done by inspection or by walkthroughs. Peers, managers, outsiders, and users if possible, sit down and review the work product of the requirements (or the design) group, and try to find the gaps, errors, ambiguities, etc. Verification is being made easier every year as the techniques for stating the requirements and design get clearer and easier.

Catching Problems Early

The idea of testing implies an end product that we now test to see if it works. We test drive the car *after* it is a car.

But it is well known that if you can test the pieces of the car *before* they are assembled, you will get a better quality product less expensively. Catching faults early avoids building them *into* the product or program. How do we test an intangible product before it is ready to run? By using new techniques categorized as verification. Verification reviews the adequacy and accuracy of intermediate results, documents, of the various pieces of the development process. The walkthroughs we will see below are verification processes. Test is a part of verification.

Testing is the activity that is performed to ensure that the finished software does what it is supposed to do. The best test of any system is its use. This is especially true for real time systems. But that is expensively late to find errors or gaps in the system. We want to find the errors as soon as possible.

The activities of the test department are:

Understand the functions to be performed

Understand the stress points in the system — time constraints and input parameter sensitivities

Design a series of exercises to force the system to perform

Configure a test system of hardware and software components

Build the test system

Schedule and orchestrate actual tests

A great deal of ingenuity is called for, and a great deal of knowledge.

Testing is subjecting the result of the development to a process to see if it does indeed do what it is supposed to do. Although testing and verification arrive in this book at this point, *after* construction, that is an accident of the serial nature of a book. In actual practice a good deal of testing and much verification occur *before* construction. We unit test each piece of software as it is declared finished by the individual developer or lowest level group.

It is worth looking again at Fig. 5-7 that depicts the development process. Note that verification and testing activities occur at the very early stages of the project.

Part of the design effort should be to make the software testable.

Inspections

With the adoption of structured programming, the program itself has become *readable*. This is in contrast to the old, unstructured code which was like a block of concrete or an unreadable bowl of spaghetti.

Structured code is indented, follows the rigid rules of structure and should be well commented. If in addition the module length is kept short, about 30 to 50 statements per module, we get very readable code. An excellent way of checking progress as the development is under way is to have code inspections called *code walkthroughs*.

Several peers, and perhaps some managers, familiar with the project and the terminology, sit down with the writer of the program who proceeds to show them his or her code and describe what he or she is doing, the flow of the program statement by statement and how much has been tested, and so on. This is new; the advent of structured programming has made it possible.

If these inspections are held regularly, nasty surprises should not be encountered *at the very end of the schedule*. Management has far more visibility and control.

The benefits are great. The "too close to see the forest" problem

The peer review, or walkthrough process, should be conducted at many times during the development process. The following chart shows the process at several stages.

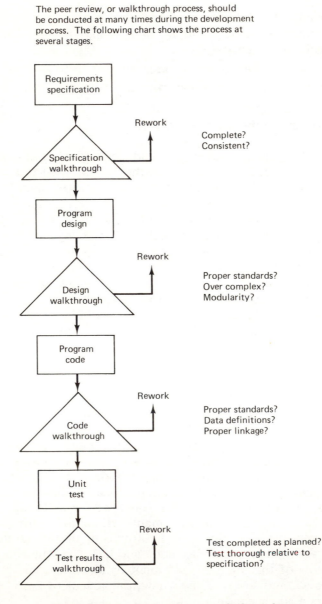

Figure 5-47.   Peer review — walkthroughs.

is eliminated as fresh minds wrestle with the problem presented. New approaches and warnings of possible pitfalls are brought out.

Pride of workmanship enters, as now the instructions themselves will be viewed, not just the results of the running program. Many programmers report that where they had tended to be cavalier and sloppy in their writing (no one ever saw it), they now take pains to make it look good. More care in the process results in a better quality program.

The peers get educated by the presenter and by the other peers in programming technique, language facilities, the application intricacies, and so on. Islands get joined. Code inspections should be a regularly scheduled part of any sizeable development. This review process is not only for the written instructions; it would be performed regularly on all parts of the development process. (See Fig. 5-47.)

On a large scale software effort, there are so many modules being developed that there should be several walkthroughs being conducted simultaneously.

Walkthroughs should catch the kind of error we hit on the space effort.

An Example of an Error

When Gemini V splashed down in 1965, the World held its breath because it was *100 miles* from the predicted splash-down point. The TV commentators led the world to believe the capsule could sink. The carriers sped toward the capsule; the helicopters got to it in one hour.

What had happened to produce such an error? The radars, telemetry, and the computers all did their tasks precisely. The program did its job correctly and precisely. But, in the calculation to predict the splash-down location, there was a constant needed. Since Earth not only spins around an axis, but progresses around the Sun, the length of time to complete the orbit around the Sun was required in one of the equations.

The specification for the calculation was correct, but the programmer took a short cut. The way to calculate was to take days, hours, minutes, and seconds elapsed since launch and calculate Earth reference points based on time on an inertial reference structure, using the Sun as a fixed reference point. This works beautifully. But the programmer thought he had a shorter approach and just deleted the number of days from the calculation (he divided total hours by 24) with the logic that a location on the Earth would be back in the same place relative to the Sun every 24 hours. This is not correct. It would be correct if the Earth only spun on its own axis, but it also orbits the Sun. The orbital movement causes a slight difference in the period of when a location on the Earth is in the same relationship to the Sun. It is not exactly 24 hours. This "misdesign" by the programmer caused the 100 mile miss of the impact point.

Whose error was it? Clearly, the programmer's; he did not follow the design. The short cut had a mine in it. But the error was not in the code; it was in the formulation of the solution. A walkthrough may have caught, probably would have caught, the mistake. It would at least have identified that the implementation was not following the design.

Testing and Quality

All new developments get tested. Detroit has test tracks to run their new cars or to find hidden flaws in construction or design. Testing can pinpoint errors, but it cannot instill *quality* into the system being tested. The process and management must put the quality there.

"Quality" means different things to different people. I mean that the software is built so that the use-phase and continued-development-phase attributes are contained in the product. Recall the attributes of a program:

Causes the computer to do something	Function
Takes memory to reside in	Size
Needs the CPU to run	Efficiency
Ease of use	Useability
Ease of recovery	Recoverability/ Robustness
Contains errors	Correctness
Is modifiable	Architecture
Exists in at least one form and should be two	Documentation

Testing can find errors but it cannot prevent them. Only a good development process with many verification activities and a good design can prevent the errors from getting in there in the first place. A system that is patched-up to fix errors is usually not as clean as a system that did not have that error in the first place.

When the software is large, we begin to hit the problem of testing very rich functionality. In other words, the product has a great number of functions it can do, in a great many sequences, and we must attempt to test the ones we'll see most often.

Extensive testing is essential, because with large complex programs there are always hidden problems and quirks. The abstractness of the product makes it exceedingly difficult to see these problems until you run the programs.

Testing a large type V is very expensive. To test the En-Route Air Traffic Control Systems, there were at the test site in Atlantic City, N.J.:

1. Over 90 air traffic controllers to work the system.
2. Over 50 part-time "pilots" — local people — "flying" simulators (hardware devices) that fed inputs to the radar simulators.
3. Over 50 observers and monitors.
4. Over 50 people in the computer room making sure the programs were ready, etc.

The monitors and controllers had scripts, large telephone directory sized books that gave for each console (display), keyboard, printer and communications device a second by second list of what was to be done and what was to show on the screen, etc.

The test ran for several weeks, tying up about 250 people per day. But — and it is a critical but — but the test is still not over. There is no way that a simulated test can ever stress the system the way the actual real-world use can.

The number of possible paths through these large programs, and the number of possible combinations of states of inputs, data, calculations, and interactions is so large that even in 100 years of use, we will only be beginning to execute the first few percent of the possible paths. Even after years of real use, there will still be bugs in the program. There were over 100 *known* errors in the software in Houston that controlled the Lunar landing expedition — none of them critical.

A high ranking officer recently demanded that disciplinary action be taken against some system developers because they stated they could never get all the bugs out of a large software system. Of course they couldn't. Anyone who insists on error-free large software systems does not understand software.

After each Air Traffic Control test, the discrepancies which had been noted in the scripts — "tag for AA 222 did not flash when squawk ID at 8:14:03 July 9, 1972" — were checked, studied, examined, and teams were sent off to discover why. Was it the program? Was it hardware? Procedures? Human error — did the No. 48 controller really enter the right ID number? Was it the interface between the computer and the display system?

The series of tests for the FAA system went on at Atlantic City for several months. When the system passed all those tests, *then* the software was moved to a field site, one of the 20 En-Route Centers around the country, and run on the midnight to 8 A.M. shift for 7 or 8 more months.

Only then, after many fixes and constant testing, only then was it brought up during heavy traffic hours in one center.

This slow, exhaustive process is necessary. As we saw earlier, the 600,000 lines of code are extremely logically intense, and the consequences of failure are very high indeed.

Reliable Software — A Misnomer

Software cannot break! It may not be correct in the first place and somehow get past the tests, but it cannot break or wear out the way physical things do. Only the world it serves can change and demand something new or different (a new tax is imposed) but software cannot break!

Yet people talk about "reliable software." The term is mischievous as it perpetuates misunderstanding about the nature of software. We should call it "correct software" or "quality software." This is software that is well designed and well-built, and well tested.

Robust software is software designed to continue to work even though other parts of the system exceed their specifications. When the letter L is typed rather than the number one, the software doesn't just stop, it displays "You entered the letter L; did you mean one? This procedure does not accept letters." Error-free software is a correct term, but it is only found in small efforts.

Regression Testing

Like everything else in computers, the testing function depends entirely on the job the computer is to do as to whether it is trivial or crucial.

To test my 100 line-of-code program to calculate annual interest, I need only enter a few — maybe a half-dozen cases — to test the program.

To test the 1,000,000 line-of-code program that is to guide a rocket, I need a hundred or so people, a year or so, a missile range, and a vast amount of machinery to test with.

Let's look at a relatively simple example, a payroll system, and examine the idea of *regression testing*. If I break the payroll system down, I get something like Fig. 5-48.

All these programs are somewhat independent, but they all feed each other. A change in the pay calculation program, due to a new union contract, for example, must be checked out not just with the check writing program, but also with the year-to-date record program, the deduction program, and so on. (See Fig. 5-49.) The fact that it works with the check writing program correctly *does not* mean it will work with the others. So several tests must be made.

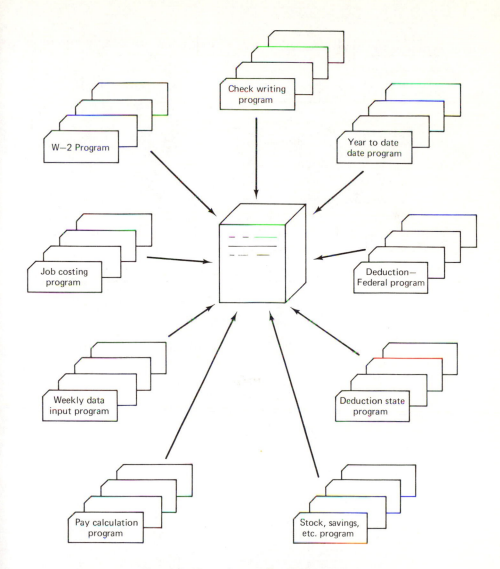

Figure 5-48. A payroll software system.

Finally, a systems test (Fig. 5-50) with *all* the subprograms is run.

Even though there is a change in only one subprogram, we must retest the entire system. This is called *regression testing*. It is not enough to simply test the changed subprogram. Lack of thorough testing of this degree is risking disaster.

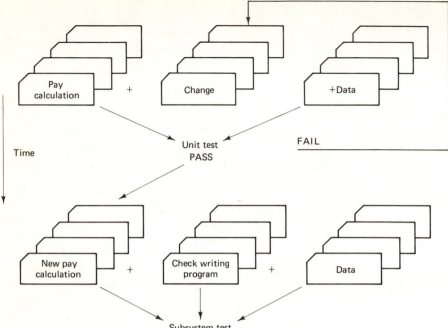

Figure 5-49.   Regression testing.

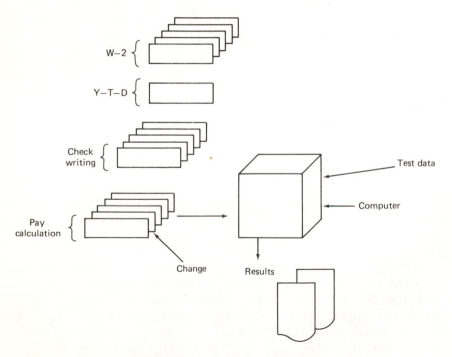

Figure 5-50.   Software system test.

Physical Security

Many times after testing thoroughly, — and passing all tests, the software system will not run next morning, because the project manager did not protect it. In a major project in Australia — and in IBM Poughkeepsie — the program managers learned they had to *guard* those working lines of code. Both in large military projects and internal IBM Operating System development, the code had to be guarded. From what? Robbers? No. From zealous programmers!

Even when you have the expensive tests, zealous programmers who are determined to put in that *last* function — or fix that little bug in their subprograms — will, at 3:00 AM in the morning, unauthorized, steal in and take the tested master disk and add their change. And run a quick test to see that their change works. And it does — for their subprogram.

At 9:00 AM the "tested" tape or disk is taken out to be used or demonstrated — and lo — there are dozens of hang-ups in other parts of the software. It doesn't run! But it ran last night! It didn't take long for management to realize that their very expensive process was being subverted — with good intentions, but disastrous results. Master files must be kept locked up and under tight security.

A sizeable expense is obviously required to perform these tests. Sizeable and expensive computers *and* programs are needed to perform these tests correctly. These computers *may* be the same as the development computer, or they may be separate computers. It depends on how big the system is, and whether or not it is a hardware-intensive system development or a software-intensive system effort. Assuming a sizeable system then we need separate computers for the development facility and for the test facility. (See Fig. 5-51.)

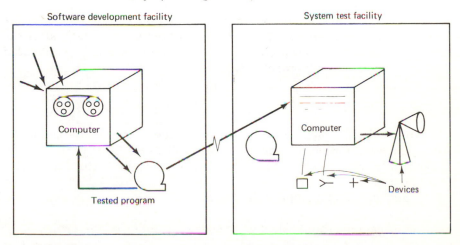

Figure 5-51.   Two computer sites: one for development, one for test.

Not only does the test facility test new or changed program modules, but it also tests hardware changes in radars, sensors, communications, displays, etc. with existing tested software.

Test — A Training Ground

Test Departments produce good, all around people. The test people must see the whole system, purpose, and structure, in order to test it. Few others on a large project get such an overview. They (the others) are building pieces, and only a few designers and managers and test people see the whole thing.

The test people purposely try to find weak spots and to do this, they must poke around the entire system. It is great training. Over the years we found that the people coming out of test often became the designers and managers of future systems. We always deliberately put the young stars into test because we knew that to shirk test meant a crash in the real use of the system. It is better to crash before you get to the real use!

Independence of Test Groups

The test organization should be as independent as possible, reporting as high up the command chain as possible. To have the test manager work for the development manager tempts human weaknesses — the test manager may feel nervous about being critical if the person being criticized is his or her boss.

Duration of Evolution

Some large development efforts have *discarded* the test data, the test tapes, the test results, the very test routines themselves — after the first release has been accepted. The whole test effort must be *recreated* by the continued development team.

Summary

In the development of large software, the testing phase is crucial. Although we know in advance that we will never be able to test the system fully, we also know that the more we test, the better the system will operate.

There are certain guideposts we can look to.

Test planning should start at the very beginning of the project.

Testing should never be shut down — the test cases and test

machines and test team should be continued into the continued-development phase.

Change in a module requires testing the new module *and* all the rest of the modules. This is called regression testing.

The latest working, tested software system should be kept under physical lock and key.

Testing requires the best of the development team people (and is the best training ground).

Testing large type V systems is enormously expensive, if it is any good.

Testing cannot make a bad program good; it can make it better.

Testing should probe at the breaking points to assure that the system will handle the full range it was designed for.

Illegal data should be fed to the system to determine results.

Long (24-hour) runs should be conducted to test for slowly developing problems.

DOCUMENTATION

People hate to document what they have created. Yet it is one of the most essential things they must do! An excellent programmer designed and wrote a program to determine orbital characteristics of a satellite. He had his program finished first; it ran correctly; and it conserved memory. It was in FORTRAN, and it was about four pages (of dense FORTRAN statements) in length. He *knew* that program inside and out. About 3 months later, he was asked to add some features to the program. He got out the documentation and poured over it. It took him 3 to 4 days to understand what was going on in that program! And it was his! Imagine how much more difficult it would have been had it not been his program! And then imagine it had not been documented.

This is the problem faced by people who do continued development. Instead of starting with requirements and design, they far too often start with an investigation of a mystery, an archeological dig. "What was the form — the structure — the plan — the path taken? Why did 'they' do this?" Then they go in and modify, delete, and add. Obviously, the clearer the trail, the easier the task, the better the results.

Surely the most repeated story in the world about programming is the one where the program is running but no one has any idea of what is in the program because the programmer is long since gone and there is no documentation. It is one of the most repeated because it is so common.

We need documentation:

1. To remind us who built it of what is in there.
2. To show others who come after us what is in there and its overall flow.

Self Documenting

Many of the new programming techniques are yielding self-documenting software, lifting much of the burden of documenting.

Documentation does not mean a machine listing of the object (machine language) program. The source listing is not enough either. Documentation for continued development purposes should be

1. Well-commented code.
2. Design diagrams and narratives.
3. Structured narratives or process diagrams, perferably the former.
4. Data descriptions.

Without these items, the programmer who must modify the existing program has a massive task on his or her hands to discover what has been done.

Structured Narrative

This is easier to read and understand than flow charts. A well commented, indented, and modularized narrative is easily grasped, once the reading structure and vocabulary are mastered. The structured narrative is not yet in code, but it is getting close. The narrative in Fig. 5-52 is a structured narrative in a program design language PDL. It is equivalent to the several flow charts that follow it (Fig. 5-53). It is better than flow charts as:

1. It fits on one page and its entire structure is visible to the eye.
2. It contains more information than the flow charts.

A different narrative with many more comments is shown in Fig. 5-54. CORP, OD, FI, and ATAD are the "close-outs" for PROC, DO, IF, and Data. Once the rules are clear, this type of document is very easy to read.

Lines like "IF * DETERMINE TYPE COMMAND*" must be expanded to go to the translatable code level, but at this level what is

```
PROCEDURE: PWARN $ display warning message
   INPUTS:
            LOTMP —time to retry after overtemp condition
            LEMI    —time to retry after EMI condition
            LACT   —printer queue overflow flag
   OUTPUTS:
            none
IF  LACT set THEN
    IF NOR less than TQR (space unavailable) THEN
       clear LACT
       set LCODE to 134
       call procedure POPMG to display operator message
    ENDIF
ENDIF
DO-WHILE LACTX is 0 thru 1
    IF  EMI is set and CSRTC is greater than or equal to LEMI(LACTX) THEN
       set LCODE to 321
       call procedure POPMG to display warning message
       store the new retry time in LEMI
       increment retry counter LRCTR
       IF  LRCTR greater than or equal 3 THEN
          clear the EMI flag
       ENDIF
    ENDIF
    IF  OVRTMP is set and CSRTC greater than or equal LOTMP(LACTX) THEN
       set LCODE to 320
       call procedure POPMG to display warning message
       store new retry time in LOTMP
       increment retry counter LRCTR
       IF  LRCTR greater than or equal to 3 THEN
          clear OVRTMP flag
       ENDIF
    ENDIF
END-WHILE
END PROCEDURE-OUTPUT INTERRUPT
```

Figure 5-52.   A structured narrative in a program design language.

happening is quite clear. With a good overall design description, this
level of documentation should suffice for continued development. This
level of design documentation is machine processable but it is not yet
at a level that is translatable to machine code.

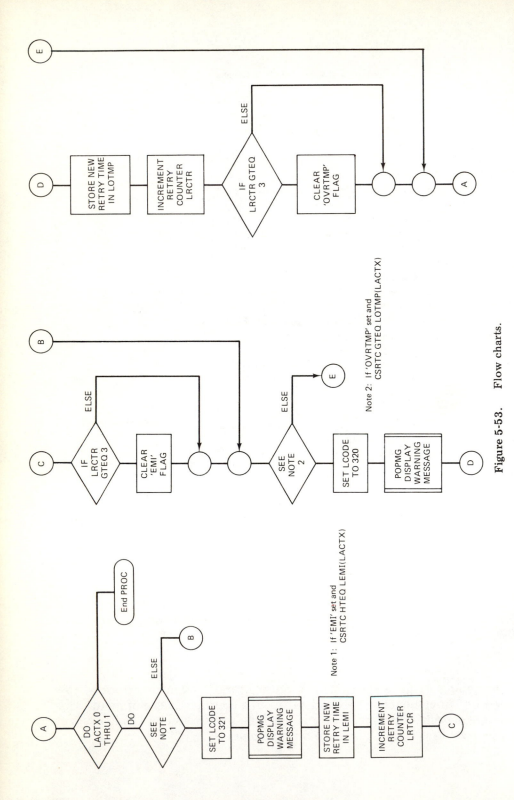

Figure 5-53. Flow charts.

```
PROC  SESSION MANAGEMENT * THIS PROCEDURE MANAGES THE
      TERMINAL INTERACTION WITH THE USER. LEGAL USER
      COMMANDS ARE MOVE AND DELETE. *

      USE     SESSION DATA

      DO      * PROCESS USER COMMANDS *

              GET    INPUT (COMMAND) * NEXT USER INPUT *

              RUN    INPUTCHECK (COMMAND, ERROR)

              IF
                     ERROR = TRUE
              THEN
                     PUT  OUTPUT (ERROR)

              ELSE   * NO ERROR — PROCEED WITH PROCESSING *

                     IF     * DETERMINE TYPE COMMAND *

                         COMMAND = MOVE

                     THEN * PROCESS MOVE COMMAND *

                         INCLUDE MOVE PROCESSING

                     ELSE * PROCESS DELETE COMMAND *

                         INCLUDE DELETE PROCESSING

                     FI

              FI

              GET    INPUT (SESSION — ON)

      WHILE   * KEEP PROCESSING INPUT COMMANDS AS LONG
              AS SESSION-ON INDICATOR IS ON (TRUE) *
              SESSION-ON: = TRUE

      OD

CORP

DATA  SESSION DATA
      *ABSTRACT DATA TYPES & COMMENTS *
ATAD
```

Figure 5-54. A structured narrative.

There are more people than just the person charged with continued development who need to know what is in the program.

- The operator, the person pushing the computer buttons in the machine room, needs to be told what to do, when, in all circumstances.
- The user, sitting at a terminal, is the one for whom the system is his or her tool. The user must be told what, how, why, when, and in enough detail and with enough clarity that the system will be used.
- User management needs a different level of documentation. What does the system do? Not do? What is possible? Easy? Difficult?
- Development management should see development status reports and test results, so as to manage the development. Much of this documentation will be discarded as it is overtaken by events — OBE.
- User management should review and study an implementation or phase-in plan.
- User management should review a data requirements plan. What must the *user* do to ensure that the data is up to date and correct?
- Continued development management needs as much and more documentation than the original developers in order to modify and correct the system.

TRACEABILITY

If we were to see the back panel of a very large computer, it would be obvious we need some diagram or listing to keep track of every wire from point XYZ to point QLR. The same is true for software. Consider every module as a circuit, and you realize one must keep track of who is doing what to whom. But it is harder to visualize software. What is a module? Hopefully it is the smallest compileable group of code, *but* it is variable and to a major extent up to the writer. And several functions can be in one module. What we need to have control of our large software is a table to trace function to module and vice versa. A chart like Table 5-5 is often helpful. (See also Fig. 5-55.)

Let's look at each column in Table 5-5 and see what it tells us.

Column 1 *The name of the function.* This should be as self-explanatory as possible.

Column 2 *Module number.* It should also be possible to call up, using

Figure 5-55.   A computer back panel. (Courtesy of Control Data Corporation)

TABLE 5-5.

Function Description	Module No.	By	Feed from	Feed to	Calls	Called By
W-2 routine	848A	Daniels	Q74	437	849	
				849	O/S	4ZM
				Printer Scheduler		
Check print routine	852	Schwartz	848A	None	Return	851
			849			
Union dues report	857	Travers	839	858	858	852
.	.	.	.	.	.	.
.	.	.	.	.	.	.
.	.	.	.	.	.	.
Cost accounting	1612	Ward	442	894	1614	1610
			857	1631		
Cost accounting print	1614	Ward	1612	None	Return	1612

this name, a textual description of the module, the source code, and even the object code for the module.

Column 3 The *source* of the program.

Column 4 What modules or devices generate the data to be used by this module; the immediate *feeder*, not its genealogy.

Column 5 What modules or devices *receive* data from this module.
Column 6 What module does this one *transfer control to*.
Column 7 What module *calls this one*.

With an automated system like this, errors can be tracked and traced in an orderly and controlled fashion. With systems that go up to several hundred thousand lines of code and beyond, the number of modules and functions can get into the thousands. An automated system is a must.

Happily there are many support programs today that will keep track of all this for us, and give us easy access to and update capability for the information. Again, the computer helps us develop.

TOO MUCH DOCUMENTATION

The documentation should fit the use to which the software is to be put. If we are going to run it on 500 machines, aboard every ship in the U.S. Navy, then that program should be more thoroughly documented than a program that is going to be used once and then thrown away. This later program may be documented on the back of an envelope.

If there are no users, do not produce user documentation. This sounds so stupid, yet it happens often. The "Standards" call for user documentation, a document that says such and such, and the program manager says produce it. So 6 feet of documentation is produced that will *never* be used.

FLOW CHARTS DISAPPEARING

Flow charts are no longer desirable for documentation, except at very high levels. They are difficult to prepare; there is a limit the amount of information one can put in a box; they spread over several pages; and are rarely kept up to date. They are useful aids in the design process, but not in documentation.

PROJECT HISTORY

Documentation of the rationale for the design decisions is extremely helpful when the time comes to change the programs. Why did they build it that way in the first place? Did they do certain things certain ways deliberately? Why? These decisions, if well documented, will help the people making changes avoid costly mistakes. A project history and notes on design decisions can be very helpful at this stage.

All in all, a large type V software system requires reams of documentation, and just as an infrastructure is absolutely required to develop the software efficiently, excellent documentation is required to keep it tuned and evolving.

"HOW" IS "WHAT"; A REQUIREMENT IS A DESIGN — LEVELS OF DETAIL

People constantly try to draw a dividing line between *how* and *what*. And they never can, because the how and the what are one and the same. It depends on where you stand in relation to it.

The documents serve two very different roles — first, they are needed to manage the development, and second, they are needed to manage the continued development, replacement, and use. In the first sense they are to some extent forward looking, showing what is to be done. In the second they are to some extent backward looking, recording what has been done. As we create the system, this dual role of the document can become troublesome. Let's see why.

When we finish our development, we will have a hierarchy of documentation, or levels, which describe the system in ever deeper detail as we go from the top-most to the bottom-most.

This hierarchy of documents exists in all technical fields. The Department of Defense has a very formal set of requirements for specifications. Basically it is what is called out in Fig. 5-56.

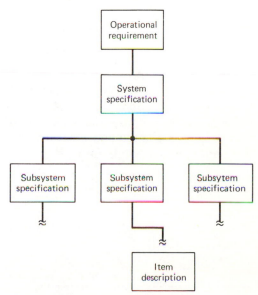

Figure 5-56. DOD documentation levels.

As we progress through the overall design efforts, we get to the point when we *are able* to write a system specification. The level of detail that should be put into this specification becomes a question. How much detail is enough?

In order to design new and difficult systems, we must go deep into detail *on some aspects* of the system, the new aspects, in order to be sure that the system will work. But that deep level of detail does not belong in a system specification. Since we have it, we are tempted to put it in there. But it is too detailed for a high level specification. It is jarring to a reviewer who does not understand nor need such detail.

On another front, what do we need in order to approve a high level specification? We may need a good deal of detail on the item that is *not* in the present document but available within the project. We may need *drafts* of future documents, or detailed drawings and descriptions contained in working documents that will eventually find their way into lower level documents.

To repeat, since *some* of the detail is available, it is tempting to insist it go into the high level document. This would be an error. The high level documents should be free of this detail. Internal work documents to support the high level specification may be called for, but the documents should be kept separate.

The requirements should be *what* is needed, and the design specification should be *how*. We must remember though that every specification is at one time both a how and a what. . . it depends on which side of them you are.

WHAT'S HAPPENING OUT THERE

The need for documentation is clear. Just as obvious is how often there is no documentation — none. Poor documentation is one thing; no documentation is another. So many programs exist with no documentation that the problem often seems to be universal. Documentation for software is more essential than documentation for hardware, as the software is intangible and abstract. A program with no documentation is an unexploded bomb. Some day it's going to blow up.

6

MANAGING SOFTWARE
DEVELOPMENT

The observations of this chapter are loosely connected, roughly according to the phases of a development effort. They are presented by time
of occurrence, when we would be likely to encounter the problem if
we were not alert. Some are early development project problems; some
are late. They are some of the lessons I learned, usually the hard way,
over the years. Some seem very simple when described, yet they are
often overlooked.

Let us step up a few levels of management and assume that we are
in charge of a very large project development. We will make our subsystem delineations and assign competent managers to each. We will
wish to review our software development effort. We are too swamped
with other subsystem activity to manage the software development in
detail; that is the responsibility of the person we carefully selected to
be the manager of software development. In this chapter and the next
we will focus on those items that are the indicators to higher management of the health of the effort. We'll look at how a software development team should be organized; how to select a manager of software
development; how to decide to develop the software in house or
contract for its development; and how to pick a contractor. We'll focus
on some areas where projects have failed in the past and where the
going is very dicey.

What is important? What do we look for? What do we discuss?
What are the indicators?

SYSTEMS, SUBSYSTEMS, AND SOFTWARE

"Muir's Law: Whenever we try to separate something, we find that it is attached to everything else in the universe."*

All Systems Leak

There is only one system, the universe. All other systems are false systems; they leak.

When we speak of the medical system of the United States, are we talking about the system encircled by the solid line in Fig. 6-1? Or the one shown by the dashed line? Or the one shown by the dotted line? Do we ever think about the fact that we are talking to someone who may be thinking of a completely different system than we are?

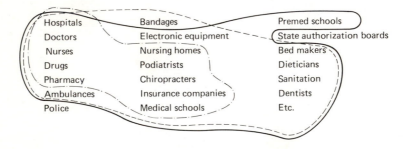

Figure 6-1. Defining a system.

Top Down Look

If I am the chairman of a sizeable company, I want the payroll done on time, or the seats on the airplane reserved correctly. I want these things done efficiently. Suppose the payroll is not getting done efficiently, or is not getting done on time. I go and check into the problem. I will go through it level by level. I will start with the person in charge of payroll and ask him or her to describe the system from the top down. He or she could break the system into five components: (1) procedures; (2) people; (3) computers/systems; (4) incoming data; and (5) distribution. At this point, I can choose to go deeper into any one of the five areas. Since we are interested in the computer area, I'll ask for the next level of break out in that area. This is shown in Fig. 6-2.

*Arthur Block, *Murphy's Law Book Two* (Los Angeles, Calif.: Price/Stern/Sloan, Publishers, Inc., 1980).

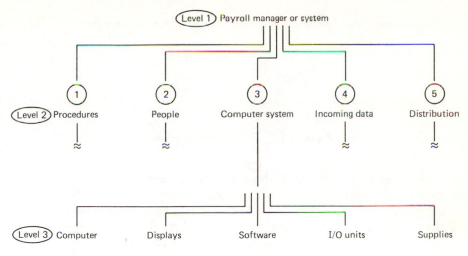

Figure 6-2. A system into subsystems.

Now, several of the items at level 2 are by necessity intertwined, inextricably, with the other four areas. What displays we buy (hardware) and what we display has a great affect on (1) procedures and (2) people and possibly on (4) incoming data and (5) distribution. Remember, there is only one system — the universe — all other systems leak! But let us continue to level 3 (Fig. 6-3). We'll drop subsystems 1,2,4, and 5 at this point but they are there in the real world (space here prohibits depicting them). The same is true as we go on down to level 4 (also Fig. 6-3).

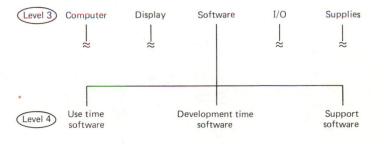

Figure 6-3. More levels of subsystems.

At level 4, as at all levels, the choice of how to break the system up is arbitrary. We could have some other classification scheme at level 4; e.g., the one we are about to use at level 5 (Fig. 6-4).

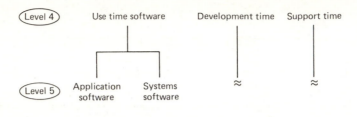

Figure 6-4. Software subsystem.

We want to look at why the paychecks are incorrect, so we want to look at run-time software, and we'll delve into the other two bodies of software only if the problems found at run time lead us back to one of the other two or both. On to level 6 (Fig. 6-5). We'll show both trails here, and in parentheses the source of the programs.

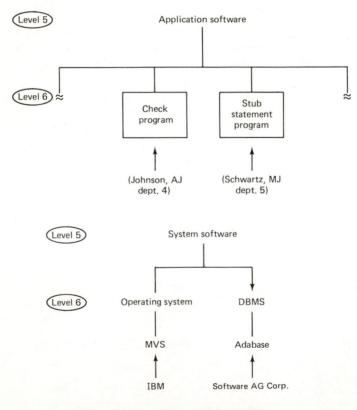

Figure 6-5. Source of the programs.

Again space prohibits listing all of the individual programs running. We could and should go on and diagram level 7 and show the modules for each program, but space again is a problem. The matrix diagram Table 6-1 shows the type of detail we want to get into. Now, if our problem is in the "net pay" area, we start examining and testing those modules affecting net pay.

Now we are at a very granular view of the world. Let's stay at level 6, only because it is easier to read and write but in practice we'd be better off starting at the more detailed level 7. We wish to depict what is running out there at run time. Let us list the programs, their source and their size. The result is Table 6-1.

TABLE 6-1.   Run Time Payroll Programs

Program	Size		Source	
Check program	8402	LOC-S*	Johnson, A.J.	Dept. 4
Stub print	462	LOC-S	Schwartz, M.J.	Dept. 5
W-2 program	892	LOC-S	Daniels, R.M.	Dept. 11
Withholding	440	LOC-S	Abadan, J.R.	Dept. 442
Year-to-date record	414	LOC-S	Withers, M.R.	No Longer Employed
State tax report	317	LOC-S	Johnson, A.J.	Dept. 4
Union dues calc	219	LOC-S	Travers, J.	Dept. 41
Union dues print	44	LOC-S	Travers, J.	Dept. 41
.	.	.		
.	.	.		
.	.	.		

*LOC-S means lines of code in a source language.

Now to troubleshoot such a system, to get it to run at all, we need people (software analysts and programmers) who understand what each program is supposed to do, and how it is to interact with the others, and how all the programs running in the machine are supposed to work as a system.

We do not expect A.J. Johnson, the author of the check writing program, to understand how the DBMS does its job. We expected Johnson only to understand what the DBMS can do, how to ask it to do its job, and how to check that it did its job.

The same is true for all other programs. Our small number of senior analysts should be able to plow through all the data, with the help of the authors and vendors, and find the error, or errors. The error could be here in this subsystem at level 6, or in any of the other subsystems procedures, people, etc. Of course, it may be in the interaction of this subsystem with one or more of the others.

Complex, very complex, But necessary. We can "do" a payroll in hours that would be impossible to do normally in a week with a hundredfold increase in people. We can control air traffic, etc.

Why do we have the vendors system software mixed in there with ours? Because it is much more efficient, much more economical to do it that way, and it runs at use time.

Many DP Subsystems Within a System

A system is made up of several subsystems — one of which is usually *the* computer subsystem, the ground control system. But all the other subsystems may have computers *and* software in them too! (See Fig. 6-6.) Each subsystem may have computers and software as a part of it. The satellite subsystem may have *several* computers and software within it. (See Fig. 6-7.)

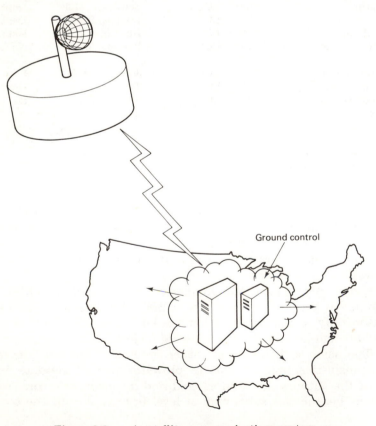

Figure 6-6.   A satellite communications system.

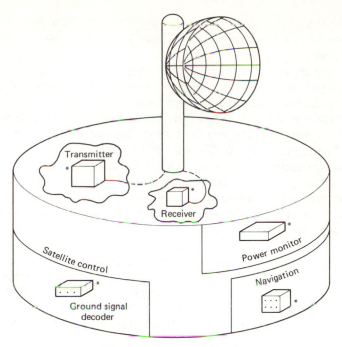

*Means a computer and software

Figure 6-7.   Satellite subsystem.

A simple question that can bedevil an organization is "Who is in charge of the software?" Well, for the software for the ground control we'll have a high level, very experienced, *project* software development manager. Should he or she be in charge of the software that goes in the satellite? Maybe. Maybe not. Should the individual manager for each of the on-board satellite subsystems manage his or her own software development? Probably not. There are no simple answers to these very important questions.

Isolating the Software

For the moment we will ignore hardware and look at only software. But can we separate software from the hardware? Yes, it is awkward at times, but we can separate the two. The separation can be very important in establishing work boundaries for organizations or audit teams.

Let's look at a banking system with on-line cash dispensing terminals. We can begin to look at the subsystems. For the sake of conceptualization we will deal only with three subsystems: the communications subsystem, the data processing hardware subsystem, and the software subsystem, which is a subsystem of the data processing sub-system. We wish to determine why there is a limitation on the overall system of, say, only 12 terminals.

Looking at the communication subsystem we may find that the lines employed to bring data to and from the data processor may be the limiting factor, in that they have the capacity (bandwidth) to carry only 12 data messages at a time. In this case we have found the bottle-neck. But assume for the moment that the communications lines are capable of carrying all the traffic we can imagine.

Then we look at the computer. It may be that the processing capacity of the computer is not capable of handling the load of the thirteenth cash terminal and still guarantee service to the network with-out losing data at peak periods. Since we are dealing with money, this is a very key fact. If this is the case, the bottleneck is the capacity of the processor.

Assume for the moment that the communications and the pro-cessor are both able to handle more than 12 terminals. It is possible the programmers wrote the programs in such a way that 12 and only 12 terminals could be handled and therefore there is no program to accept a thirteenth terminal — even though all the hardware is fully capable of doing so. If this is the bottleneck, the programmers can be asked to go in and modify the program so that it will handle extra terminals. This is fairly simple and should not take much time — if the programmer who did the job in the first place documented the program, and is still with the bank, and is not busy on some other crisis.

Some systems have bottlenecks in many areas, in many sub-systems. The point is that the bottleneck may be a hardware limit or it may be a pure software limitation. "Balancing the system" means to not have any subsystem much weaker than the rest. As we mentioned earlier, good software can make poor hardware perform well, and vice versa. The example on page 131 of the query handler is another ex-ample of where the hardware is perfectly capable of doing the job in several ways. The software determines the system use characteristics.

A Hardware Subsystem Overload that Looked Like a Software Problem

When the Navy added the Link 11 communication software to the Navy Tactical Data System (NTDS) the system kept stopping, or giving garbage for results. There was something wrong with the new program!

No, there wasn't. It was just that the addition of the new function overloaded the machine. It had too much to do, it began to fall behind, the inputs "overran" the ability of the machine to process them, because they had finally added too much to the computer for it to do in the time available.

They searched for a long time, scrutinizing the new program, before they found that the machine was simply overloaded.

INABILITY TO FORECAST DEVELOPMENT COST OR SCHEDULE

Development is such a common word and we do so much of it that we are sometimes misled into thinking that we have our arms around the process. Everyone quickly agrees that we cannot predict research costs and results. And everyone quickly agrees that production of even a complex product can be controlled and forecast. But what about the D in R & D? The dictionary says that development is (1) "a gradual unfolding," or (2) "to bring into being." Development is *not* a known, estimatable activity — either in software or other fields. No field of technology can forecast the time and cost required to develop new things. We can forecast *production*, but production is repetitive by definition, and there is a learning curve that we know will be followed, making the last unit less expensive to produce than the first. Writing in a massive work that studies living organizations and organisms, James Grier Miller in *Living Systems** cites a study by Joan Woodward performed in England and comments on it.

> Another investigator who recognizes the importance of producer processes is Woodward. In one of a relatively few researches which have collected data on a large population of organizations, she analyzed 100 industrial organizations in South Essex, England. ... Within the commonly used categories of "jobbing," "batch," and "mass" production, Woodward made further divisions to yield 11 types of producer subsystems. "Integral products" refers to products that are manufactured in units — singly, in batches, or by mass production, "Dimensional products" are measured by weight or volume, as chemicals, liquids, and gases are.

Woodward in her book comments on the various types of process in the table shown in Fig. 6-8.

> Moving along the scale from Systems I to IX, it becomes increasingly possible to exercise control over manufacturing operations, the physical limitations of production becoming better known and understood. ... However well-developed production control procedures may be in batch production firms, there will be a degree of uncertainty in the prediction of results. Production

*James Grier Miller, *Living Systems* (New York: McGraw-Hill Book Co., 1978).

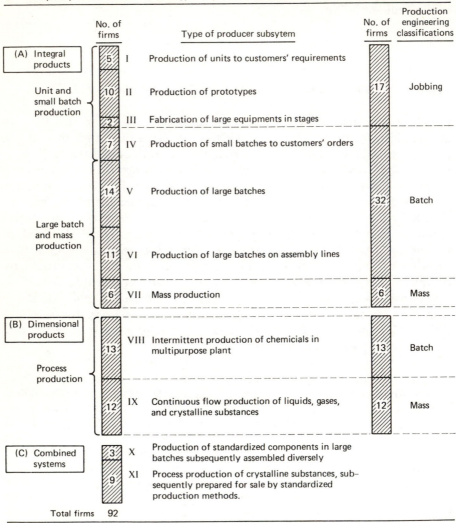

Figure 6-8. Production systems. (Joan Woodward, *Industrial Organization Theory and Practice* (London: Oxford University Press, 1965). Reprinted with permission.)

proceeds by drives and a continuous attempt is made to push back physical limitations by setting ever higher targets. The difficulties of exercising effective control, particularly of prototype manufacture, are greatest in unit production. It is almost impossible to predict the results of development work in terms of time or money.*

*Joan Woodward, *Industrial Organization Theory and Practice* (London: Oxford University Press, 1965).

Let me comment on what all this means to me. Woodward is saying that the hardest of all the manufacturing processes to control is the one that produces things in units. A program is a unit. She describes the "production" process as hard to control and then comments that "It is almost impossible to predict the results of development work in terms of time and money." How much truer these statements are for the development of programs, which are units, *and* which indeed are *intangible* units. Development by definition can not be pinned down in terms of costs and schedule and results. If it can be, it is not development; it is some other process to which we will have to give a name depending on what is being done.

THE "ABANDON FUNCTION PHENOMENON" OF LARGE SOFTWARE DEVELOPMENT

Ignoring our lack of knowledge of requirements for the moment, there is another overriding reason to adopt the evolutionary approach to software (and, therefore, system) development. There are few if any techniques or teams in the world that are capable of creating in one pass the complex systems that we are putting into service today. The systems are too big and too complex to permit one pass development.

We encounter the "abandon function" phenomenon here. Some roughly defined set of functions is to be delivered. As the delivery date approaches, the development managers see that there is no way to deliver *all* the promised functions on time. Like a balloon losing altitude, the development team jettisons all "unnecessary" functions. The schedule is "made;" the effort a "success," even though a number of bright people are hurriedly put to work in the back room doing some functions that were to have been done by the computer. It now is a job for the continued development team to add into the system these abandoned functions. Since the development phase of the Big Bang approach is over, this effort gets lumped into "maintenance." The number of people on that job is usually a lot less; the "maintenance" team is in reality a development team. (See Fig. 6-9.)

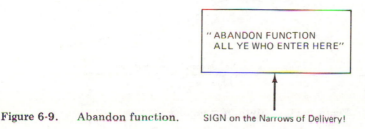

Figure 6-9.   Abandon function.   SIGN on the Narrows of Delivery!

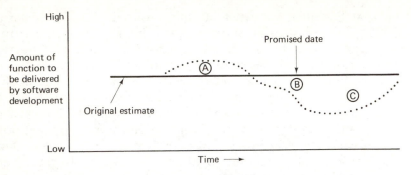

Figure 6-10.   Function versus delivery.

As a software development effort moves forward, the amount of function that is supposed to be delivered varies. At first, a sense of euphoria causes even more functions to be promised by the software developers. (See Fig. 6-10.) Reality sets in only as the promised delivery date nears. Schedule rules, and functions are thrown overboard.

The project is declared a success, even though much of the function that was to have been done by the computer is being done by very capable people with sharp pencils in the back room.

The function that got "dropped" to make the date is still to be done (Fig. 6-10, Ⓒ). It is done by the Operations and Maintenance (O & M) people and money since no one is anxious to admit what really happened. This is not desirable; it is what happens. "Custom" said Mark Twain, "is to have a place for everything and then keep it somewhere else."

"We mount to heaven on the ruins of our cherished dreams, finding in the end, our failures were successes." Amos Alcott.

Figure 6-11 showing staffing is a myth for large complex software. This diagram is true only for small, simple programs. Yet we still see this depiction of the software development effort!

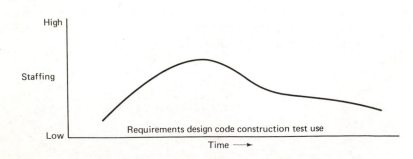

Figure 6-11.   Myth of manpower decrease.

PLAN TO EVOLVE

If we know that the requirements will change, then how do we design to evolve? There are at least nine guidelines to be followed here:

1. We must design our software to be *as modular as* we can make it. Even though this will cost us more lines of code at use time, and more time in development.

2. We must group the modules so that the interactions are as few as possible.

3. We must practice information hiding, even if it raises the number of lines of code. Thus, when we must change, we will have to change fewer modules. Information hiding is the result of high cohesiveness.

4. We should use table-driven techniques of logic. Change an entry in the table, you've changed the logic. We used this technique in the FAA En-Route Air Traffic Control System. Rather than change logic from one center to the next (for the 21 centers), the structures of the airways were defined by tables. Thus, we had *one* program and 21 tables for 21 different sites.

5. We must establish and insist on programming standards. This is unpopular, but necessary.

6. We must impose rigid and detailed control. We will cover this in the section on Project Management.

7. We must plan to keep key members of the team for ensuing releases or versions.

8. We must plan to keep the test and development facilities for continued development.

9. We must budget for all of these.

The penalties for not investing in a system that can easily evolve are often not obvious; in many cases they are completely hidden. The frustration they produce is felt, but the cause of the frustration is vague.

For example, a product in the market needs new functions to make it more saleable. All the new functions can be done with software, and should be done with software. The estimate to field the software is a year. "A year!!" is the reaction. "That's crazy." But the year stands.

The reason is that the software that is out there is like a block of concrete! There was no "investment" at the front-end to make the software easy to modify.

Worse, there was no investment at the front-end to make the software "understandable"! That is, only a few, very low-level people understand what the software looks like — and *they* make *key* decisions.

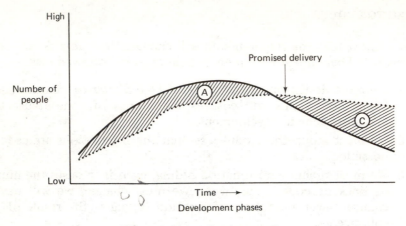

Figure 6-12. Getting people.

Staffing

The availability of programmers is not only low, it is negative — which is to say, if you are not looking, someone is hiring *your* programmers away from you. The shortage of programmers is both severe and grim. The shortage of software developers is grimmer and going to get much worse. The typical project looks like Fig. 6-12. The solid line depicts the number of people planned for the effort. The dotted line is the actual number of people on the project. The shortfall (A) is made up by the extra man years in (C).

The developer *always* forecasts fixing the shortfall in (A) "next month," but that is almost always impossible to do.

As we have seen, the more true model of what is happening on the large efforts looks like Fig. 6-13.

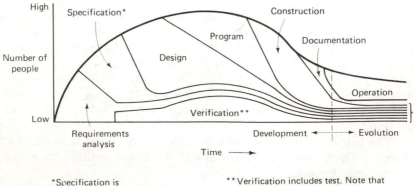

*Specification is
requirements documentation

**Verification includes test. Note that
verification overlaps—is concurrent
with-programming and construction

EVOLUTIONARY DEVELOPMENT OF LARGE SYSTEMS

The one overriding lesson of all the foregoing is that for a large software development effort, we *must* plan an *evolutionary* development, and construct a system that will evolve over time.

If we do not, we will patch and use bailing wire to hold the system together and have a fragile structure — or we will have a system that will be ignored and unused by the user.

The first thing that must be done to develop a system that will evolve is *to budget to keep the development team in place.*

This is perhaps the most striking difference between the NASA Manned Space Effort and the FAA En-Route Air Traffic Control System, on one hand, and many other large systems on the other. Both NASA and the FAA planned and budgeted to have the development team stay in place *for 10 years*! Both realized that they would be evolving the system over that long a period.

The staffing diagram we saw in Fig. 5-6 is wrong for these kinds of systems; the down turn in the number of people after delivery *does not occur* on big systems; those development people should stay in place for the next versions or releases.

This idea that "releases" are necessary was driven home to me in 1970 when a Congressional Committee was about to have a public hearing on the En-Route Air Traffic Control Development effort. One of the Congressional aides reviewed with me that FAA and IBM would be criticized as "the fact that the seventh release of the program has been delivered *proves* that the team did not know what it was doing." I told him I'd reply to the charge in a few days.

As it happened I visited my Houston team a day or so later and was told that they were on "release 14.7" — or a total, if one ignores the decimal notations — of at least fourteen releases — and we had just put the man on the moon!

"Why so many releases?" I asked. Two reasons, I was told. First, the hundreds of operators monitoring consoles and interacting with the computer *could not absorb* changes in operating procedures in big doses — they had to absorb it a piece at a time. *And* they just couldn't predict so far in advance what the users would want or what would be needed in the control system.

I related all this to the Congressional aide. He seemed to accept the logic of it. But either he never got to the Congressman or the Congressman didn't want to hear it, because the public hearing castigated us as the number of releases of the program showed that we did not know what we were doing!

What we have — or should have — from a software point of view, is two very different sets of programs that will run together in the first software release:

1. A set of *systems programs*, that will schedule the machine and the application programs to be run and control the environment.
2. A "starter set" of applications programs so that the user can begin to use the system and (a) derive benefit from it and (b) discover new and better modes of operation that can then be added to the software in the next release or version. This process of adding new function continues over the life of the system.

Why is this approach often rejected? There are at least three things preventing this evolutionary approach from being undertaken.

First, it appears to cost more. To put all that infrastructure into the system programs so that they can easily accept new functions in the applications programs costs money, and the benefits of the infrastructure are not seen *until* the continued development phase of the life cycle, and even then they are seen usually *only* by the insiders. They do not *show* in any sense, and top management can only vaguely appreciate what their technical implementers are telling them. Only secure management will invest wisely here. It does cost more in development to build a flexible system; however, the total life cycle cost is much less.

Second, the infrastructure programs eat up some machine cycles in the use phase; they use memory and computer time. Both of these resources are often scarce.

Third, it is not an easy technical task to design this infrastructure. It takes top talent to design such a flexible structure.

PROJECT MANAGEMENT TASKS

Managing software development is a difficult job. So many small yet crucial tasks must be performed and controlled. The following list is the table of contents from the U.S. Navy's Military Standard 1679 — Weapon System Software Development. We have covered the major items already, and yet the smaller ones can take on big consequences now and then. This list is evidence of the difficulty of the development task.

GENERAL REQUIREMENTS
    Software development management
    Design requirements
    Program generation
    Quality assurance
    Configuration management

Subcontractor control

Deviations and waivers

DETAILED REQUIREMENTS

Program performance requirements

Supporting information for program performance requirements

Computer program performance analysis

Mission areas

Functions

Applicable documentation for program performance requirements

Weapon system description

Functional description

Detailed functional requirement

Adaptive parameters

System resources

Program design requirements

Supporting information for program design requirements

Computer program design analysis

Applicable documentation for program design requirements

Functional allocation

Program functional flow

Resource allocation and reserves

Design constraints

Data base design

Intersystem interface

Programming standards

Control structures

Included/copied segments

Entry-exit structure

Program traceability

Self-modification

Recursive programs

Size

Branching

Relocatability

Indentation

Programming conventions

Symbolic parameterization

Naming

Numerical conventions

Symbolic constants and variables

Mixed mode expression

Grouping

Significant digits
Narrative description
Abstracts
Comment statements
Source record format
Execution efficiency
Source code segment includes/copy
Source statement
Flow charts
Program production
Program production organization
Resource management
Language
Library usage and control
Sequence numbering
Listings
Program listings
Cross-reference listing
Load maps
Program regeneration
Program operation
Program operation analysis
Nonfunctional operation
Functional operation
Program test
Module tests
Subprogram tests
Program performance tests
System(s) integration test
Software trouble reporting
Software trouble report category
Software trouble report priority
Software trouble report disposition
Quality assurance
Quality assurance organization
Reporting level
Participation in audits
Design reviews
Program design
Program coding
Tests
Deliverable items
Reporting
Authority
Program acceptance

Reserve requirements for program acceptance
Software quality test requirements for program acceptance
Test environment
Software to be tested
Software quality test documentation
Software quality test program operation
Software quality test duration
Software quality test input data
Software quality test stress testing
Software quality test reduced capability testing
Software quality test and maintenance support programs
Errors during test
Software quality test limitations
Error limits
Patch limits
Configuration management
Configuration identification
Baselines
Documentation identification
Configuration control
Software changes
Documentation changes
Software configuration control boards (SCCB)
Configuration status accounting
Management control
Management organization
Resource requirements
Status reviews
Status review subjects
Status review subject items
Documentation reviews
Special reviews
Inspections and audits

The list is by no means complete. Any list more than a year old will be out of date. However, it is useful, to show the scope of the effort in a short space, and to check for things overlooked.

OUTPUT OF THE PROCESS

What is the output of the software development process? The main outputs are:

1. The *programs* that will run, certainly; but what else?

2. *User's Guides.* The instructions and descriptions that will make the system usable by and understandable to the user.

3. *Continued development materials.* Materials to use in order to continue development are the same items that we need to develop the software in the first place. Test plans, test results, specifications, and all the things we have been using, and good documentation.

The items shown in Fig. 6-14 are *all* outputs of the software development process. This figure is not in complete detail. For example, as a subset to System Design we could list simulation and modeling programs written to help us arrive at the correct design. These programs, valuable for the continued development team, are also results of the software development effort.

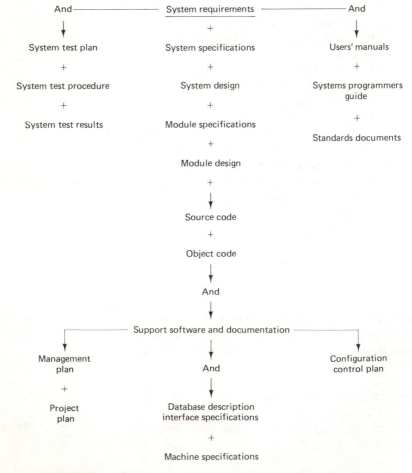

Figure 6-14.   The output of the software development effort.

DEVELOPMENT OR PROJECT PLAN

Every major project should have a development plan. Today these plans should be machine processable and should reside in the support computer.

The development plan contains a great many things, and in great detail. It must be kept current if the project is to be kept under control.

The project or development plan contains:

1. Requirements specification
2. Work Breakdown Structure with schedule dates
3. People assignments
4. Budget
5. A standards document for the effort

The manager of development iterates from results to the plan, updates the plan and continues. Fig. 6-15 is simple; following it is very difficult. The little box on the left, Revise schedule, budget, or function, is *the* critical activity. When things go awry, something must give — and

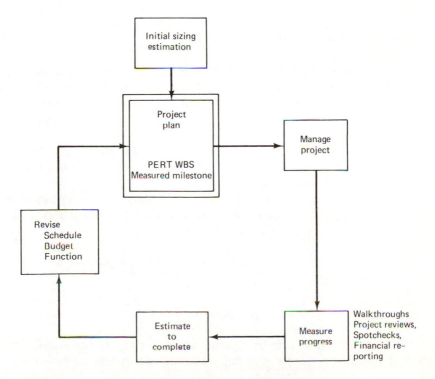

Figure 6-15.   Planning/controlling cycle.

it must be one of these three items. Management is usually slow to admit that the plan must be changed.

Note that the entry to the Plan box is initial sizing, or estimation. Let us now look at estimation and its predecessor, productivity.

PRODUCTIVITY AND ESTIMATION

Productivity is the rate of producing finished programs, ready for use. It is the output of the development process per unit of time. Usually it is measured in lines of code per man-month (or man-year). We'll look at the many problems with this metric in a moment.

Estimation has two parts. First we must estimate the size of the thing that we are about to build, and second, we must estimate the rate of production that we can achieve, in terms of time, dollars, and staff. To estimate the second part at all, we must have some idea of the possible and usual rate of accomplishment on the type of effort that we are going to undertake, i.e., some estimate of productivity. Therefore let us look at productivity first, and then move on to estimation.

PRODUCTIVITY IN SOFTWARE DEVELOPMENT

We do not know how to measure productivity in programming or software development. We are just beginning to develop the vocabulary and the metrics. There are still many areas we do not understand. To describe the difficulty of a job we say "hard," or "very hard," "big," or "huge." These words do not help much.

More useful is the metric of number of instructions or lines of code (LOC). What this tells us is that this job or function — say a payroll — takes 50,000 lines of code.

This is the only real metric that we have today. Yet it is obviously a flawed one. It rewards poor developers who take more instructions to do the function.

	Programmer A	Programmer B
Time	2 months	1 month
Lines of Code	2000	900
Productivity	1000 LOC/man-month	900 LOC/man-month

Our lines of code per unit time measurement is rewarding the inefficient design or sloppy writing. Programmer A has a poor design and "fat" code, yet he or she produced more lines of code per unit time.

Productivity Database

The field has few useful statistics. Those who claim to know productivity averages are mistaken; there is simply not enough data to state productivity averages.

Lines of code can be likened to the number of strokes a house painter uses to paint a house. The fact that one painter uses fewer strokes than another is a meaningless fact *until* we compare the results.

When I wanted to give Outstanding Contribution Awards for the great productivity accomplished in the New York Times Project, I found no productivity data within IBM.

We decided we would start to measure lines of code. We already had, in our contract accounting, a record of hours per person, per job per day, their job catagory (manager, analyst, programmer, configuration control, etc.) and their pay. We had it all — we thought. We discovered almost immediately that no one had a definition of a "line of code"! Nor of "man-month"!

Definitions of Lines of Code and Man-Month

There is a great confusion in the field as to what constitutes a line of code.

Two Meanings of Line of Code

It is useful to know the number lines of object code so that we can estimate how much memory we need to store the instructions — the *object code*.

It is useful to know or estimate the source lines of code so that we can measure and estimate productivity, or numbers of programmers, we need to accomplish the job. Source code usually is in a higher order language.

Even though a higher order language line of code is usually called a "statement," we usually never see statements per day as a measure of productivity; we see lines of code as the standard measuring meter. Both source and object lines of code measures are useful, but we should take care not to inadvertently mix them. They are useful for different reasons.

Therefore there are two meanings to line of code, and both are useful.

- As a measure of productivity of the programmers in development, a *high order language line of code, source code*.
- As a measure of *object code* in use. How much memory is required, and how much effort is needed to support these object language lines of code.

We are still in deep water, even with this distinction.

Source Lines of Code Definition.   A line of code is any source record up to 80 characters in length (executable and nonexecutable) written by a programmer or used in our use time software system. There will be at least two types of such statements. There will be those *not* for retention, which are statements written, debugged, and used and not kept (possible examples of not kept code: some drivers, some simulators, some test programs) and not run at use time. There are comments and data definitions. And then there are statements that will generate object code to be run at use time.

Should we not include comments in the count as lines of code, programmers may not write comments in order to raise their productivity. But this is wrong; we want comments as they will make the continued development phase of the project much easier to perform. On the other hand, we do not want programmers writing two pages of comments for a 30-statement program. Some established norm for comments must be in place. But a comment is a line of code.

We must count *all* lines of code, statements, written or used by our developers whether they run at use time or not. They are integral pieces of the project. And we must count object lines of code as well in order to understand our use time system.

Object Lines of Code Definition.   An object line of code is a single machine language instruction that is either written as a machine language instruction, or generated by some translation process from a different language, or "lifted" from some other project but constructed into our system. The number of all these must be tracked.

Software Categories

There will be a diversity of types of software that will be developed:

Operational software — both system and application, which run at use time

Support software — software for development; software for test

If there are multiple computers in the system, the software for each, if different, should be tracked separately. We should measure separately the LOC created for:

1. The use time or operational software.
2. Supporting the operational software development, including "discarded software" such as drivers.
3. Supporting the hardware development for the system.
4. Performing the test for the system.
5. Supporting design; e.g. modeling software.
6. Management control; e.g. PERT; cost tracking.

We should expect far, far more lines of code per man-month in the later categories than in the first. A diagram showing these distinctions is in Figure 6-16.

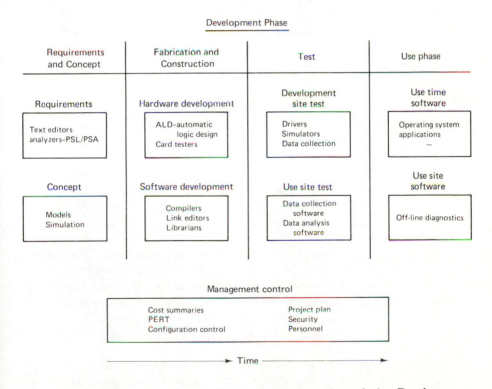

Figure 6-16. Software used/created at various times during Development/Use Phase.

Definition of Man-Month

Counted in the man-month (MM) are *all* personnel that support software development from the beginning of the project until the project has delivered an operational system. Requirements analysts, designers, secretaries, managers, librarians, guards, (as apportioned to the software effort) must be counted in the man-month estimate. Some percentage of systems engineering man-months should be counted as software expenditure, as determined by the manager of systems engineering and the manager of software development. All hours charged to the project from start to finish must be counted.

Variability

We do not expect the LOC/MM to be constant for different types of software. It should be easier to deliver LOC for use at development time than it would be for operational use. Control or systems software (operational) should be more difficult than application (operational) software. Initial deliveries are expected to be more difficult than later deliveries, as a learning curve is experienced and the software team works more efficiently as a team over time.

The Productivity Questionnaire

Let's look at the report data we collected in the productivity data base. We wanted to find out what affected the production of lines of code, so we wanted a lot of data about the effort. We wanted to know the customer environment. Had the customer had much experience with the application? Had the customer much experience with data processing or automation in general? Did the customer participate in the design specification? In the definition of requirements? In the development of the program? Was the interface with the customer very complex, or of average complexity?

We wanted the "project value," the estimated cost. Was there more travel required than necessary? Was the development team near the customer? Was the development location a "good" one? Or poor? In one large job we had to bus the programmers 50 miles in the morning and 50 miles in the evening so that they could gain access to the development computer and customer. Was computer time only available from midnight to 4 AM?

We wanted to know the percentage of development programmers who had participated in the design. We wanted to know the turnover rate, and how good was the programming team — good, average, poor. Was the requirement documentation meager, average or extensive? Was the design "stable"? Where were the changes originating — with the user or with the development team? What languages were being used? What run time computer resources were available? What development time computers were available? Was the use time computer hardware being developed concurrently? Then we wanted to know about the management procedures:

Was there a plan — and was it used, for:

- Evaluation and implementation of system design changes
- Evaluation and implementation of software design changes
- Testing (all levels)
- Notification of program error, detected, corrected
- Use of computer facility
- Back-up development computer facility
- Protection of vital records
- Cost control
- Management control
- Documentation
- Standardized coding techniques

Was the unusual I/O or display-equipment? Or unusual uses of such equipment? Had the programming group worked on this machine before? With this language? With an application of this size and complexity? Had the key programmers worked together successfully before? What was the development environment like? An open shop? Time sharing? Remote job entry? Did programmers ever get hands-on? What was the turnaround time — interactive? Less than 2 hours, 2 to 7 hours, 8 to 24 hours, more than 24 hours? What percentage of code was developed with:

A program support library
A programming librarian
Structured programming
Code review
Top-down programming
Chief Programming Team

Then we looked for an estimate of complexity for:

Application
Program flow

Interprogram communication
External communication
Data base structure

What percentage of code was:

Nonmathematical application and I/O formating
Mathematical and computational programs
CPU and I/O control programs
Fallback and recovery programs

What were the constraints on design?

Main memory
Timing
I/O capability

Was the program classified? How many modules were there? How many classes in the data base? The number of pages in the documentation? Internal? To be delivered? How much storage was being used by the operating system at run-time? We wanted a chronology of errors found, with counts by categories. We wanted, of course, the number of people, by

Management
Administration
Programming
Analysis
Operations

We wanted a list of computer resources. We wanted to know the amount of effort on simulation or modeling.

Obviously the data gathering was an added burden to already burdened software development management. Often I was told by my subordinates that I had a choice — I could make the schedule, or I could get the data asked for in the survey. Very often I did not get the data. But slowly over the years the data came in. The reason for listing most of the questions is to show that there are so many variables and different options that to pinpoint any one of them as *the* determinant of productivity is an over simplification. We need to gain a vast volume of data about software development, from hundreds and hundreds of efforts, before we will be able to use a data base of such figures as a productivity predictor and management tool.

LOC Mistakes

The most prevalent mistake made in the lines of code area is to ignore ingenuity and to measure and reward lines of code per man-month! So many managers get mesmerized by this detail and ignore invention and creative people.

Many people make the mistake of measuring the man-months part of the equation as only the time spent by the programmers. We have already seen that in the very large projects more than 50 percent of the effort is performed by support people and management. These are direct costs and must be counted.

Measuring LOC per month in the middle of the development is a bad mistake. If you have estimated the total number of lines of code *and* the average number of lines per man-month, and you have a "commitment" to perform to, do not fall into the "measure in the middle" error. Do not make a rate of production at any instant the constant you use to calculate future productivity.

We had a contract on the West Coast on which we had under-estimated the number of lines of code by a factor of two. We had changed managers — and the new one did not want to "be hung" with the old errors. One cannot argue with that.

Our productivity numbers were also wrong, argued the new manager. He was taking the rate at that specific time X (See Fig. 6-17) and stating that it was *the* rate that would be experienced on the entire project.

That is as wrong as trying to use the rate at (Y) as the one we would experience from day one. We must use *the average* rate.

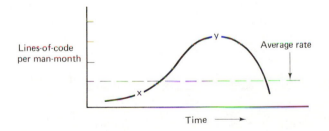

Figure 6-17. Lines of code per month on a project.

To take a rate at any one time is to fall into deep error! The *only* way one can measure lines of code on a project is at the end, after it is finished. There is no number that can be reliably derived until the end. Only the total makes sense, not instantaneous rates.

Indeed, on the West Coast project, we had predicted that the first produced software (systems software) would take far more time and effort per LOC than the last delivered programs. The counterargument was to keep the early rate, at point X in the figure, as the *constant* rate.

The instantaneous rate of software production at any given time is not to be used as a constant to project the future production. Lines of code produced is not a constant rate. It starts very slow (zero), zooms to a high, drops to zero again.

Law of Large Numbers.   It is obvious from these questions that the number of variables that are at play here is very large. Because of this the real meanings to be gained from this data base will not be learned very quickly. The data was clearly fragmentary when I left IBM in 1977. I had kept the data 'company private' to avoid misleading articles and conclusions, with one exception.

Misinterpretation of the Contents of the Data Base.   In early 1977 I allowed one article to be published in the *IBM System Journal* by C.E. Walston and C.P. Felix with the provison that only part of the data be published and that it be clearly stated that our analyses were preliminary. Yet that article is frequently quoted as though it were a final report, and it is often misquoted.

The article cites the following:*

Sixty completed software development projects had reported data. Twenty-eight different languages had been used. The 28 languages are for 66 different computers. The efforts range from 4,000 source lines of code to 467,000.

The article ignores object code; it *reports* on only source code. The article lists 29 of 68 reported variables had the most effect on productivity. The article states that interactions between the cited 29 variables are ignored. It states, "this analysis was performed on each variable independently and does not take into account either the possibility that these variables may be correlated, or that there may be interrelated effects associated with them." Table 3 of the article lists the first entry as follows:

	Median 50%	Quartiles 25-75%
Source lines per man-month of effort	274	150-440

Now let me comment on this. There is less than one completed project per computer used. There are 2.1 projects per language used. The range of scale is even greater than the 4,000 source lines to 467,000

*C.E. Walston and C.P. Felix, "A Method of Programming Measurement and Estimation," *IBM Sys. J.*, 16, No. 1 (1977), 54-73.

lines implies. The space effort from Houston was broken into several 'programs,' each reported separately. They did not run separately.

One table uses the *median* lines of code per man-month; the table that shows the 29 most important variables uses the *mean*. Table 3 above cuts off the bottom and top 25 percent of the figures. This makes the data look more regular than it is. The figures on page 239 under Estimating Productivity show the *wild* range of productivity — which *we did not understand*.

The article does not treat object lines of code. This is the product of the effort, not the source code. Object code counts are in the data base. To ignore object code is to also ignore the productivity multiplier of High Order Languages. Language is not one of the 29 most important factors listed. This is due to the article, not the reality of the situation. As an aside, one of the things that shocked us all when we first saw the data base was the percentage of projects that were still using Assembly level languages. It was well over 50 percent.

Many of the 60 projects were repeat implementations, the second time through for the same team.

The article says that no interaction of the variables is considered. Clearly these variables interact!

The article implies, if not directly states, that the variable that most significantly affects productivity is "customer interface complexity." A table contains the item and the numbers; the text does not comment on them. We knew that the reports coming in were from all over the world. The data base was in Gaithersburg, Maryland — the big efforts were in Houston, Texas; Atlantic City, New Jersey; Los Angeles, California; and Morris Plains, New Jersey. We recognized that "more than normal complexity" of customer interface was not a measurable variable. We could not match a manager's judgment in Texas with a manager's judgment in Los Angeles, or Saigon, or Tokyo. It was a very personal judgment.

I do not believe that the complexity of customer interface was or is the most important variable affecting productivity. The data is simply too sparse to draw any such conclusion.

I have seen *three* documents — a book, a copy of a presentation and an article that cite the article incorrectly! These articles state that 'IBM says such and such.' IBM had said no such thing.

Yet the data base of IBM is a most valuable resource. IBM should continue to publish more and more of their findings, despite the risk of misinterpretation.

I approved this article in 1977; I am responsible for much of the confusion I relate above.

In retrospect it may have been a mistake to publish the article. It

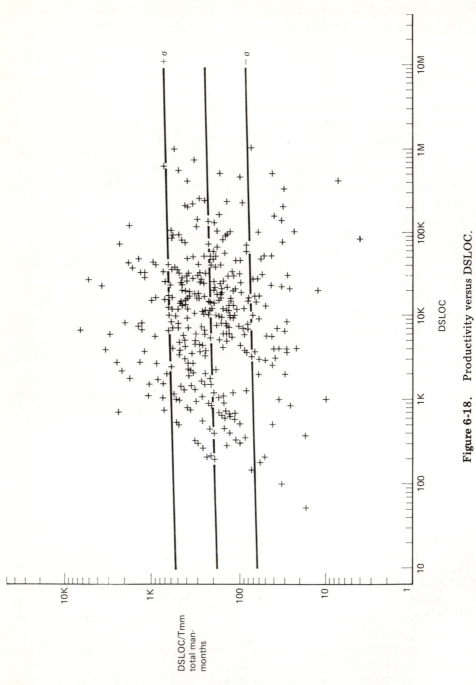

Figure 6-18. Productivity versus DSLOC.

was meant as a progress report of *incomplete* but valuable research. It is being misinterpreted but perhaps cooler heads are drawing valuable insights from the data, *recognizing* how preliminary it is.

There does not exist today a good data base from which to make judgments. The data that does exist ranges wildly in productivity achieved, and we do not understand why. Productivity rates over 1,000 LOC per man-month and of 60 LOC per man-month can be seen on similar efforts. We do not understand yet all the reasons for this range.

These measurement activities are expensive, and yet we must continue to collect this kind of data if we ever hope to fully understand the dynamics at play in software development. Until data in large numbers and great detail are collected, we will not have our minds around the software development process.

Until that is done, the idea of using "data bases" of project history to predict costs and effort is naive. It is meaningless; there are too many variables.

A Set of Numbers Signifying Wild Randomness. Figure 6-18 comes from a US Government study on lines of code delivered (DSLOC — Delivered Source Lines of Code) versus productivity (LOC/MM). Note that the scale on both axes is logarithmic. The only thing this data shows is that we cannot make any valid estimates from it. The variability is wild.

It is meaningful only in showing that we do not yet have a useful set of data. For a 100,000 LOC program, I have, on the chart, within the sigma deviation, projects that got 80 DSLOC/MM and some that got 800. Such a range is useless for forecasting!

Warning. Lines of code as a productivity measure and estimating technique is prone to gamesmanship at this time. There is no known way of coupling functions and lines of code. If management insists that lines of code per unit time be high, programmers may deliver "loose," "fat" code, which makes their productivity look good, but which is absolutely *not* desired as a product as it takes memory and CPU time to execute that code. I have seen many examples of 'good' programming managers insisting on so many lines of code per month from each programmer.

Report Format — Lines of Code

The type of report desired on a project would be something like the following:

<u>Title</u>: Missile Engagement Program: Mathematical; Overlayed; Time Critical

<u>Functions</u>: Calculate heading, speed and all control signals needed to guide a missile in flight to intersect another missile.

<u>Not Including</u>: a) Tracking of all missiles; done in another program
b) Transmission and reception of all signals; done elsewhere

Total LOC OPERATIONAL — Object	36,441
Written LOC (operational) — HOL	7,014 written
MACHINE LANGUAGE	1,314 written
Not written — operational	8,424
Man-Months (direct charge)	340 man-months
Code* written not retained (thrown away)	26,584
	8,144 Test
	11,240 drivers
	3,100 simulation
	4,100 misc.
Code* written and retained but not operational	50,445 total
	22,814 test code final version
	18,416 comments
	1,114 simulation
	8,101 data reduction
Time to Deliver	18 months

Time to *first* iteration of Requirements Specification   4 months
of Design Specification   8 months

*Object lines

This sample report is placed here to illustrate some of the concepts in the previous pages. Some, but not all of the concepts. We should include in a full report the detailed answers to the many questions we have stated we are interested in — what kind of computer is being used for compiling, etc.

Some Results of the Record Keeping

The net of all the effort to date is that no one knows yet how to predict productivity for a randomly selected large software project. There are just too many variables, too many qualitative items that have a great effect on the results. For a specific effort, with a tested team on a well understood application, we can come close.

Below are some interim results of the measurement project at IBM. The efforts are grouped under the management forecasted difficulty of easy, medium, and hard. Look at the wide divergence in lines of code (LOC) actually produced per month!

	Productivity Experienced
Small/easy* (300-900)	
1	517
2	615
Medium/easy* (200-600)	
3	199
4	39
5	100
6	286
7	524
8	28
9	109
10	167
11	274
12	1071
Medium/hard* (100-300)	
13	562
14	403
15	128
16	81
17	68
18	400
19	253
20	227
21	250
22	163
23	198
Large/hard* (50-150)	
24	186
25	68
26	284
27	182
28	229
29	46
30	120

*Productivity predicted by management.

ESTIMATION

Estimating the Size of the Program

If we knew in advance the size that the program was going to be, we would be in much better shape at the start of all large development projects.

For jobs that are comparable to already programmed jobs, we can get a good estimate of the number of lines of code that will be needed by having a knowledgeable developer look at the running system.

We are obviously in the midst here of the old circular discussion of: "You can't have the job because you have no experience." "How can I get experience if I can't get the job?" But that is just where we are. We want our estimate to be made by some one who has done it before. Or done something close to what we are trying to do.

Here the categorization of five uses of a computer and our taxonomy comes in handy. Just because an individual has developed large *application* software does not mean that he or she is equipped to estimate the effort to develop *systems* software. In fact, such a situation should be a red flag. Do not let applications people do estimates for systems efforts! Do not allow people who have been developing batch programs do the estimating for a real time system. And so for all the other categories.

Factors that Determine Development Difficulty

Many factors combine to make a development job harder or easier. We will list 27 of them before we end this chapter. They break into three major categories:

The function to be done
The use-time environment
Development time factors

$$\boxed{\text{Software Development Difficulty} - F \times UTE \times DTF}$$

Development/Difficulty Chart. Table 6-2 can be used as a list of what to watch out for as you begin your system development. The indicators, a +, ++, or —, tell you whether or not the task to develop gets easier (—) or harder (+) as the effort moves from a type I or II, to a III, IV, or V. You would get more productivity if the task is a (—), less if it is a (+). First the chart, then the explanation of each of the 27 delineations.

TABLE 6-2. Developmental Difficulties

Function	I	II	III	IV	V
Functions to be done, amount					+
Functions to be done, complexity		+			+
Functions to be done, clarity					+
Interaction of humans with the system			+	+	++
Number of different users of the system			+	+	+
Number of times the program will run			+	+	+
Number of machines on which the program is to be run					+
Functions to be done, interrelationships					+
Data elements			+		
Expected frequency of change to the program					+
Interaction with other systems					+

Use-Time Environment

	I	II	III	IV	V
CPU	—	+		+	++
I/O	+	—			+
Main memory	—				+
Auxiliary memory			+		
Reliability/availability			+	+	++
Real time					++

Development-Time Factors

	I	II	III	IV	V
Operating system adequacy			+	+	++
Time available to create the software					+
Availability of development tools; languages, debuggers, etc.					+
Availability of machines to develop the software					+
Experience of the development team with the hardware					
Experience of the programmer team with the support software					
Number of modules					
Stability of the software tools					+
Stability of the computer					+
Experience of the user					+

—	Easier	+	More difficult
	Normal difficulty	++	Much more difficult

Function Factors

1. Functions, Amount

The more functions to be done, the more programs to be written to do them. The difficulty of software development rises nonlinearly with the size of the program to be written.

2. Functions, Complexity

The program to calculate the orbit insertion for a lunar rendezvous is 50 or so times more difficult to do than the programs to add tax to a sales bill for a monthly credit card. Control programs are logically complex, and logical complexity is more of a problem than scientific complexity.

3. Functions, Clarity

Some functions (payroll) are clear and well defined. Others are in the heads of the old masters and mischief can break loose when people try to write them down so they can be programmed. Type V systems are particularly difficult to pin down.

4. Open Loop, Human Interaction with the System in Operation

A system that has a person in the loop is a much more complex system than one that does not. The person must be given information in a certain way; his or her response must be accommodated; variability of the response must be expected; further information must usually be given, and the sequence of requests cannot be so rigid as to cause him or her to reject the system.

5. Number of Different Users of the Program

Different users will stress the computer and its software differently. It is axiomatic that the more users a program has, the more errors will be found in it. Users does not mean the number of sites. A missile computer and program can be used in hundreds of different sites, but the use is one use.

6. Number of Times the Program Will Run

If the program is to be run constantly then we will be concerned about the efficiency (how much hardware it must have to run) at use time. If it is to be run only once, we will not be concerned at all about the efficiency of the program.

7. Numbers of Machines the Job Will Run On

If we are developing a program to run on one machine we can be a little less concerned about how much machine resources we use up. A radar program that will run on hundreds of computers on hundreds of ships should be honed and squeezed. An extra memory will be multiplied by hundreds.

8. Functions, Inter-relation of

Some complex jobs have little interaction with the other things that are going on in the computer; others are intricately connected so that the jobs are almost intertwined.

9. Data Elements

The number and length of the elements of data, their variability, their interrelationships, their volatility can have a big impact on the size of a program and on the difficulty of its design phase. Brooks states, "Show me your data and I can tell more about your program than if you show me your flow charts."

10. Expected Frequency of Change to the Program

If I have a stable program that will not be changed very often, I can build my program in a very different way than if I expect my program to be frequently changed.

11. Interaction with Other Systems

If our computer system is to be at the the beck and call of other systems, we must program it to respond to those kinds of interruptions.

Use-Time Factors

12. CPU Power Available

Every program uses the CPU to get the job done. Some programs use this CPU time more efficiently than other programs. When the CPU resource is scarce, then the programmers are asked to do design work that is aimed, not at getting the job done, but at getting it done within the prescribed limits of the tight CPU resource. And they try, and test and try again -- and again. It works; it is expensive in terms of programming time.

13. I/O Paths Available   This problem is logically the same as the scarce CPU usage, but the big requirement here is for the number of input/output paths to and from the machine. The programmers may have to go to great lengths to squeeze the flow of data into the small number of "ports" that exist on the machine.

14. Main Memory Available   Again the same problem, but now from the memory side. Programs take memory to reside in and if there is a scarcity of memory the programmer must "roll in - roll out" the programs to be run into the main memory and back out again to an auxiliary memory. This takes running time *and* memory space. Or they squeeze and design and squeeze again. In 1946 von Neumann wrote that memory was the key to performance. He is still correct; memory speed and size are critical.

15. Auxiliary Memory Available   The problem is again the same; now it is with the auxiliary memory.

16. Reliability/ Consequences of Failure   A 2-day failure in a type I system can be tolerated. Inconvenient, yes; catastrophic, no. But an hour or 10-minute outage cannot be tolerated in an air traffic control system, or in a system to control the flying space shuttle, or in a system that is doing antimissile defense. If the consequences of failure are high, a standard operating system (supplied by the hardware manufacturer) cannot be used. The same problem arises with real time systems. In these cases, either a new or modified operating system must be created.

17. Real Time Constraints   If a payroll takes 2½ instead of its normal 2 hours, who really cares? It's an annoyance. But if the radar return comes every 6.4 seconds, the computer better be ready to take it and to have finished the processing of the previous radar return. If not, the system can be overrun. In a real time system, a standard operating system will not suffice. How many things can be carried on at the same time? How many jobs must get finished before another task is started? The more that can and must be carried at the same time, the more systems programming that must be there to control the flow and keep it in order. Examples: Time sharing systems; command and control systems, en-route air traffic control systems.

Development-Time Factors

18. Operating System Adequacy	Computer manufacturers usually deliver or lease or sell a large software system with the hardware that schedules and runs the various hardware units of the computer. However, these operating systems may not support the software development very well.
19. Time Available to Create the Software	Schedule becomes the dominant factor in most advanced type V systems. The reason for this is that the computer and its software are usually only a component of a complex system. Satellites, ships, weapons, missiles, buildings, businesses -- any one of these may be the "pacing" item -- and the software must be ready when the rest of the system is ready. What normally happens is schedule is met -- at the expense of the function to be done. Less function is delivered than planned, and the original function is added into the system at a later date.
20. Availability of Development Tools	Software tools, like all other tools, are essential to productivity. New machines are usually lean at first when it comes to tools. A rich set of powerful tools greatly enhances productivity.
21. Availability of Machines to Develop the Program	There are two aspects to this item. First, the people who build systems are so fa-

miliar with this need for a *development machine* that they take it for granted. When it is not there or not powerful enough, all slows down. Yet people who are not familiar with the process do not understand that the computer is *the key* development tool in the process of creating software. The computer is used at development time as fully as it is used at use time. The computer is also needed of course for testing the software.

22. Experience of the Programming Team with the Hardware

There is a learning curve in every field of endeavor, and this is true in programming. If we have a team of programmers who have worked with this hardware before, the learning curve has been mastered in the past and we will get more productivity from the team.

23. Experience of the Programming Team with the Development of the Software

The same learning curve experience that we saw with the hardware is at work with the support software.

24. Number of Modules

The number of modules and the interconnection between them are factors that greatly change the complexity of the job to be done. This area is close to the "functions, interconnectivity" but it is different in the sense that the two may not always be interrelated because this area — number of modules — depends to an extent on the design of the program, whereas the other is inherent in the job to be done.

25. Stability of the Software Tools

If the tools used to create the programs are unstable, then random problems are introduced into an already difficult creation process. Example, a compiler that has errors in it may cause errors in the object code.

26. Stability of the Hardware

If the computer to be used at use time is still being shaken down, then the programmers cannot tell whether a difficulty is with their programs or with the hardware. It is a simultaneous confusion.

| | This is the worst situation a software development team can face. |
| 27. Experience of the User | The user is the real customer and an important part of the development team. A user who has used a type V system in the past, who has been through the process, makes a far better development partner than one who has not. Naive users can bring a good development team to a standstill as new users often grope their way forward in fits and starts. |

Brooks wrote in *The Mythical Man-Month* that systems programming is three times more difficult than compiler programming, and that is three times as hard as application programming. Systems programs that must operate in a real time fashion are three times as hard as normal systems programs. Programs that cannot fail are two to three times as hard as systems programs. Programs that must operate in an interactive way are at least twice as difficult as those that are not interactive.

The major contributors to the cost of software development are:

1. Scale. The amount of function to be developed.
2. Clarity. The degree to which the functions to be developed are understood.
3. Logical complexity. The number of conditional branches per 100 instructions.
4. Consequences of failure. How much design and effort must be accomplished to meet the reliability and recovery requirements.
5. People interaction. How often and how intensive is the user interaction with the system.
6. Real time requirements. How fast must the functions be done.
7. Stability of the support software. Is the support software stable and mature?
8. Stability of the use phase computer. Is the computer to be used at use time stable?

These are the most critical of the 27 factors that we have reviewed.

Let us use these 8 factors and demonstrate how the cost of a line of code can go from $1 per line to $32.50 per line. When we use all 27 factors and have a worst case in all factors, we can get to $200 per line of code.

The numbers I am about to use are *not* based on any survey or study. They are representative numbers based on my judgment, and I show them not for their values but for the concept of escalating costs per line of code and for the relative value of each. I show that the worst thing that can happen to balloon the cost per line of code is to have an unstable use phase machine. I assign this factor a multiplier value of 20.

I postulate a base cost per line of code as $1 per line. I wish to ignore for the example efforts that cost less.

It will cost me more to develop a program that can not fail than it will cost me to develop the same function without regard to failure. How much more is the question we are after. I assign to this factor, reliability, a multiplier of 15. Therefore if it were to cost me $1 per line of code for the "unreliable" program, it would cost me $15 per line for the reliable program.

I assign multiplier factors to each of the eight major contributors to cost as follows:

Scale	1 to 8
Clarity	1 to 10
Logical complexity	1 to 10
Consequences of failure	1 to 15
People interaction	1 to 5
Real time requirements	1 to 5
Stability of the support software	1 to 10
Stability of the use phase computer	1 to 20

If we had the worst case for each and every one of these eight, then the cost per unit line of code would be the *sum* of the highest value of each of them, or $83 per line.

But in a real situation, we would rarely have the worst case for every one, and I would have to estimate the relative difficulty of each factor for my particular development task. Figure 6-19 shows the result of my judgments, for let us say a 10,000 line of code missile control software package that can not fail, must accept radar data every 4 seconds, has no user interaction, stable support software, and a "fairly stable" use phase computer. The logical intensity is minimal and the clarity is excellent.

My cost estimate is therefore $32.50 per line of code, and it was arrived at by adding the costs shown on the diagram. One dollar per line is my base; now I want the multipliers.

I have made the following judgments:

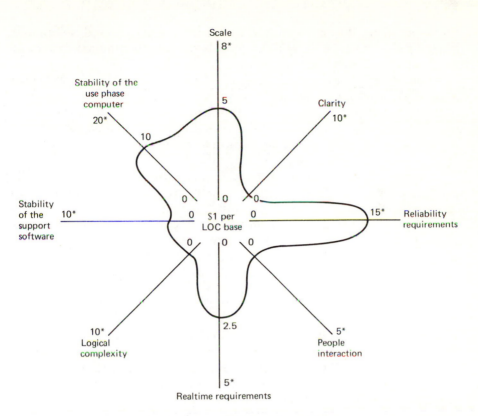

Figure 6-19. Pieces of an estimate.

no multiplier for logical complexity
no multiplier for clarity
no multiplier for people interaction
no multiplier for software stability, support
5 times multiplier for scale
2.5 times for real time
15 times for reliability
10 times for use time computer instability

This yields a cost estimate of $32.50 per line of code. To repeat, the individual factors are multiplicative; the overall cost is additive across the factors, not multiplicative.

I am presenting a methodology here, not the numerical factors themselves. Two judgments must be made if this type of cost estimate is to be made; first the maximum multiplier for each factor and then the location on the range of each factor for the particular development effort. I also am presenting in the numbers I use here my assessment of the relative difficulty introduced by each factor.

The methodology here ignores the fact that the difficulty in reality *is* multiplicative across factors.

If I were going to use this method in a real situation, I would not use all the 27 factors that contribute, but only those that contributed heavily in my judgment to the situation at hand.

Some of the best estimators in my experience do this whole process backwards. They estimate how many people they need to do such and such function and how long it would take those people to do the job, then estimate how many lines of code per day their people could create and then arrive at the total lines of code for the function. I say this method is backwards. Perhaps it is the forward way and the more prevalent method of estimation is the backward way.

How to Estimate

Conservatively! With all the things that can go wrong, many will. The estimate should be done by the most experienced person in the area to be automated. If necessary, outside consultants should be used. Outside consultants should check any important estimate. No estimate should be believed if done by someone who has never developed *this type* or *size* of program.

Making the Right Estimate versus Making the Estimate Right. Estimation will always be with us. But after we estimate, we budget. And after we budget, we develop. At this point, making the estimate right is more important than delivering all the functions in the first delivery. It may be that we must revise the cost estimate upwards, the delivery schedule outwards, or the function to be done downward in order to meet the estimate. It was only an estimate, after all.

Assumptions for Estimating

A good software development manager will state clearly the assumptions on which the estimate is based. The development environment is one key assumption. The availability of people to do the job is crucial, not only in terms of numbers but in terms of quality.

The state of requirements definition is crucial. At this point the overall systems manager sometimes states that requirements are firm. The good software manager knows that on large projects this is usually not the case, but that at this stage he or she can not prove the point. So what he or she should do is embed in his or her estimate a factor for new work. We'll comment on other assumptions as we go through this management section.

Success Schedules.   Success schedules are those that are based on *everything* coming in on time — the new radar, the satellite, the computer, etc. It never happens, but if you want to win a competition or get your project approved you may have to bid this way. Just do not believe it! This is the "society" aspect in play again! We plan for success schedules in order to get the award, to get the project past a review.

ORGANIZATION OF THE SOFTWARE DEVELOPMENT EFFORT

Organization is the key to so many of our marvelous accomplishments, and yet so often we somehow muddle into selecting the right organization structure. Peter Drucker in his 1945 classic, the *Concept of the Organization,** points out that the marvelous production achieved by the U.S. during WW II was not primarily a technological achievement but an achievement of human organization.

There are but a few organizational principles that are significantly different for software than for any other development. Organization will differ markedly depending on size and type of software being developed, and the organization will evolve as the software development phases are completed.

We'll use the organization chart of Fig. 6-20 to make the points.

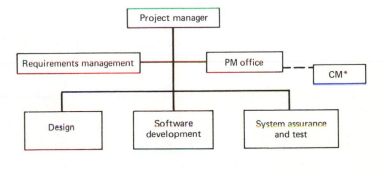

*CM is configuration management

Figure 6-20.   Software development organization.

*Peter F. Drucker, *Concept of the Organization* (New York: The John Day Co., Inc., 1972).

Some Key Points for Large Projects:

1. Requirements Manager. This position is rarely seen in software organizations, yet it is a critical function. When I once asked the project manager for a 100 million dollar effort "who is responsible for requirements?" he was puzzled by the question. He was, he said. Which meant that no one individual was responsible! When times get tough, who will represent the user?
2. The Project Management (P.M.) Office keeps track of costs, schedules, equipment, property, etc. A strong forceful group here will uncover many problems.
3. There should be a Manager of Design, a Designer, or Chief Architect. This person should *not* be the Development Manager (Production Manager or Implementation Manager). Design is a most creative endeavor and is critical to the success of the large software development project. Designing and managing are very different activities.
4. The Software Development Manager should control all groups that deliver code.
5. Configuration Management (CM). A permanent committee — with at least the development manager, the requirements manager, and the project management manager — should meet weekly to review all proposed changes, test results, and the state of the system. *This is the way to keep on top of what is happening in a large development effort.*
6. The System Assurance and Test Group must be started early and be kept separate from the development group.
7. Organizations should mirror design as much as possible. If the design shows a separate input subprogram, then there should be a separate input group (assuming the task is large enough).

The most common mistakes I encountered in organizations are the following:

1. No designer. "The design will evolve!"
2. No independent test group.
3. No independent requirements group.

We will cover corporate organization for software in Chap. 8, stating what every large organization should do if it is serious about managing software.

MONITORING PROGRESS

No large software development job is kept under control without tight, close monitoring. Scheduling dates for the completion of *every* subprogram and module, and tracking progress and effort expended are essential to understanding whether the project is on target, ahead of plan, or behind.

There are many ways to track the myriad of completion dates that are found in large projects. PERT or GANTT charts both work well — if worked at — and that means people and dollars. The computer and software are useful tools to help keep track of these details.

There are dozens and dozens of "Project Control" systems that are perfectly adequate to track the development — *if* they are used. But the management must check and recheck that the reports are accurate, and that the system is not being subverted. These systems will give early warning signals when things begin to go wrong. At this point, the lower level managers in the project will try to "explain away" the deviations as mere aberrations, hoping to fix their problem next month.

The good program manager knows his or her tool *and* what it is telling him or her. It is probably telling him or her bad things — and he or she, if competent, will pay attention.

All large projects should have a mechanized project reporting system. Every week there should be a computer printout that shows what's been happening. Management *must* study the printout. Remember: Effort expended is *not* a measure of progress.

CONTROL

To allow people to do what they want is usually acceptable if we are not trying to achieve something on a schedule or within a budget. To let people do what they want is insanity in most work situations. Yet most work situations also provide, in themselves, the visibility to allow the manager to see what is going on.

Software development has been invisible for 30 years. It is rapidly becoming more visible. People have been able to do what they want. For small, relatively standalone programs this is fine. For a large number of interconnected programs this is an invitation to bad trouble.

Management of the large software development wants predictability and control. Everything must fit, and therefore freedom to choose from alternatives must be reduced to the absolute minimum, once the design is set. The implementor must be kept *under control.* (For an example of how individuality, no matter how well motivated or conceived, can rise up to thwart the efforts of thousands, see An Example of an Error, page 187.)

Short Cuts

Short cuts are welcome on small unimportant software development projects. They are *deadly* to large development efforts, and to the groups assigned to continuing development.

A short cut means not following the standards, and standards and rules are what allow us to build large, complex systems. A short cut is quicker because it ignores at least part of the strictures. Short cuts cost money and grief over the life of a large software product or project.

Configuration Control

We need rigid and absolute control over what the system is and what it is going to be, what changes we are going to put into the system, and what the effect of those changes will be. This is how to develop hundreds of thousands of lines of code by hundreds of programmers. There are many automated (computerized) systems that are available to help us keep control, but the essential item is management commitment and time.

A weekly meeting of the key managers is essential. No delegation should be allowed. This is the place where the key decisions are to be made regarding schedule, cost, function, and people assignments. Priorities must be worked out at this meeting. Figure 6-21 shows the sequence of events. The key is management.

Automated Module/Function Matrix

We saw with the payroll system (towards the end of Chap. 5) that many sizeable programs can be a part of a system. Of course, each of the programs we listed is made up of many smaller modules of instructions.

In a small system the number of functions and the number of modules is small, but as the system gets to be even of moderate size the number of modules and functions gets very large indeed. To keep track of what instructions are performing which functions, a simple matrix that lists modules on one axis and function on another is a very useful tool to aid the configuration control group. Programs to update these matrices automatically are available from many vendors, even when the number of functions and modules runs into the thousands.

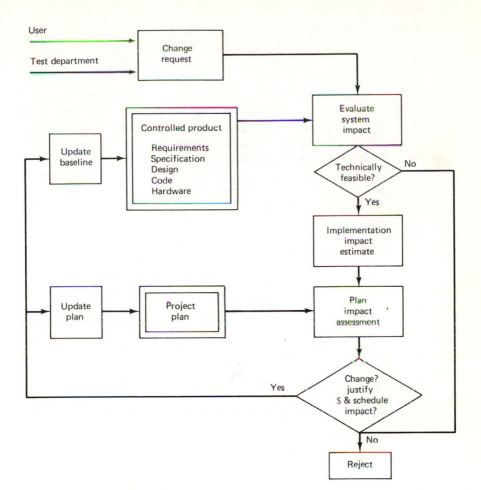

Figure 6-21. Configuration management cycle.

THE KEY TO SUCCESS – THE MANAGER OF SOFTWARE DEVELOPMENT

I have learned over the years that all the support tools and checks and balances are important, but *the* most critical item to success is the manager in charge. I've seen some projects run by "great" companies fail, and some by "so-so" companies succeed beautifully, due to the software development manager. Let's look at the software manager and how to select her or him.

CHOOSING THE SOFTWARE DEVELOPMENT MANAGER

The first trait to look for in selecting a manager of the software development is not technical capability or even experience, but emotional maturity and "toughness." The good software development managers have handled the crunch of objectives versus reality, and have stood firm and said "no" to the incessant requests for a "little more" function, just a little more here and a little more there. This accretion of function is called "creeping elegance" and can be fatal. They know that the time to do $n+1$ trvial things is two times as long as for n things, for n sufficiently large (Logg's rebuttal to Gray's Law).* They know that Brooks was correct when he wrote in *The Mythical Man-Month* "How does a program get to be a year late? A day at a time." They know that *requirements* are the first line of defense. Keep the "enemy" at bay here and things are controllable.

The second trait to look for is attention to detail. Most of the good software managers spend a great deal of time understanding the minute details of the effort. They know.

The third thing to look for is just good management traits in general.

Next, look for knowledge of the job to be done. Then, experience. Has he or she ever done anything this big before? Beware the Peter Principle here. Many great number two people can not be a number one! Putting out a million lines of code is a lot harder than just ten times the effort to put out a hundred thousand lines of code.

What traits to avoid?

Avoid "salesy" managers. Those who are good on their feet are often too willing to compromise. I have rarely seen the manager who can span the range of traits from sales to project management. The salesy manager is often too anxious to compromise, to please everyone.

Technical Training

One need not have a technical degree to be a programmer. But to manage the large structures of complexity in software, to arrange a close to optimum "fit" of hundreds of pieces, to schedule the work of hundreds of technical developers, to do all this, a person is far better prepared if he or she has a technical degree. A look at some of the new tools to structure this complexity shows that they are in the advanced mathematics and engineering fields.

*Paul Dickson, *The Official Rules* (New York: Delacorte Press, 1978).

The Software Development Career

If we look at the major activities of a software development manager. we find some disturbing things. Estimating is imprecise and personal. Experience is the only "good" methodology and estimating is still a black art. Measuring progress is a problem. Only with a good automated development and tracking process system can one even begin to estimate how near to completion the project is. There is no good way to predict, measure, or even quantify productivity.

1. It is hard to tell how big the job is.
2. You can't tell how productive your workers will be (or even were).
3. You can't quantify the percentage of work completed.
4. It is hard to tell where you are going!
5. It is hard to tell how fast you are moving!
6. It is hard to tell how far you've come!

With this set of problems, who would ever want to take on such a job?

FIVE STAGES OF ALL NEW PROJECTS

1. Euphoria
2. Disenchantment
3. Search for the guilty
4. Punishment of the innocent
5. Distinction for the uninvolved

Every project manager should be aware of the stages of a project and should know that the first management team often is removed as the difficulties set in. It is the risk you take for getting in the game.

Pioneers Get Killed a Lot

Enough said. A study of new developments will show that the first and second managers to run the effort usually get "shot." Only after one or two "bloodlettings" does upper management get realistic. Why would anyone ever want to be a manager of large software development? Because it is the fast lane, the express to the top — if you can hold on. It is exciting and richly rewarding if you succeed.

There is tremendous accomplishment possible, with all its psychic rewards. Some of the best software development managers I've known speak of "Christmas morning" - when all the lights go on and the entire, nationwide system works!

When managing a large effort, it should be obvious that as few breakthroughs and new techniques as possible should be used.

Obvious? Not as obvious as you might think! In 1961, the committee appointed by President John F. Kennedy after the N.Y. mid air collision recommended what should be done in the automation of Air Traffic Control. It reported that the Federal Aviation Agency should buy "off-the-shelf" computers for use in any new system. This restriction was put in place because in the late 1950s the FAA had begun to fund computer development — and the money disappeared into that endeavor rather than into the development of an air traffic control system.

The same thing happened in the mid-1970s in a hospital system. The developers took their eye off the objective of getting a system that would be acceptable to the doctors, nurses, administrators, professionals, and staff — and began to develop a "network" of minicomputers, with a distributed data base.

Neither the FAA nor the medical system needed innovation in the data processing hardware area. The systems problems were formidable enough without the computer innovations. Do not let your innovators loose on large systems. Send them to the laboratories.

A small consulting company lost $300,000 — several years' profit — trying to finish a contract on which they were using IBM's Series 1. The hardware was fine; the system software and support software were a shambles. Yet it always appeared that the breakthrough was just around the corner. The software was new! Just because it is IBM doesn't guarantee it. And the contract was ironclad in IBM's favor.

WILL THE REAL USER PLEASE STAND UP?

It is critical to manage the requirements all the way from the user to the programmer. This sounds so simple, but it can get off the track at several different points. There are so many people and organizations in the loop in large systems.

Figure 6-22 shows the typical organization for a large project. The real requirements of the ultimate user can and do get garbled as they go along the paths A and B. Two paths are labeled 1 deliberately. Which is the "right" path? They are often in conflict.

Paths 2, 3 and 4 are not "clean." How many projects got into trouble because the designers or programmers decided *they knew* what was needed? That "those people" in the chain of command ahead of

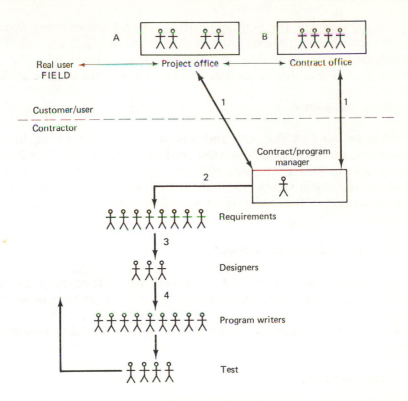

Figure 6-22. Organizations involved in a project.

them were all wet? Too many! I have seen systems where the programmers knew more than the designers, so they did the system their way. Systems where designers "knew" what was required. Systems where no one really spoke to the eventual real life user. In short, things can go awry at A or B, 1 or 2 or 3 or 4 and things do go wrong.

It is the job of the project manager on large software developments to check and check and check again, to be *sure* that what is being built will be used.

Getting people who have been doing the function in the real world to participate in the design and configuration control is a major step towards getting a useable system.

AUDITS

I have seen all kinds of audit results — those that said everything was fine, and it was, and then some that said everything was fine and it was a disaster! Some said there would be a disaster, and there was! And then sometimes the predicted disaster never materialized.

In other words, the audits are often wrong! Those being audited say, "We know more than the auditors; *they* are wrong." And often the auditors are wrong. How does the manager know who is right? And do these errors in the audits mean that it is not a good idea to have audits?

Audits are Essential

Despite the fact that the auditors are frequently wrong in their assessments, the audit is an essential tool of management. Whether the audit is right or wrong, the very process of having an audit imposes discipline on the organization. Ideas on organization, design, and process are interchanged. Often the project improves because of the intensified attention.

What Should be Audited — When?

All efforts of a certain size should be audited once every 6 months. Any effort that is showing signs of distress should be audited as soon as possible. Signs of distress may be schedule slippage, inordinate overtime, low utilization of the host computer, inability to staff the project, etc.

What is an "Audit"?

Audits are not the same as reviews or inventories. An audit is a spot check on key points of a product or process. It is a formal check, usually done by people not working on the effort. A walkthrough is a detail review, and is a microcosm of an audit. A review is more cursory than an audit, and does not go into as much detail. An inventory is a lising of what exists and is close to an audit, but usually is done for different reasons.

Who Should the Auditors Be?

The best, experienced people available should perform the audit. They should be experienced in the area they are auditing. To send batch people to audit a conversational system does not make sense. Developers between jobs make the best auditors. Long standing audit groups tend to become obsolete.

Why Not Have Audits?

Audits are disruptive. The project manager will tell you flat out that he or she is going to slip the schedule 2 days for every day the audit lasts. The disruption is too great to absorb will be the thrust of the argument. Have the audit; do not accept the slip. "We'll see." is management's reply.

Audit Reports — Always Have an Oral Report

Both oral and written reports are essential. Time after time I found my auditors were willing to state verbally the depth of the problem, confusion, or incompetence, yet they were unwilling to put it in writing. Putting it in writing tones down the report to the extent that the message sometimes gets lost.

First Visit of an Audit or Inventory Team

When the team doing the audit first visits the development or support team, there are several guidelines I find useful.

1. Ask no leading questions. What the development manager chooses to present to you tells a great deal.
2. Listen for at least a day; interact the second or third day.
3. Note who does the presenting. Is it a salesy V.P., or *the* software manager?
4. Note the vocabulary being used. For example, does the word "modular" get used? "Information hiding"?
5. Insist that all terms be defined.
6. Ask to see the current organization chart, *and* the resumes of the key players.
7. Ask to *see* the standards documents; note dates and updates.

PEOPLE AND TOOLS

The software development manager must plan many things, but two things are overiding — the people to do the job, and the tools to do it. People planning falls into two main parts — the quality and the quantity. On large developments we need both! The key to success is quality. The right people make or break the project. They are worth whatever you pay them; they are rare!

Once the plans and designs are in place, then the quantity of people are needed. Here again we run into trouble. The world suffers an acute shortage of software developers. Do not underestimate the severity of this shortage. If you plan on 120 man-years over a three-year period, but can never find more than 20 qualified people to hire, your

120 man-years may require 6 years. Software companies are experiencing the same problem, so contracting out your programming does not guarantee avoiding this problem.

Tools can make or break a project, as they have a great effect on the productivity of the people. We have covered tools in the previous chapters.

The most critical tools are the computers to generate the object code, the software to run on those computers, the people who understand how to keep the tools running, the test system, and the configuration control mechanisms.

We frequently encountered problems with too little horsepower in the CPU of the support systems, resulting in poor turnaround and poor production. Poor tools can usually never be overcome; schedule slips and costs rise.

Being among the first to use *new* languages or operating systems is usually a frustrating and very expensive experience.

BUY IT OR BUILD IT

The decision as to whether to buy or build your software is a most critical one. Let's look at the decision first, and the directions it leads us in, and then look at the components of the decision. (See Fig. 6-23.)

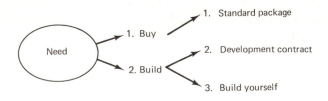

Figure 6-23.   Buy or build the software.

Any decision to build or buy rests primarily on the availability of software development people. If my organization does not have people, then there is no choice but to buy. Even if we have people, we may need to decide on which projects to use them.

In general, if a standard package can be purchased that will work on my system, I should buy it. This conserves the scarce, and getting scarcer quickly, resource of software developers. It may waste hardware, but that is usually acceptable.

A standard package has advantages and disadvantages, as shown in Table 6-3. Despite the disadvantages, if we have the chance, we should use the standard software.

TABLE 6-3. Standard Software Packages Pros and Cons

Advantages	Disadvantages

• Available now
• Updated and corrected by seller
• Saves my software developers
  for other efforts
	• General, therefore not tuned
	  Wastes some computer resources
	  Does not quite fit application
	• Dependent on some other organization

Develop Ourselves or Contract Out

If the software must be developed, should we do it ourselves or contract it out? Let's list (Table 6-4) the pros and cons and then look at them.

TABLE 6-4. Develop Software Ourselves or Contract for It?

	Develop In-House	Contract Out
Pros	More control Less cost Continued-development team in place	Saves people resources More skilled and experienced developers
Cons	Uses up people resources	Continued development more difficult

How to Contract for Software Development

First, a *good clear* description of what you want is essential — for you and for the bidders. If you need help developing this, buy it. It will save you tons of money down the road. Then you want written proposals, with prices, the approach, the design, people commitments, and contractual terms. Note the word commitment after the word people. Demand to know *who* will work on your job if they get the contract. Then you want oral presentations from the few finalists you select.

Here you want to evaluate the program manager — the highest level, full time person on your job. He or she will make the project a success or failure.

How much of the presentation of the orals is orchestrated and run by the program manager? Is he or she crisp? Articulate? Knowledgeable? Does he or she avoid questions or hit them head on? All the characteristics listed above for the program manager should be carefully looked for. If they do not come out, ask nasty questions and watch the reactions as well as the answers.

Then you want to evaluate the corporate organization *and* its top manager *and* their commitment to this project. With the dearth of programmers, top management support is usually essential to a successful project, and your project is in competition with all the others this organization is performing.

Is top management *at* the orals? What *precisely* did they state? Record the oral presentations. This usually makes people more careful in their statements.

Is the organization large enough to do the job? Does it have reserves of people and technology to draw on when the crises hit? Have they been through similar projects?

Can you push them around with your tough questions? If you can, worry. You want managers, not salesmen, on your project. Then, and only then, get into the design, understanding, and other aspects of the proposed approach.

Who are the other managers for your project? What is their availability? Are they on other projects now? Are they bidding for any other projects? Are they committed to *this* project?

Does this organization have software standards? Published? When published? Updated? Used? Consistent? Or are they a smooth bunch of talkers, who know all the buzz words?

What project control methods do they employ? Is the program manager familiar with them? Has he or she used them? Does he or she have examples of where they applied?

Does the program manager know the pitfalls of software projects? Does he or she know that requirement confusion is the biggest danger? Be careful not to put words in his or her mouth.

Regarding the contract, is the company resisting being pushed into a more binding written agreement? Hopefully yes, as this indicates they have experience and know the pitfalls of large scale development. To be too willing is often ignorance, or worse, a buy-in.

After the contract is signed, you lose much of your clout. Your contractor is your partner of sorts, and you dump that partner only with a great deal of pain. You and the performing organization become a team. Your leverage sinks. It costs *you* to change contractors, to sue, to go to court.

One technique for keeping your leverage high is to call the top person in the performing organization once a month and ask to review the project with him or her, or just have lunch. This ensures an internal review at high levels, and this shapes up the project overall. The project manager may fume that you are going over his or her head but it is worth it.

These techniques are summarized in Table 6-5.

TABLE 6-5.   How to Select a Contractor

1. Oral *and* written Proposals required
2. Contract form is very important
3. Program manager, *not* the company, is key
4. Standards — do they have them?
       Published?
       Followed?
5. Availability of people
6. Commitment of management
7. Experience
8. Staying power/reserves

The Type of Contract

The cost-plus contract is the only way to contract for a large type
III, IV or V, with one exception which we'll get to in a moment. The
cost-plus contract has been a standard in development work in the US
Government for decades. It has withstood the test of time because it is
fair to both contractor and buyer. It is used when it is not possible to
state the requirements or development processes with enough precision to go with a fixed price. The one exception is when a buyer can
purchase a large type III, IV or V *that is exactly* like a system now in
use. This happens, but rarely.

I advise my clients *not* to insist on fixed-price contracts when the
requirements are not precisely and exhaustively spelled out. To do so
drives away responsible developers and opens the door to novices or
worse.

WHAT TO DO WHEN IT GOES TO HELL

When it is clear that the software development is in trouble, the first
thing we want to know is why. It is often because of misestimates; it is
often due to confused requirements, and it is sometimes inadequate
management. We have already commented on how to manage requirements and on estimation.

Changing managers is easy enough to do, but not always productive. It is always a major disruption. And the new manager often
doesn't work out either. Yet there are times when there is no other
choice. Often I found managers with very successful track records who
simply had run into a dry spell in their lives and were not the same per-
formers they had been last year. Sometimes they had simply hit their
Peter Principle level of incompetence — this job was the one too big for

them. Removing the manager always sent shock waves through the rest of the team. "If it happens to him or her, it can happen to me." So this is the last solution that should be tried.

Before that, try to beef up the staff of the project manager. Add a manager of requirements. Add a design manager. Add a production manager! Sometimes — often — this does the trick.

When it doesn't, and we have to put in a new manager, we want to be right. We don't want to come back the next year and change the top person again.

Finding a Replacement Manager!

There is a scent of failure about a project where the top person is being changed. It has already "got" one top person; there are serious problems. Why should anyone wish to walk into that environment? Anyone with a reputation and track record knows that that environment is risky, slippery, and full of land mines — and that it is full of 80-100-hour weeks, trauma, friction, and sheer struggle. *New* people may see it as a chance to make a name, to leap ahead, but they are *new* — untested, untried. There are in this day and age too few good proven software development managers. It is not a simple problem.

The Out-of-Control Big One

The *out-of-control-big-one* seems like a moonless, midnight, parachute drop of half-crazed Watusis! People are in chaos! Sleeping in the office; crazed; explosive; fighting; quitting — dedicated to making the Watusi drop in total darkness work — but obviously unable to control anything but the most immediate action. This is not a *rare* occurrence. Schedule is met by throwing away function. The *operators* then *do* much of the functions by feel, by brilliance, by guess. But it works! And it is declared a success. Sometimes it doesn't work and the project is either delayed a year or so or abandoned. Many projects have been abandoned after expenditures of *$50 million or more.*

And sometimes, even though it is a success, the software is such a mess that is must be redone. The development team starts anew immediately after delivery of the software.

SOFTWARE STANDARDS

Every large software development group should have a set of standards for software. Every corporate entity should have a set of software standards, hierarchically structured so they do not impose restrictions not needed. Every large corporation should have a Director of Software. Every set of standards should be documented, distributed, and *enforced* by audits. Continuous education is essential.

Any sizeable software group not doing these things is not going to produce quality software consistently. It may do so accidentally at times, because a few managers really know how to do things, but it will not be consistent. Software development can be greatly improved by the imposition of engineering disciplines.

In software, techniques that are commonplace elsewhere are looked upon as radical innovation. IBM gave one of its employees a $75,000 award for the idea of having in-process-work reviews by peers and management (called "walkthrough"), a process commonplace in industrial activities.

Rapid advances have occurred in software development practice, so rapid that most software development shops have been left far in the past. It requires investments, commitment, and strong management to move an established programming group into the realm of good commercial practice.

Standards should be hierarchical. The standards for a hardware-intensive software should not be as stringent as those for software-intensive products.

A consistent vocabulary and a consistent set of guidelines go a long way to maximizing the output of the scarce resource of software developers.

The following set of "standards" (Table 6-6) is a set for a large product or project development effort. There are exceptions to all rules, but this would be a start. Are they in force? Published/Followed? Understood? Updated? By whom?

The standard modularization of software (e.g., operating systems) has entered the everyday work of data processing and, although we do not think of them as standards, they are in effect just that — a standard way of doing things and a standard division of work to be done.

The most important reason to use a data base management system is to facilitate change and to save programmer effort.

No Free Lunch — Standards Cost in the Early Phases

The software development phase will take longer and cost a bit more, perhaps even a lot more, because of the standards that we are insisting on. So might the use phase. We may have to burn a few more CPU cycles to execute overhead functions that we have added in order to get our modularity and our readability. We may take a bit more memory. Then why do it? For the savings in the continued develop-

TABLE 6-6.   Software Engineering Practices

1. Operating system software
2. Data base management systems software
3. Communications system software
4. I/O software
5. Display software
6. Inquiry software

Standard modularization of software

7. Configuration control used
8. Quality assurance
9. Documentation showing program function by subprogram
10. Block diagram of equipment and program relationships with internal and external data flow
11. High order languages
12. Use of analysis and estimating resources needed (CPU, memory)
13. Use of structured programming
14. Module size — small, strong-functionality, information hiding
15. List of design constraints and design principles
16. Frequent walkthroughs
17. Use of librarian
18. Patches in object *and* source
19. Use of automated support tools
20. Design for performance: a. Functional: percent of stated requirements met
    b. Technical: accuracy; approach, proof of algorithms
    c. Operational: failure recovery
    d. Performance: (time) meet time constraints

ment phase. We gain so much in this phase that it outweighs the cost of the other two.

A Weakness for Fads

Perhaps because the field is so new it is prone to accept the latest fad as the new marvelous advance that will solve so many of the problems. Perhaps it is the media, in their race to sell magazines, that ballyhoo this or that as *the new method.* Perhaps it is the practitioners, — or is it the researchers — who want their names in the magazines, who write the articles that say such and such is the new touchstone of success.

Probably it is all of these. But the wise manager knows that pioneers get killed a lot, and the wise manager waits until the latest whizbang has been thoroughly understood and well supported before utilizing it.

The manufacturer is not an adequate measure of reliability. How many users suffered when IBM mangled the first releases of OS 360? TSS for the Model 67? The software for the Series 1?

Networks, universal compilers, and distributed data processing are but few of the fads that have swept through the industry.

Often it is the higher management who rush to the fads. At the opposite extreme, the technicians, the programmers, resist the new techniques. Yet within their own area, programmers must sometimes be restrained! Or else, like children with marvelous building blocks, they'll have fun and build in delightful, intricate, involved, and undecipherable ways. They will write three-page nested DO-LOOPS!

A three-page nested do-loop is a logical nightmare. It represents something much more complex than:

> LITOTES, a double negative, or multiple negative, as in a sentence by Harold Laski: "I am not, indeed, sure whether it is not true to say that the Milton who once seemed not unlike a seventeenth-century Shelley had not become, out of an experience ever more bitter each year, more alien to the founder of that Jesuit sect which nothing could induce him to tolerate."*

Now the three-page nested do-loop may work beautifully. And if we have a tooth pick or hammer program, no problem. Pat the programmer on the head. But if we have a program that we must return to and modify, shoot him or her. We have a logical nightmare to untangle before we can modify or add.

Resistance to Change

The programmers and managers often resist the proven new ideas. They are uncomfortable. The people doing the work seem to prefer known sloppy slap-dash methods than the rigorous ones. They prefer to be magicians, not mechanics.

A commonplace occurrence is that the very idea of software standards is rejected by the incumbent software manager. He or she dismisses the standards with either the comment "I'm already doing that," or "We don't need that kind of overhead." The incumbent is often an "obsolete-producer." The key here is that he or she *is a producer*! By some means or another — he or she *gets* the thing running. He or she became the boss, the leader, by success — and these new ideas are strange and threatening. They may take away some of the magic that he or she has performed. They may seem likely, these new techniques, to create competition for the top job.

The big boss knows nothing about all these strange words. Given a choice, the boss sticks with the producer, obsolete or not! And the new techniques await some other management team.

Resistance to change is not always wrong. As we have seen, this

---

*David Hackett Fischer, *Historians Fallacies — Toward a Logic of Historical Thought* (New York: Harper & Row, Publishers, Inc., 1970).

new field is prone to snake-oil solutions. Prudent management does not rush in and adopt the latest technique being featured in the media. But prudent management does not resist the new *proven* techniques that have been stabilized and in use for two or three years.

Humpty Dumpty said, regarding words, "The question is, who's to be in charge"? He may well have been speaking of software development, and who is in charge? Management, or the troops? Because the field is so new, and practitioners so scarce, the troops often make the key decisions.

Are the inmates to run the asylum? It takes tough, strong management to *force* the adoption of proven new techniques. The established resist new technologies. These new technologies threaten their positions. Who needs these new things? They're not proven! "Boss, you don't understand these things!" See Table 6-7.

TABLE 6-7.   The Natural Enmity of Programmers and Managers

Programmers Want	Managers Want
Beauty in the program	Performance of the program
"Neat" solutions	Understandability of solution
Intricacy	Simplicity
Tightness	Easy to use software
Artistic solutions	Easy to change software

Change Is Initially Expensive

We issued an edict in the early 1970s that all new programs undertaken within the 4400 person IBM Federal System Center would be performed using structured programming. We found that we had to educate the 2600 or so programmers and managers. That was 5200 man weeks or 100 years of effort and expense, not to count the logistics, trainers, materials, etc.

We had a control center where we reviewed once a week with the Director of Structured Programming Training the progress, the plan, the schedule, the resources, the needs. We provided consulting help to projects adopting the new techniques. Classes are not enough to effect such a change.

Then we had to audit *all* projects to ensure that the new techniques were indeed being used. It was a massive effort, without which we would have accomplished only lip service to the technology of structured programming. Was the effort worth it? Absolutely. It is not easy to introduce structured programming or any new technical methodology. It takes money and people and resources and dedication — and it is fiercely resisted by the practitioners.

Lip Service.   No one today would think of arguing against structured programming. They did in the early 1970s, as we saw. But now many organizations claim to be using structured programming and they are not.

Overuse of the Word "Structured."   Structured programming has done so much good for the profession of programming that I hesitate to write anything against it, but structured programming is primarily a tool for programming in the small. It does not help as much on the design of the system in the large. It makes programming visible and more manageable for the reasons that we enumerated but it is most useful in the design and programming efforts.

We must take care not to confuse methods that apply in one of the parts of software development with other methods that are to be used in other parts of the process. Marketing people have pinned the name "structured" on just about any technique in sight for just about any purpose or use. If it is "structured" it sells.

Structured design has nothing to do with structured programming. It does not naturally fit with structured programming any more than with any other way of programming.

Structured requirements is yet another term entering the field. It is entirely separate from structured programming and from structured design. And now we see structured documentation, structured English, and on and on.

If we can *define* the term, as Mills, Linger and Witt did for structured programming, then *perhaps* it may be a useful term. In general, it smacks of too much salesmanship, which is unfortunate as the technique often has some merit — it is just not 'structured.'

This is not to say that these new techniques are bad. Many of them are very good. It is just that the name implies a compatibility that does not exist.

DEVELOPMENT OR CONTINUED DEVELOPMENT AS THE DOMINANT COST PHASE

The total cost of a software system is often broken into only two parts — the cost of the original development and the cost of the continuing development. (See Fig. 6-24.)

The continued development (maintenance) can cost by far the majority of the dollars, up to 70 to 80 percent. But it also can cost a very, very small percentage. This swing obviously depends on several factors. The most critical are the length of time the software will be in use — 1 year or 20 years; the stability of the external environment affecting the

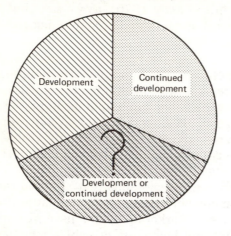

Total cost of software development

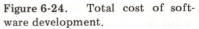

Figure 6-24.   Total cost of software development.

software; and the quality of the software produced in the development cycle.

Too many people show charts stating that "70 percent of the cost of software is encountered in the support phase." This is an over-simplification! There are many software systems where this just is *not* true!

ONE REASON FOR OPTIMISTIC ESTIMATES

Why do we estimate optimistically? Too often we fear that if we stated our real estimates, management would kill the project. So we estimate optimistically, based on everything going right. Once committed, management will probably see it through, and they do not understand software anyway. So we continue our practice of missing schedules and budgets.

Of course, all of this is true of hardware projects as well! Does software have more than the normal number of grave problems that beset all complex activities? Yes, because it is new, and therefore un-disciplined, as most new technologies are. And it is abstract.

When a total complex project is in jeopardy, and perhaps about to be canceled because of cost, the developers sharpen their pencils and do optimistic estimating. Software gets cut the deepest because it is usually the least understood. To cut the satellite cost by the percentage that software gets cut would be too obvious.

RESEARCH IN SOFTWARE

Software R&D from the early 1950s to the late 1960s was aimed at helping the programmer. Software R&D since the 1970's has *begun* to be aimed at helping the software manager. Software R&D must begin to help the system manager, specifically in the requirements definition and in the design for evolution.

There are beginning to be tools that help in the front-end of the process. For design, we have the tools of finite state machine notation, design languages, formal grammars, abstract machines, and research is beginning in the requirements definition area. There is a start in this area, but much more is needed.

The majority of the money to be spent in software research for the next several years should go into these front-end areas of the development process.

The language area of the development effort gets too much money. It is funded as heavily as it is because it now has a constituency — there are a great many language experts.

THE INABILITY OF THE TECHNOLOGY TO DEPICT SOFTWARE

A *program* is a list of instructions that will cause a computer to do work. A program can exist in a static state — written or printed — or in a dynamic state as electrons in a memory device. This point is significant.

Many people tend to think of the program in its static state, where it looks much like many other written lists. It is, to an extent, palpable and tangible.

Other people think of a program in its dynamic form — *in* the computer, where it is in violent progress, being executed at the rate of millions of instructions per second. *And* the path, the choice, of the instructions to be executed, is constantly changing as the data and events present to the running program different situations which the program recognizes and chooses its course of operation accordingly.

A pale analogy is between a series of photographs, a film, and a moving picture. A printed program is a totally inadequate representation just as a photograph of a jet fighter, or a list of its parts, is an inadequate representation of the plane and as a number of still photographs is an inadequate representation of a movie film.

The fact that a program can be in several forms simultaneously is a source of confusion. Not only a source of confusion to the newcomer,

Time →

	Design			A Program	A program	A program	A program
	x or x or x						
	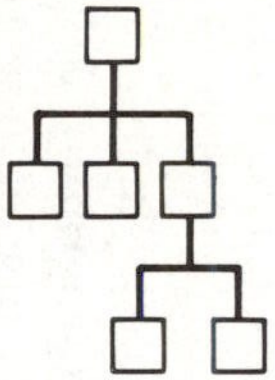	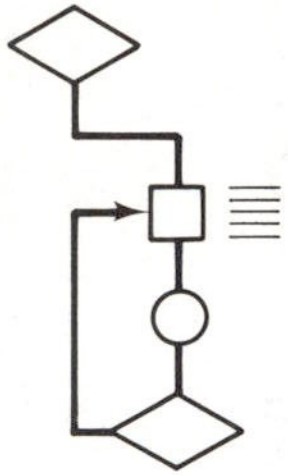	Start CALC Gropay DOX FIND	GP = Hours* Rate 1 (GR 2,000, Then EXCEPT	CLA GROPA add bonus sub	011011011101111 101110111 – – – – – – 101111011111	
In neurons	Drawn + text	Drawn + text	Written	Written or printed or in memory	Written or printed or in memory	Written or printed or in memory	In elecrons, in machine
Concept	Design HIPO or charts	Flow charts	Design in program design language (PDL)	Compiler statements	Assembly code	Object code	Object code
Concept	Design not a program	Design not a program	Design not a program	A program	A program	A program	A program
	Not machine processable	Not machine processable	Machine processable not translatable	Translatable by machine to object code not executable	Translatable by machine to object code not executable	Executable by machine	Being executed by computer

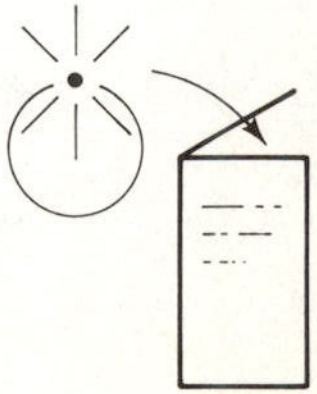

Figure 6-25. The various embodiments of designs and programs.

but a source of errors in real systems as one form often gets modified and the others do not. Over time there can be great confusion as to *which* version of the program is *the* version. (See Fig. 6-25.)

DEVELOP SOFTWARE AS WE DEVELOP HARDWARE?

Why is it that we can build large, incredibly powerful computers that are very reliable, but we seem to have major difficulties every time we build a large software system? There are major differences between software development and hardware development. Basically, there are two major differences:

1. Hardware benefits greatly from the production phase; the long, systematized manufacturing cycle that follows the development of the hardware. Hardware *development* suffers from the same difficulties as software development. No one makes money on the development of hardware.
2. Software is unconstrained in its interconnections; hardware has the laws of physics as constraints. You can only interconnect so many things to so many other things. Not so with software.

The *development phase* of a product does what it's name implies — it causes change to occur in a desired direction. It is a creative activity; not a disciplined, predictable activity. Surprises are expected. This surprise-filled phase is true of both hardware and software development. Hardware developers cannot predict time and cost, and they usually lose money on development contracts, and make it up on the production run. Software developers never get a production phase.

Engineers, in frustration over software, wonder aloud as to why software people can't manage the way hardware people do. There is some validity to this, and we'll get to its truth in a moment, but first we must show that the idea is more wrong than right for large software.

Hardware can be touched, felt and seen. Software is abstract. One can never physically see or touch large software programs. Holding a listing or a tape is but to hold a representation of the program.

Software is invisible. It is even more invisible than moving pictures. Consider a motion picture, made up of millions of individual still photos that are moved at high speed past a light and projected onto a screen. Seeing the film itself — the 35 or 70 mm strip or stills — is not to *see* the movie. The result is the measure of the movie film, and the result is the movie seen on the screen.

The same idea is more true of the program or software. Seeing static instructions written or printed is useful, but it is *not* the result.

The end is the *working* program, not the static representation of the working program.

We cannot *see* the program with even a thousand glimpses, if it is large. A million lines of code is over 8000 feet of paper! Even with Superman's eyes all we would see is a static representation. Until it is *activated* or run, the flow, interactions, connections, boundaries, etc., *cannot* be seen.

The running program, like the running movie, is perishable and not capturable. It is a series of events over time. We need its static representation to reproduce it, to study pieces of it, to modify it.

We would not need a static representation of the program *if* we knew it was correct *and* if we knew it would never be changed, and if we had a way of being sure we could reproduce it from its storage medium at will — that we would not lose it. We need new techniques to help us visualize large running software systems.

With a stored set of instructions, there is no limitation on variations of sequences, on interconnections. I can switch from anywhere to anywhere. I have *completely variable interconnectivity*. And since I can read in new instructions from tape or disk, I have no real limit on the number of instructions. Sequences of instructions numbering in the millions are becoming more and more common in our work-a-day world.

The tyranny of physical interconnections is gone. Up until stored instructions, machines were told what to do by their physical construction. If these machines could conditionally branch, they were special-purpose computers. Jon von Neumann's 1946 memo calls this point out, that before the general-purpose computer, its predecessors *"were instructed what to do by their construction."* (Emphasis mine.)

Physical limitations inhibit the number of possible paths or sequences that can be selected. The piano is hardware, it has 88 keys. The music sheet is the instructions to the player to follow if he or she wishes to make music and the number of different sheets is unlimited. And the idea of "correctness" is subjective. What is pleasant to one person is not to another. But it *is* music.

Another analogy is the dictionary (the hardware) and a novel — the interconnection of the words. The dictionary is precise and bounded, even if very large. But with a limited number of words we can write instructions to do anything, or unlimited fiction. (See Table 5-7.)

Engineers are trained to build complex machines; programmers are often not technically trained and do not know the advanced tools to handle complexity. Software developers often put complex system development in the hands of people not trained to the task. This should be corrected. To build large operations/process systems, we should have managers trained in the technical disciplines.

TABLE 6-8.   Differences between Hardware and Software

Limited Connections	Unlimited Connections
Hardware	*Software*
Piano	Melodies, music
Dictionary	Novels, poems, etc.
Film and Projector	Movies
Computer	Programs

Software is a new human endeavor. It has not been practiced for any length of time and its practitioners are still learning how to control it. Its vocabulary is still far too small and confused.

Software is soft and can be changed. People will undertake to modify a program when they would never dream of modifying the hardware already installed. We rarely produce hardware in a fashion to make it easily changeable, yet this is precisely what we want to do, and can do, with software. Software is fundamentally different from hardware here, except for hardware-intensive software.

Recall, or reread at this point, page 39 where we pointed out the pervasive differences in the life cycle of hardware as opposed to the life cycle of software.

Software has no production piece in the life cycle. It sometimes has a support piece in its life cycle. These two facts have a profound effect on the economics of software in the everyday world.

Similarities between Hardware and Software

Reliability.   To achieve hardware reliability in the environment that Department of Defense computers must operate in, the computer manufacturer must build the computer differently, test it more, and use different components. Usually this reliability/environmentalization doubles the cost of the commercial version of the same computer. The same is true of software. It costs far more to deliver the same function if it must be fail safe.

Space.   When the computer will go into space or be airborne, in addition to ruggedization it usually must be as small and as light as it can be made. Again different components are selected. And again the price is approximately doubled. The cost of software is substantially increased if the size of the instructions (the number) must be shrunk because of lack of memory space to house it.

7

SOME ADVANCED
COMPUTER CONCEPTS

The software field, like all new fields, is easy prey for the half-baked idea, for the neat-sounding new, better way. *Why* should people go to distributed data processing? Why go to multiprocessing? Few people can define these ideas, much less list their benefits! Our first reaction to all such neat-sounding new approaches should be skepticism.

When I was general manager of my IBM group I was told by my manager of internal data processing (we did a payroll for 15,000 people nationwide) that we should "buy" a remote computer to use as a device to off-load the central computer, and do "remote computing." I said "Fine, show me the dollar savings." Three meetings — a total of 4½ hours later — we agreed that there were no dollar savings and there was indeed some extra cost, and there "might" be some operational efficiencies. The efficiencies were nonessential (my judgment). It should never have taken so long. It proved to me that my manager of internal processing was not a crisp thinker.

MULTIPROCESSING AND MULTIPROGRAMMING

Multiprogramming is a systems software technique that manages the computer in a way to switch from one program (payroll, for example) to another (inventory, for example) without loading and unloading either program. It *increases* CPU utilization. Dozens of programs can be in memory simultaneously, and run intermittently. It greatly reduces CPU idle time caused by waiting for disk access or I/O actions.

Multiprocessing is the use of more than one CPU, attached to a common memory or memories, *with one operating system in control.* A multiprocessor is almost always multiprogrammed.

There is a master-slave way of using two CPUs. There is a front-end, back-end use of two CPUs to increase throughput, but here two operating systems are used, and it is not multiprocessing by our definition. A high performance CPU may be coupled to a slow CPU with a lot of I/O units. The slow CPU would do all the I/O functions, leaving the large fast CPU to chew up the queued-up work. This is often called an ASP system, for attached support processor system. This type of system has declined as multiprogramming operating systems have appeared.

Performance of Multiprocessing

If every CPU in the multiprocessor was a 1 MIP machine — each could perform 1 million instructions per second — and there were four CPUs, then we should have a 4-MIP system, right? Wrong. There is a blocking effect that occurs when more than one CPU is attempting to access a bank of memories. There are lock-out requirements of some applications that must be adhered to to protect data integrity when more than one CPU tries to access the same data file or the same physical memory. There is a degradation in performance that occurs that is not well measured or understood. (See Fig. 7-1.)

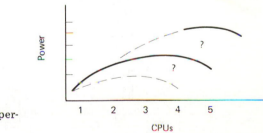

Figure 7-1. Multiprocessing performance.

When someone states that such and such multiprocessor has 16 CPUs, it is a good bet that either (1) it is performing on a very specialized problem with very defined boundaries or (2) the computer is a laboratory curiosity that will not see much use in real application. There is too much interference in a 16-CPU system on general data processing problems.

There are some wonderful examples of multiprocessors in use in real time systems. The FAA En-Route Air Traffic Control System has four CPUs, four programmed I/O channels, and dozens of separate memories. It began operating in 21 centers in a multiprocessing mode more than 6 years ago. It is very expensive software development and the fail-soft features (continuing in a degraded capacity mode when a hardware unit fails) are not yet programmed in full by any means. But multiprocessing does work.

Availability

Before multiprocessing, the way we assured reliability was to duplex — to put two complete systems side by side and have each run the entire job. This was done on dozens of systems and it worked just fine. The Air Force BMEWS — the Ballistic Missile Early Warning System — and most of the NASA Space Flight installations of the early 1960s were built this way. There are still some systems being built this way, but many fewer in overall percentage.

Why? What is the drawback to such an approach to assured performance? Cost, primarily. The second system is really not doing anything unless the first one is disabled.

There is a fascinating technical exercise we can plow through to try to determine if duplexing is more reliable than multiprocessing. To take a simple case, consider a multiprocessor with only two memories and only two CPUs, and let's ignore the I/O channels, etc. (See Fig. 7-2.) The only difference in the system is that the memory units are shared by (or accessible to) each processor. Therefore, one could lose the CPU from system 1 and the memory from system 2 and yet the system would still operate. Now we must realize that we are discussing the *probability* of the availability of the system for use.

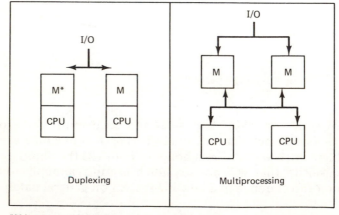

*M is memory

Figure 7-2.   Duplexing — Multiprocessing.

We must take into account the mean time between failure of each *unit* and the probability of *simultaneous* failures, *and* the added circuitry to handle the switch from one unit to the second, and the failure rate of this added circuitry, and the mean time to repair each unit.

It may seem intuitively obvious that the multiprocessor has a higher availability, but such is not the case — at least not always. Research and calculation — extensive calculation — must be done. In 1963 a deep study of this by a special group in IBM research, called together by Vin Learson (V P of IBM, later to be Chairman of the Board) to answer this exact question with respect to the FAA RFP then out for the En-Route Air Traffic Control System of the United States.

The Engineering Division of IBM was arguing vehemently that duplexing gave more availability — that it yielded a system that was more available. As proposal manager for the FAA bid, I was arguing that the multiprocessor was more reliable (because the RFP called for a multiprocessor specifically). We spent many hours with the Research Committee. They reported — to my astonishment — the duplex as the more available system. I could not believe my ears that wintry day in Poughkeepsie, N.Y. in 1963. Learson was about to decide that IBM would bid a duplex system. "But the RFP asked for multiprocessor!" For some reason, I had never made this point this clear to Learson. He asked if all assembled agreed that the RFP asked for a multiprocessor. All did. Learson decided to bid the multiprocessor. We won the bid.

Reasons for Multiprocessing

There are three main reasons for multiprocessing — the first two are easily achievable, the third is extremely difficult.

The first reason for multiprocessing is *increased power* (internal and throughput power) at the highest performance levels of computer technology. If we can not build a faster computer, we can put two CPUs into one configuration.

The second reason is *non-disruptive growth*; to have the ability to add power without ripping up the room and disrupting operations pulling out one CPU while installing a more powerful, software compatible CPU.

The third reason is to achieve *fail-soft operation*. Not fail safe, but fail soft. Fail safe means to have one back-up unit for every critical unit you have in the system, and if there is one failure, then the back-up unit is brought on-line and operation continues. Fail soft means to have multiple failures modes, using the multiple CPUs and memories as back-up units, discarding pieces of the function after each successive failure is encountered. Fail soft is easily achieved in hardware, but is almost impossible to achieve in software. The possible combinations of failures mounts to very large numbers very quickly. One memory failure isn't hard to program for, but when the second and the third fail, we are confronted with hundreds of possible combinations and we must program for each. The recovery program becomes unlimited very quickly. If we define one level of back-up as fail safe, that is doable. If we define two levels of failure as the condition we wish to protect for, and we have dozens of different units that can fail, we are in deep trouble.

DATA INTEGRITY

If I alone use my bank account, and I have several checks to deduct from the amount that was there as of last night, I simply do them in sequence with one computer. But if there are only two checks, I give you one, and I keep one, then we must not both be at different terminals up-dating the account at the same time or we will get the wrong result.

If I have $575 in checking and my check is for $75 and the one you have is for $100, and I go look up the balance and see it was $575, and sit down and do the subtraction, and you go get the balance and get $575 and begin to do the subtraction, we have trouble. I get $500 and you get $475. Whoever *writes* the new value into the master record *last* has written an incorrect balance. The integrity of the process has not been protected. *We cannot allow up-dating of a master record by more than one up-dater at a time.* We must lock up the balance value while anyone is up-dating it. This is true for many types of data — airplane positions, medical data, etc. The same thing is true of multiple computers. Whether the multiple computer is a multiprocessor, or a distributed processing system, or a network, we must protect the integrity of the data.

How do we do that? With systems programs.

Distributed processing is easy to accomplish; to have a distributed data base in real time use is *very* difficult.

The hardware solutions for these advanced configurations have been available for decades. There is just no problem in these areas with the hardware.

The problem in achieving the use of computers in these configurations is in the software development in real time systems. For normal usage, vendor delivered systems software is perfectly adequate. We must be careful here as to how we state this software difficulty. It is not that difficult to create the software to make these configurations work — it is *very* difficult to create the software so as to achieve fail soft degradation in performance.

The most important question to ask about these advanced configurations of computer is *why* are we going to use them. Too often people will accept, or even demand, these configurations without any idea of why they are taking on the added burdens of implementing unusual systems. Far too many users who want to use the latest popular, advanced configuration cannot even state the supposed benefits.

NETWORKS

When a number of computers — usually geographically dispersed — are connected to each other via communications lines or channels — we have a network. There are basically two reasons for a network.

1. As a communication mechanism. In this mode the computers are a means to an end, and the network exists to pass information.
2. As a computer network. Here the reason for the network is computing, and the communications serve the computing function.

Obviously there is overlap between these two types. The FCC has struggled with the overlap for decades.

The first type — the communication network — should be cost justified on its own terms. It is either worth its cost or it's not. And if there is a less expensive way to control the system, computers should not be used. In the computer network, it is not easy to show that such a network is economically justified. The Advanced Research Projects Agency (ARPA) Network of the Department of Defense is a marvelous technological achievement, which proved that a network of many diverse computers could be connected together and the protocols written to make it all run correctly. But there are few, if any, such computer networks that are in profitable use in the private sector. Some big time sharing companies have found it more economical to use a central computer installation, with many computers at one site, and use a communication network to feed the data to the centralized site. Only one set of management, operators, guards, etc., are needed. There are other reasons for distributing the computers, besides economics. Reliability, protection from disaster or sabotage, and avoiding the burden of huge, complicated systems software are some good reasons.

The General Motors Network Bid

In mid-1974, I received a call from the IBM Data Processing Division: Would I have my best people spend a day reviewing the state of the proposal DPD was going to submit to General Motors? I would.

It was unusual for DPD to ask for assistance. Whoever named the parts of organizations "divisons" was prophetic! The GM proposal already had a mythology about it — its scale and complexity were said to be unprecedented.

So I, with four of my best designers and most experienced people, spent a day with the DP people struggling to respond to the GM request for proposal.

The RFP *was* big — 6 inches or so of paper — and the response was *big* — and complex. We spent hours going through networks — stars, rings, packets, SNAs — and hours of techniques to make these huge collections of dozens of millions of dollars of computers work together.

The DP people briefed us — and there were two things very obvious (1) technical competence and (2) confusion in goals.

Why should a large computer doing inventory, payroll, and production scheduling in city 1 interact with a large time sharing system in city 2? And why should both of them interface with a large scientific computer in city 3?

Because the RFP asks that we do! Presumably for load leveling, for sharing data, for. . . ?

There was no clear answer! How you interconnect and the protocols used depend on *why* you are "melding" all these computers together. The how follows the why.

Indeed, GM never awarded a contract! Even though IBM — and several others — had each spent a million dollars or so on the response.

General Motors was no newcomer to computers. Yet even this experienced user had been lured from safety by the siren call of the "new" techniques, "new" uses.

DISTRIBUTED PROCESSING?

There is and has been a role for distributed processing. But it must be justified; it is not a panacea, a new miracle drug. It has its place, but it must be justified. There is too much blind acceptance of these "new" approaches.

SUMMARY

All the rules and lessons we've seen thus far are still valid. The imperative to limit interactions is true for software modules, people, hardware modules, computers, distributed processors, or computers in a network.

If we are not very careful to estimate the size of the program to do intercommunication, we can find that the resulting system is used up

80 or 90 percent of the time to communicate — not to do work. Every time we add an independent executor (a computer or CPU) into a network, we increase the communications burden on the rest of the network. We must take care not to let this burden grow to the point that it cripples the processing.

The benefits *and* drawbacks to these *new* approaches must be carefully assessed *before* adopting them. The drawbacks are real. If they were not, the bulk of the systems being used today would be multiprocessors and distributed. They are not, for good reasons.

The developer who wants to automate with the newest and most newsworthy is an adventurer.

A PERSPECTIVE

Let me try to make some summary comments, without being too repetitious. And let me venture some predictions and some guidelines.

USE OF INDUSTRIAL TECHNIQUES IN SOFTWARE DEVELOPMENT

Software development is being controlled more and more, and some of the most powerful tools brought into play in the last several years are tried-and-true techniques used in the manufacturing world for decades. Some of these are:

Work breakdown structure
Configuration management and control
Traceability
Inspection (walkthroughs)
Quality control
Verification
Testing
Spot-audits
Project management

Software is slowly being inched out of its invisible state by the imposition (painful) of standards, rules, practices, standard parts (systems software), and other good management practices. The imposition of these techniques involves initial cost, but yields such significantly better results over the life cycle that every serious creator of software should embrace them as soon as possible. As we gain more and more control over software, I believe we will see even more industrial techniques being used.

The Director of Research of a Fortune 100 Corporation in the information business made a beautiful analogy recently about the state of software and the industrial revolution. Let's look at this analogy, as there are lessons to be learned from it.

Pre-Collectivization	Cottage industry. Each pottery maker did it all, in his or her cottage.
Collectives	Economy of scale in support functions. No change in basic manufacturer process. But now a central clay gathering group supplies clay to all pottery makers. A central sales group sells the products. But pottery is made the same way. This step is independent of the following steps.
Specialization of Labor	Certain functions given to people who are good at the function. Trim is done on all pottery by a special group of Trimmers. Adam Smith wrote in *The Wealth of Nations* that 10 unskilled men, each working independently, would be hard put to make one pin each in a day, but 10 men with the labor divided, can produce more than 48,000. This is the beginning of the concept of the assembly line.
Automation	Economies of scale allow funds to be expended to change from the basic processes done in the cottage. Furnaces and kilns are used on a scale undreamed of. Stamping processes are automated by windmill or steam-driven power.
Assembly Line	The separation of the total process into a series of processes that are done to every product at a set certain time.

Interchangeable Parts   In the late 1790s, Eli Whitney undertook to build 10,000 muskets in 2 years. Absurd, it was said. By 1807 he was producing 2000 a year, six times as many as the US Armory in Springfield, MA. The secret was the interchangeable part, made possible by the progress in metallurgy and machining. The interchangeable part became *one* of the fundamental practices of the assembly line.

These processes revolutionized production.

Software development is still in the early phases of its industrial revolution. We have collectivization, and some specialization of labor has occurred, and some automation, but we do not yet have fungibility, the interchangeable part. It is on its way; it is inevitable, even with software, but it is not here yet. (See Fig. 8-1.)

We are still learning how to organize to "produce" software. We are developing the tools and technologies simultaneously. We are proceeding at a great rate, faster probably than most imagine.

Yes	Somewhat	Beginning	Beginning	Not yet
↑	↑	↑	↑	↑
Collectivization	Specialization of labor	Automation	Assembly line	Interchangeable parts

Figure 8-1.   Software versus the steps in the Industrial Revolution.

VOCABULARY

Recently, I was introduced to a new Deputy Assistant Secretary of the Navy for whom I had been chairing a committee on computers. "The only thing I hate more than computers is software," he said. His antipathy was no surprise and such a reaction is usually in response to the utter incomprehensibility of software to most intelligent people. The software field is semantic swamp. There is no generally accepted vocabulary.

There are many striking names, and they are good; they stick in the mind and are easily remembered. But when they get misleading they are just plain bad.

"Inverted files" sounds like it is a clear label, but it is not. It is not a *file* at all, but a table *about* a file. It contains a logical description of the relationship between some fields of the file. "Operating System" and "Data Base" are not very descriptive. "Access Method" is not a method.

As technologists, we deserve the scorn of the practitioners of the more stable disciplines *only* if we do not *attempt* to be precise in our statements. That we know but do not take the trouble to delimit is inexcusable. Precision and clarity are the trademarks of understanding.

ORGANIZATION IMPERATIVES

This is what every serious information system organization should be doing. Software is becoming *the* differentiating item in the information systems arena. Up till now we have been talking about the project or product organization. What should a large corporation do organizationally with respect to software?

What To Do

Several important actions should be taken:

1. Create a corporate Director of Software.
2. Embark on a company wide project to educate key executives.
3. Establish software standards.
4. Avoid decisions at too low a level.

The Corporate Software Director

There should be a Director or Vice President of Software in every large corporation. Software is too important and the supply of practitioners so far short of demand that *every* large organization should have a lead software official. The organization that is *in* the information handling business is not going to fare well without a software official.

This person would have the following duties:

1. Set corporate level software standards.
2. Review and appraise division level software standards, plans, personnel, and review actual software development.
3. Conduct audits.

4. Control the expenditure of R&D dollars in software.

5. Advise top management on business opportunities and trends affected by software.

This is not a technical role. It is not a job for a software giant brain. That talent should be used elsewhere. This is a senior management job that requires business acumen, software knowledge, and managerial judgment. A software-only background is inadequate for the task.

When I visit a large corporation, I ask to see their software standards. I ask who is *the* person who looks over software the way the Vice President of Engineering oversees that function. Far too often the answer is blank looks; there is no such function being done. My conclusion is that the organization is not serious about software. Too often this is the result of ignorance on the subject.

Standards

Without standards at the corporate level, we allow splinter groups to charge off in all directions. They encounter the Tower of Babel problem when they attempt to talk to each other.

The key decisions about software should be made at the appropriate level, and must be reviewable and implementable. This demands standardization at a corporate level of *certain software practices* and *nomenclature*. Without this standardization, the fiefdom structure of software domains will continue for a much longer time. Any corporation that does not have *enforced* software standards is not seriously in the information business, whether they know it or not. Yet we must not let standards be imposed without study and senior judgment. There should be corporate, division, product, and project software standards. They should be compatible but not identical.

Low Level Decisions

Whether or not new functions can be added, whether the user should have selection options or functions, which functions, how many, how soon? These are the kinds of questions we expect product managers to make. And if you asked them, they'd tell you they certainly are making them. But audits of several products show the opposite. The product manager *asks* the software manager "when can we do such and such?" In most cases, the software manager goes two levels or more lower and asks a senior programmer. He or she "decides" whether or not a product improvement can be made, based on his or her set of criteria and work pressures.

Why? How did we get to this pass? Because there is no documentation in a form that can be read by anyone but the senior programmer!

This is clearly a management failure, and the problem is almost universal. Even the form of what constitutes adequate documentation is at issue in the software field.

Yet management will tell the auditors that all is well, a few problems exist, but nothing serious. They are not hiding the facts; in most cases they do not realize how bad things are. The idea that senior programmers are making key product introduction decisions would be rejected at once. Management does not understand what is happening to them.

A Painful Change

The changeover to a software orientation is a painful effort for two reasons. The first is simply the newness of the field. Most executives are ignorant of its dimensions and features. The second overlaps the first, but may surprise many. It is that most software practitioners are obsolete! *They* must be upgraded, or overlaid. The field is moving so rapidly that most of the producers of the software are still using 20-year old techniques. It is the middle-ages in software development for 90 percent of the developers.

Most will stoutly deny this and resist change. To some extent this reaction is defensive ("What is this new stuff?") and to some extent based on the expense to upgrade ("I can't afford the time or the money"). There is, of course, merit in this last point. Hence the need for the Corporate Director of Software.

The expense is not only in dollars, but in the pain of forcing valuable producers into new techniques that are strange to them. Many of the new techniques are technical, to handle the complexity of the effort. These new techniques are being taught in the good computer science college courses, but they scare "established" practitioners.

Educate Key Executives

We do not want to make software experts of all executives. We couldn't anyway, and it is not efficient. We *do* want to make *all* executives software conversant, able to absorb and judge presentations to them by expert subordinates.

This is eminently possible, and critical to the information systems company. Any executive who is not knowledgeable about software is in grave danger of becoming extinct.

A series of seminars and workshops, graduated in length for various levels of executives, should be underway at all times. A standard vocabulary for the corporation should be in place.

PREDICTIONS

1. Software will become *the* distinguishing factor between large information systems vendors.
2. The shortage of programmers will retard the use of the "chip." Today's shortage will get much worse.
3. Machine cycles will be so inexpensive that a "systems constructor" will appear. He or she will link quasi-general purpose programs into a "processing system." Crisper and more accurate interface mechanisms between programs must evolve first, but that is happening. The resulting system will be far from optimal — but it will work well enough indeed. It will be a *profligate* user of machine cycles, but no one will care!
4. The collision of the momentum of microelectronics and the inertia of software development will be the famous irresistible force and the immovable object, respectively. The result will be that software development *will* make tremendous advances. It must. Major breakthroughs in software development will occur.

New user languages will evolve; not the kind of language that Ada and Pascal represent, but what QBE — Query by Example — represents. Ada is very intricate, and difficult to learn. A user "instructs" the computer system through commands to get a result — a seat reserved, a missile fired, a course heading. A programmer "instructs" the computer system through statements to get an object program.

The gap between the high level languages used by the programmer and the languages used by the user is narrowing rapidly. It is a small change in concept to "capture" the user commands and generate object code, as opposed to simply process the commands.

Language will get progressively higher level. Users will become programmers, but not in the sense we use the word programmer today.

PROGRESS

We should not be surprised that software development is so hard. As we saw, *all* development is very difficult by definition. Were it predictable, it would not be development.

When we looked at bridges, plain, old, prosaic bridges, we found that 40 *per year* in the U.S. fell down in the 1870s. New technologies yield to human control very slowly.

Software is not only the latest very complex undertaking but it is made much more difficult as it is "invisible" and not apparent to any human sense. In addition, it is susceptible to hundreds of acceptable solutions or constructions.

Like all new fields, software suffers from the interconnected problems of semantic looseness and an abundance of charlatans and amateurs.

There has been great progress in software development in the past decade. Much more than anyone has stopped to identify. Huge systems work — and work well and reliably. Systems software, structured programming, languages, librarians, cross-compiling and hosting, have all been developed. We made programming visible. This sounds so trivial, yet it is so vital to controlling, to managing, software development.

Structured code can be read. A marvelous change.

Librarians keep code records. Programs belong to the organization, not the programmer. We can see what programmers have been doing. We can perform code inspections.

By making software visible, we've begun to make it more manageable. We've increased productivity.

We use the common code of operating systems and DBMSs. A vast amount of programming has been avoided by use of this body of programs by thousands of users.

We have thousands of computer science graduates who know the theory of many of the new techniques and tools.

It is only when we look back 10 years that we see how far we've come.

Management must not permit technological obfuscation. "You can no more explain what you don't know than you can come back from where you have not been." Far too often management allows themselves to be bullied by technologists using big but vague words. It is in the best interests of everyone to enforce meanings on *all* software words.

INDEX

A

"Abandon Function," 215
ACP, 58
Ada, 154, 171
Alexander, Christopher, 112
ALS, 10
American Airlines, 5
Apollo Project, 22, 67, 77, 120-1
APSE, 171
ARPA Network, 283
Assembler, 150
ATT, 4
Audits, 259-61

B

Baker, Terry, 140-1, 146, 168
Balancing a system, 33
Batch, 58
Benchmarks, 33
Big bang development, 43, 98-9
BMEWS, 280
Boundary conditions, 80
Bronowski, Jacob, 156, 158
Brooks, Frederick, 29, 70, 142, 247, 256

C

CARA/CLARA, 62, 110
Chief Programmer, 141, 168
Church, Alonzo, 156
Coder, 135
Compile, 163
    cross, 160
Compiler, 150
    selection, 175-7
Computer, definition, 14
Computer, general purpose, definition, 15
Concept of the Organization, 251
Configuration control, 254
Construction, 170-83
    automated, 172
Continued development, 7, 42, 45
Contract, 263
Cost of software:
    development, major contributors, 247
    development vs continued development, 271-2
    of O/S, 55-6
    of support software, 63
    per unit, 26
Cross compiling, 160

Cycle, life, 7, 35-6
    hardware, 39
    software, 35-46
        continued development
            phase, 36, 45-6
        development phase, 36,
            45, 89
        use phase, 36-7, 43-4,
            89, 118

D

Data base management systems, 52-4
Data integrity, 262
DBMS, 52-4
Department of Labor Directive, 135
Design, 111-48
    compromise, 143
    concurrent, 145
    detailing, 144
    device independence, 134
    documenting, 145
    embodiments of, 274
    information hiding, 132
    iterative, 143
    levels of, 128-30
        compartmentalization,
            130
        high level, 129
        interlevel mechanisms,
            136-8
        lowest level, 135
        macro, 130
        micro, 131
        middle level, 130
        triviality, 136-8
    module, 132
    new techniques, 147-8
        difficulty to introduce,
            147
        structured design, 147
    parts and process of, 122
    robust/user friendly, 145
    synthesis of, 126
Development of Software (see Soft-
    ware, development)
Device, independence, 134
Dickson, Paul, 256
Dijkstra, Edsger, 119, 156
Distributed Processing, 282, 284
Documentation, 92-3, 195

    embodiments of, 274
    flow charts, 202
    level of detail, 203
    self documenting, 196
    structured narrative, 7, 8, 196
    traceability, 200
DoD Instruction 5000, 31, 154
Douglas, Donald, 65
Drucker, Peter, 251

E

Error, example of, 187
Estimate, how to, 250
Estimating, 226, 240
    assumption for, 250
    optimistic, 272
Evans, Bob, 67
Evolutionary Development, 98-9,
    219-20
Evolve, plan to, 217
Exxon refineries, 73, 106, 111

F

FAA, 5, 58, 67, 69, 105, 111, 142-3,
    189, 217, 219, 258, 279-81
Ferrentino, Andrew, 42
Fischer, David Hackett, 269
Fixed schedule, law of, 97

G

Garage programs, 81
Gemini V, 187
General Motors bid, 283-4
Gies, Joseph, 70
Gödel, Escher, Bach, 157

H

Halprin, Lawrence, 123
Hardware intensive software, 82
Hardware, life cycle, 39
    versus software, 275-7
HIPO, 110, 147
Hoare, C.A.R., 155, 157
Hofstadter, Douglas, 156-57
HOL, 150
Hosting, 160-1, 163

I

IA, 62, 110, 147
IBM, 4, 18, 95, 97, 235, 270, 283
    Series 1, 258
    system 138, 4
    System Journal, 51, 234
Industrial Organization Theory and Practice, 214
Information hiding, 132
Instruction set architecture, 32
Introduction to Modern Linguistics, 149

J

Jackson method, 147
Jensen/Tonies, 142
JPS, 106, 111

K

KIPS/KOPS, 29

L

Languages, 149-77
    language, 149
    parole, 149
    power, 152
    proliferation, 154
    requirements documentation, 103
    selection, 175-7
Laski, Harold, 269
Librarian, 141, 169
    automated, 167
Lines of code:
    definition, 227
    mistakes, 233
    report format, 238
    warning, 237
Linger, Richard C., 138, 142
Litotes, 269
Living Systems, 213
Logic of the Mind, 156
Lowes, John Livingstone, 127
Lucas, F.L., 155
Lunar landing, 189
Lyons, John, 149

M

Manager of software development, 255
Man-month, definition, 230
Manning diagrams, 96-8
Martin, James, 65, 70, 71
McLuhan, Marshall, 16
Mealy, G.H., 51
Meier, Robert, 140
Miller, James Grier, 213
Mills, Harlan, 138, 140-2, 144, 168
MIPS/MOPS, 29
Mixes, 28
Module/function matrix, 254
Multiprocessing, 278-82
    availability, 280
    data integrity, 282
      vs duplexing, 280
    performance of, 279
    reasons for, 281
      fail soft, 281
        non disruptive growth, 281
Multiprogramming, 278
Mythical Man-Month, 70, 142, 247, 256

N

NASA, 144, 280
Navy, U.S., 63, 108, 288
    NTDS, 212
    Link 11, 212
Networks, 283
New York Times, 140-2, 168-9, 227
Nova, 16
NSA, 10-11
NSDG, 108, 146

O

Operating system, 7, 46, 49, 129, 166
    OS 360, 51, 129, 268
Organization, 251

P

PARS, 58
Physical security, 193
POL, 152
PPMC, 95
Predictions, 292

Principles of Mathematics, 156-57
Production engineering, 39
Productivity, 226-39
    data base, 227
    questionnaire, 230
        vs DSLOC, 236
Productizing a program, 79
Program, attributes of, 88
Program, definition, 2
Program, embodiment of, 274
Programmer, a professional?, 135
Programmer variability, 167
Project management tasks, 220-3
PSL/PSA, 62
Psychology of Computer Programming, 159

R

Real time, 58
Recipient, 44
Repertoire, 32, 160
Requirements definition, 12, 100-11
    requirements definition language,
    103
Resistance to change, 269
Response time, 31
Road to Xanadu, 127
RSVP Cycles, 123
Russell, Bertrand, 18, 156-7

S

SADT, 62, 147
Sarnoff, David, 17
Sense of the Future, 156
Short cuts, 254
Skylab, 22, 163, 167
Smith, Adam, 287
Software:
    application, 35, 46-7
    buy or build, 262
        contract, 263
        selecting a contractor,
        264-5
    complexity, 68-72
    continued development phase,
    36, 45-6
    corporate director of, 289
    cost, 86
    "definition," 2

development:
    career, 257
    difficulties, 240-1
        factors, 242
    environment, 3, 171,
    178-82
    evolutionary, 219
    manager, the key to
    success, 255
    organization, 251-3
    phase, 36, 45, 89
    plan, 225
    planning cycle, 225
    process, 93
    versus production, 213
engineering, 39, 142
inability of the technology to
    depict, 223
industrial techniques for, 286-8
intensive, 82
isolating the, 211
'maintenance', 6, 9-10
organization imperatives, 289
product, 35, 76
project, 35, 76
reentrant, 131
reliable - a misnomer, 190
research in, 273
scale, 35, 64
standards, 266-271
    at the corporate level, 290
    cost of, 267
    weakness for fads, 268
support, 35, *61*
system, 35, 46-7
    benefits of, 59
    disadvantages, 59
taxonomy of, 23, 34-5, 83, 85
two roles of, 11-2
versus hardware, 275-7
vocabulary, 288
use phase, 12, 36-7, *43-4*, 89,
    118
    design of, 118
Sprint, 31
Staffing, 216
Strange Loops, 157
Structured:
    design, 147
    overuse of the word, 271
Structured Programming, 138-42
    acceptance of, 142
    benefits of, 141

Structured Programming, 138-42
  (continued)
    change is initially expensive, 269
    change to, 270
    introduction of, 140
Style, 155
Subsystems, 112-13, 206, 210
Success schedules, 251
Synthesis of Form, 112
Systems, 206-13

T

Tarski, 156
Testing, 184-94
    duration, 194
    FAA, 189
    independence of, 191
    inspections, 185
    physical security, 193
    and quality, 188
    regression, 190, 193
    training ground, 194
'THE' Multiprogramming System, the structure of, 119
Throughput, 27
Top down, 178, 206
Traceability, 200
Translation,
TSS, 268
Turing, Alan, 6, 156
Turnaround, 27

U

Univac, 23
Use phase, 36-7, *43-4*, 89, 118
    memory map, 51
User, 44, 103, 105, 166
User guides, 224
User, real, 258
Uses of the Computer:
    five, 18
UYK 20, 163

V

V and V, 184
Verification, 184
VLSI, 15-16, 24-5
Von Neumann, 15, 30

W

Walk-throughs, 141, 186
Walston & Felix, 234
Warnier-Orr, 147
Wealth of Nations, 287
Weinberg, Gerald, 159
White, Henry, J., 140
Whitehead, A., 256-57
Wirth, Nicholas, 156
Witt, Bernard, 138, 146
Woodward, Joan, 213-15